# REA

D0602426

# The
# Sacrificial
# Mother

# the Sacrificial Mother

## Escaping the Trap of Self-Denial

### Carin Rubenstein, Ph.D.

HYPERION

New York

All names and identifying characteristics of
persons in this book have been changed.

Excerpt from Thomas J. Bouchard, Jr., reprinted with permission from Thomas
J. Bouchard, Jr., David T. Lykken, Matthew McGue, Nancy L. Segal and Auke
Tellegen, "Sources of Human Psychological Differences: The Minnestoa Study
of Twins Reared Apart," *Science*, October 12, 1990, pp. 223-228, copyright,
1990, American Association for the Advancement of Science.

Library of Congress Cataloging-in-Publication Data

Rubenstein, Carin.
The sacrificial mother : escaping the trap of self-
denial / by Carin Rubenstein.
p.  cm.
Includes bibliographical references.
ISBN 0-7868-6262-9
1. Mothers—Psychology. 2. Motherhood—Psychological aspects.
3. Self-sacrifice. I. Title.
HQ759.R82 1997
306.874'3-dc21   97-12076
CIP

Designed by Christine Weathersbee

First Edition
10 9 8 7 6 5 4 3 2 1

# Contents

*Oh! There is an enduring tenderness in the love of a mother to a son that transcends all other affections of the heart. It is neither to be chilled by selfishness, nor daunted by danger, nor weakened by worthlessness, nor stifled by ingratitude. She will sacrifice every comfort to his convenience; she will surrender every pleasure to his enjoyment; she will glory in his fame, and exult in his prosperity; and if adversity overtake him, he will be the dearer to her by misfortune; and if disgrace settle upon his name, she will still love and cherish him; and if all the world beside cast him off, she will be all the world to him.*

—Washington Irving, from "The Widow and Her Son,"
in *The Sketch-Book*, 1848

For David and Rachel and Jonathan

# Acknowledgments

Here are the people who listened to my ideas, lent me support, nodded their heads with great patience while I complained, or came to my party: Karen Adair, Penny Cassar, Laura Copland, Harriet Fier, Lenore Glickhouse, Andrea Glickhouse, Kay Brown Grala, Michael Hume, Sarah Kahn, Andrea Kott, Stephen Mantell, Mark Levine, Shelley Markowitz, Ken Neufeld, Nancy Porter, Michael Pressman, Annegret Rice, Berkeley Rice, Rick Routhier, Rebecca Scarpatti, Phillip Shaver, Laura Spitzer, Deborah Doyle Swartz, Carol Tavris, Litsa Tsitsera, Harvey Zachem, Beth Zolkind, and Neil Zolkind. Special thanks also to Pamela Moore and Annette Steiner.

I must also thank my original sacrificial mother, Trudy Rubenstein, and my father, Alvin Rubenstein, for their lifelong encouragement and faith in me. Thanks also to my sister, Joann Neufeld, for her stories and her jokes, and to my brother, Steven Rubenstein, for taking all the risks.

I'm indebted to George Sharrard, for all of his quick and efficient computer help, and to my crackerjack researcher, Nancy Margolin, and to Stacey Lutz. I'm grateful to my agent, Barbara Lowenstein, for her early enthusiasm and support. If it weren't for my friend and colleague Stephanie von Hirschberg at *New Woman*, I wouldn't have had so much rich survey material to work with. I must also thank Susan Ungaro, the editor of *Family Circle*, who gave me the chance to put my sacrifice ideas to the test. Finally, I have to thank my editor, Leslie Wells, who very gently but firmly put me on track and kept me there.

I'm grateful, too, to the nameless thousands of women and men who have answered my surveys over the years, opening their lives and pouring out their hearts in the hope that somebody would pay attention.

I did.

I have my children, Rachel and Jonathan, to thank, for coming along and making me a sacrificial mother in the first place. They are my miracle babies, the ones that the doctors informed me I'd never be able to have. Then there's my husband, David Glickhouse, who has been my best cheerleader. He read every first and second draft, threw me that great party, and best of all, learned to share my sacrifices.

# The Sacrificial Mother

# Introduction

I'd like to tell you about my pickle revelation.

In my family, we all love pickles, just about any kind of pickle. But if there's only one pickle left, if it's the last pickle in the jar, I always give it to my children. They each get half a pickle, I get none. This is how it always has been and, I imagine, how it always will be.

My husband laughs about this, about my willingness to give up the last pickle in the jar.

"I would never do that," he says, and it's true. Faced by a last pickle, he simply eats it and recycles the jar. It does not occur to him to deny himself a pickle for his children.

"That's a mom thing," he says.

Thinking about it, I realize that many mothers I know would, in fact, give up the last pickle for their children. In a nutshell, this book is about mothers who give up pickles and what happens to them when they do.

It was the sight of the pickle in the jar—the one I didn't get to eat—that jolted me into a sudden awareness of my own surprising and relentless ability to deny myself for the sake of my children. It's an ability that goes way beyond pickles, of course.

My transformation to sacrificial motherhood, my path to the last pickle, began on the day my first child was born. As soon as I had a baby, I eagerly gave up my self. She was more important than me because her needs were more immediate. She needed to be fed right now, changed right now, held right now! Once I was handed this ultra-demanding newborn, I caved in. I was negated; my needs vanished.

During those early, high-maintenance years, when my daughter was a dependent and perfect little person, and then my son came along and needed me too, my life quickly became a sleep-deprived, sacrificial blur. For me, sensuality was a dim memory, fine dining a laughable relic of another life. *Anything* that gave me pleasure felt taboo—I existed to service them. Like many mothers of small children, I felt an enormous amount of both tenderness and frustration, delight and depression. I really believed that this stage of my life— Baby Slave—would last forever.

And, in a way, it did.

I stopped buying myself new clothes. I began to wear socks with holes, baggy sweaters, nightgowns without buttons, winter coats so far past their prime that they let in a breeze. I refused to use makeup or comb my hair, often running out of the house without even a glance in the mirror at myself. It didn't really matter what *I* looked like, as long as my children were dressed and fed and warm. For years I was secretly proud of how old and ratty my clothes were—they were my red badge of courageous self-sacrifice. They announced to the world: "Look, I haven't bought anything for myself in years! My clothes are older than my children! I don't matter, but they do!"

I earned my own scarlet letters: not an "A" for adultery, but an "S," for Sacrificial Mother, a letter that should have been stamped on my forehead.

I was baby-obsessed, child-possessed. My two children had become my only passion. Even when my children were no longer infants, I still gave them the best piece of meat, the first choice at the video rental store, and, of course, the last pickle in the jar. Wherever I went, I was thinking of their needs, their desires, their fears. But my feeling of complete devotion to them went way beyond food and entertainment.

I considered my children first, last, always.

They became so much a part of me that I am no longer the person I was before they were born. My allegiance to them is so fierce, so complete, that I cannot imagine myself without them.

As time passed, I became more sacrificial, not less so. It was a habit I had fallen into. No one told me to do this or forced it on me. I just did it, as if on autopilot, as if I were careening down a rapids on a raft or shooting down a steep hill on a fast sled. I went where I was taken, to new extremes of maternal sacrifice, to levels of sacrificial thought and behavior that I had never thought possible in my pre-motherhood life.

I spent ten years living not for me, but only for my children. I spent ten years on hold, waiting to be me again.

My devotion to my children is not without rewards, as most sacrificial mothers will acknowledge. Both of my children have brought me, and still bring me, unimaginable joy and fulfillment. I would never, ever want to undo them.

That said, I certainly gave up more than I ever anticipated. There's a lot more to babies than babyhood, mostly because they get bigger. Now that my children are no longer babies, I don't need to carry them everywhere in my arms. Instead, I carry them everywhere in my car.

During one week in springtime, this is what I did:

Every day I drove my fifth grader to rehearsal for her ballet recital. I had a writing deadline to meet that week, so I'd race to drop her off, race back to work, race to pick her up, race back to work. One morning at seven-twenty I drove her to school, in the rain, with her relief map of Australia, which, because it was made of Ivory Snow, absolutely *could not* get wet, or it would have been transformed into a project on the unknown continent of White Bubbles. Then I raced to work.

It was kickoff week for spring sports, so I also accompanied my third-grade son to the annual Spring Baseball Parade, in which every child enrolled in T-ball, minor leagues, major leagues, or softball convened in a school parking lot with their parents so that we could all march to the high school auditorium, proudly stopping traffic as we followed our police escort. After that, I raced back to work again.

While trying to meet my deadline, I also made phone calls to try to track down a local classics scholar for my son's Greek myth project. I had to find one who was up on Zeus and Aphrodite and willing to explain deities and ancient rituals to a third grader who would rather be playing baseball. One who was also nearby, so that I could race to the interview, sit nearby while my son asked his six questions, then race back to meet my deadline.

I know I am not alone in my sacrificial approach to family life, because I see other sacrificial mothers wherever I go.

I see a divorced neighbor, a woman who works full time, dropping off her daughter and the girl's violin at school, tenderly sheltering both under an umbrella from car to door. I see another working friend en route to her volunteer job as stage manager of the dance recital, where she has to be every evening this week. She gets her work done by commuting to her job at dawn. I see another who has to attend several humiliating meetings every month with school officials who try to withhold the costly services that her severely disabled son desperately needs.

These women are not particularly noble or supremely self-sacrificing. They do what many of us do, or would do, or will do, when and if we have to.

During my hectic, though typical, week, I altered my needs and my work schedule to fit the shape of my family's agenda. It went without saying, without thinking, that my priorities came last, after I'd sorted out and satisfied everybody else's.

I'm not bragging or whining here, I'm just stating the facts of sacrificial maternal life.

Well, so what? Big deal.

This is what mothers are supposed to do, and we have to do it for only ten or twenty years. Why not just *give in* to the necessity of sacrifice?

Because it is harmful to our health and our sanity.

Because many of us reach a point at which we have nothing left to give.

Because, to paraphrase Gertrude Stein, we are in danger of having no there there.

Because we can simmer for years with an internal stew of anxiety and irritation and anger and despair—a reaction to all that we are not doing or being, for the sake of the children.

Not long ago, I hit a sacrificial wall. I had a life-changing epiphany that I had to do something, and fast, about my sacrifice problem. I was in Los Angeles with my children after an exhausting ten-hour trip. I couldn't fall asleep because I was stricken with a terror that would not leave. In a stuffy, mildewed room on the

Pacific Ocean, I was surfing: not real waves, but waves of pulsing anxiety. Who was I, outside of my children and family? I couldn't remember me, because I couldn't find my self.

The next morning, bleary but determined, I decided that I had to figure out what I wanted for me, where I wanted my life to go in the next ten years. I had to figure out my needs and understand where my impulse to sacrifice had come from.

Was I trained by my own sacrificial mother to replicate her kind of mothering? Or was I brainwashed by society into believing I had to sacrifice in order to be a good mother? Or did I have some kind of female sacrificial gene that kicked in when I had a baby?

How many other mothers sacrifice so much for their children, and who are they? Why do they do it? How does sacrifice affect women's emotional well-being and physical health? Do men benefit from their wives' sacrifices? How about the children—does mothers' sacrifice actually do them any good?

I'm in a unique position to answer these questions, not only because I'm a mother but also because I am a social scientist. I do research in which I conduct surveys, the kind that appear in magazines and are carried out in national telephone polls. My research probes deeply into how women and men think and feel about themselves and their lives. I've written on topics ranging from sex after babies to mothers-in-law to infidelity. In this book, I've included the results of fifteen of my most recent surveys. They include information from about 55,000 women and men—a huge sampling of mothers and fathers, wives and husbands. I have compiled their responses in this book, and I have conducted extensive interviews with several hundred people. (For the purposes of privacy, all of the names and some details have been changed.) The results that I am presenting here are original and have never been reported in this way.

Assembling all of these responses and gathering the relevant results, I'll spin a web of evidence about maternal sacrifice, using my original research and personal interviews as well as research from other social scientists.

How can you tell if this book might be useful? Here, in no particular order, are some signs that you might be a sacrificial mother:

- You spend at least one-third of your day thinking about something your child needs or wants, or agonizing about what you should have done or wish you'd done or said to your child.

- You can't remember the last time you spent more than one hour by yourself.

- You and your spouse have not had an evening out by yourselves since at least your last anniversary.

- When your daughter is devastated by something someone said to her at school, so are you.

- When your son forgets his lunch box at home, you drop it off at his school before noon, even if it's the third time this month. Working mother corollary: If you can't take his lunch to him because you're at work, you feel guilty about it all day long.

- You'd rather buy your children new overalls than find yourself a new pair of jeans.

- Hearing about a single neighbor who's away on a business trip for a week, you are slightly annoyed that she's left her child home with the baby-sitter.

- If you go away for several days, you tape-record yourself reading stories to your children. Or you leave little notes. Or you shower them with presents when you return.

- Your children don't know how to turn on the washing machine or how to fold clothes. (Applies to any child over the age of eight.)

- You give the last pickle in the jar to your children. (Applies only if you like pickles.) Can be generalized to any other food you really love.

In this book, I'll examine women's urge to sacrifice and explore the potential harm that this longing may present. I'll also show how women's sacrifice helps the men in our lives but makes very little difference to children's well-being. Finally, I'll suggest ways in which women can balance their need to deny themselves for their children with a desire to focus on themselves and their own dreams. This includes learning how to be what I call "selfist," paying attention to yourself—not to be confused with self*ish*, which is focusing on yourself at the *expense* of others.

Women who are selfist know how to pamper themselves in very much the same way that they indulge their children and husband. Being selfist means that a woman takes care of herself the way she cares for her family, showing as much concern for herself as for them. And it means doing all of this out in the open, so that everyone else sees it and understands that she values her self as much as she does them.

# One

# Women and the Tradition
# of Self-Denial

When I was growing up, I had a close friend who lived up the street. I liked to play with her because she always let me decide what to do. If I wanted to ride bikes, she'd come along, even if she really wanted to play kickball in the street or Barbies on the patio. If I got picked to be captain of the dodgeball team and didn't choose her for my side, she said she didn't mind. If the big girls down the block were looking to put a handful of Japanese beetles down someone's back, she was the one.

She was a dutiful, self-denying friend.

Later on, as a teenager, she had a few boyfriends, but all were the kind she could take home to meet Dad. When her parents couldn't afford to send her to an Ivy League college, she went to a cheaper local one instead. She didn't make a fuss over it. After graduation my friend got a good job near where her family lived and visited them every Sunday. A few years later she married a local boy whose religion matched hers, a decision that thrilled her parents.

She was a dutiful, self-denying daughter.

As newlyweds, my friend and her husband lived in her little bachelorette apartment, close to where she worked. But after he found a job in a nearby city, they moved so that he would have the easier commute. It took her more than twice as long to get to her job.

When my friend got pregnant for the first time, she couldn't wait to be a mother. She longed to stay at home with her new baby, but she and her husband couldn't get by without her salary, so reluctantly she went back to work. From then on she spent every waking minute when not at work with her little girl. She felt guilty for leaving her daughter with a baby-sitter, but she never told her husband because she didn't want him to feel bad.

She was a dutiful, self-denying wife.

Eventually my friend moved to a house in the suburbs, complete with a backyard, swings, and a sandbox. I didn't see much of her during those years, because she was so preoccupied with her daughter and her second baby, another girl. She spent every weekend with her children. The last time I heard from her, a few summers ago, my friend had taken a vacation from work and had spent most of the week shopping for, buying, and hanging new wallpaper for her seven-year-old daughter's bedroom. When the girl saw the pattern of horse heads that pranced around near the ceiling of the room, she was so happy she hugged the wall.

My friend was a dutiful, self-denying mother.

What she has never been is dutiful to herself. My friend has spent years trying to please other people, ignoring her own dreams in the process. A feminist revolution may have been debated, updated, and won, but she never noticed. She always did what she thought she should, which never happened to include doing things for herself. Her duty, as she sees it, is to take care of other people—even if it's at her own expense.

The message my friend sends to me, to her family, and to herself is that *she doesn't count*, that her needs don't matter, that nobody should worry about her because she'll be fine.

But my friend is *not* fine. She gets headaches. She doesn't sleep very well. She's a bit overweight, full of self-doubt, and sometimes inexplicably sad. She looks too old, too soon.

Since my own revelation, I'm burning to set her straight, to tell her that *her needs matter*, that the worst thing she can do to her young daughters is to pass on her self-denying message. The lessons in sacrifice that she's giving to her girls can only harm them in years to come, just as they have subtly but undeniably corroded her own sense of self.

When I try to envision a typical sacrificial mother, this friend is the one I think of, a woman who has submerged her true self so deeply, for so long, that it has nearly vanished. After all these years, I wouldn't know how or where to find it; it would be like trying to discover a stack of gold coins somewhere on the bottom of the Atlantic Ocean.

My friend's path to self-annihilation is a direct result of being sacrificial, a personality trait that is especially common among women. Being sacrificial means having an ability to put other people first, and it's usually accompanied by an aptitude for self-denial. This talent becomes most obvious when women become mothers, a time when their sacrificial tendencies expand and soar like so many hot-air balloons.

When women give birth, they're primed to use their expertise in the art of sacrifice. They become professionals at compromise, queens of concession. For many mothers, self-denial feels good. They feel righteous giving of themselves: They are Joan of Arc, Florence Nightingale, and Mother Teresa, all rolled into one tightly wrapped sacrificial package.

Why are mothers so especially sacrificial, so much more sacrificial than men?

Mothers sacrifice because they are compelled to do so by both nature and nurture. Women are predisposed to have an enormous capacity for empathy and to be willing to sacrifice. When they give birth, new mothers are infused by a wave of hormones that stimulates them to nurture selflessly. But they also spend a lifetime absorbing a strong cultural message and learning that it's best if they put themselves last. For thousands of generations, then, mothers have obeyed their biological destiny and heeded social signals by becoming sacrificial.

In fact, the words "mother" and "sacrifice" are practically synonymous. Honey is sweet, a kitten is soft, a mother is sacrificial.

Of course, not every woman on Earth feels a primal urge to sacrifice for her children. There are dysfunctional and seriously disturbed mothers, those who abuse or even murder their own children. But women like these—the Susan Smiths of the world—get so much attention precisely because they are *so* aberrant, so far out of the realm of what is normal.

The vast majority of mothers are willing to sacrifice whatever is necessary to make their children's lives easier, happier, better. They give up sleep, they give up their friends, they give up buying themselves clothes and doing things for fun. They give up solitude, the simple pleasure of just being alone sometimes. They give up going out with their husband, because the children don't like baby-sitters.

My research shows that about eight in ten mothers say they often sacrifice their own needs and desires for their children. And nearly as many believe that this sacrifice is their duty as a mother. They sacrifice so much, so often, because they feel certain that their sacrifices will ultimately benefit their children. But as we'll see, it's possible that mothers who sacrifice too much harm both themselves and their children in the process.

## What Women Sacrifice

Mothers deny themselves for their children just about every day. Some sacrifice by staying home all day when they'd really rather go to work. Others sacrifice by going to work when they yearn to be at home.

Whatever their situation, many mothers sacrifice naturally, automatically, and without question. They sacrifice not just for their obviously needy newborns but for their rambunctious toddlers and inquisitive six-year-olds, for their newly independent fifth graders and their moody teenagers.

Examples of the trivial ways in which women sacrifice for their children are humdrum, unexceptional, *expected*.

I always end up with the hard end of the loaf of fresh bread so that my children can eat the chewy middle. I take the apple or the peach with the soft, brown spot. I choose the strawberries halfway fuzzy with mold, the somewhat-shriveled blueberries. I eat leftover jelly beans, the colors that nobody else wants. I hold back from eating too many handfuls of fresh popcorn, picking out the unpopped kernels instead.

My sister's friend always offers her children the chicken wing, even though it's her absolute favorite part, with that tender, teeny bit of meat. A Kansas woman always gives her little girl the last homemade brownie, even though she covets it for herself. Another mother denies herself a cherished soda in the morning, because she doesn't want her four-year-old daughter to see her drinking an unhealthy beverage at such a bizarre hour. A California mom unconsciously stops eating fruit, although it's the only food she likes, so that there will always be enough for her fruit-crazed son.

Giving children the choicest bits of food is only one minor symptom of sacrifice. For most women, true sacrifice goes far deeper than these everyday examples. It means always thinking of the children's needs first. It means always worrying about what is best for the children, what will make them happiest, smartest, most secure. It means feeling guilty for not always being the most giving, supportive, caring mother. It means making sacrifice a way of life.

Sacrificial mothers have, in fact, become a new serving class. Few families have servants anymore, but many have a sacrificial mother who performs similar duties.

Kathy Vecchio, thirty-six, a mother of three from a small town in New York, is a member of the sacrificial serving class. She doesn't consider it possible to put herself first, ever: "I'm always thinking of everybody else's needs before my own. I'm so involved in thinking of what should be done for my husband and children and then maybe me, the wife, the mother," she says.

Kathy's job is to do everything and be everything for everyone in her family: She exists to serve them. This chubby lady is funny and lusty, and she loves, loves, loves to talk. She yaks at a New York, mile-a-minute pace, like a machine gun stuck on automatic. In less than three minutes of conversation, I find out that her husband is a home-improvement contractor, that she works part time as a clerk at a dialysis center and as a hairdresser, cutting hair in people's homes, and that she just lost thirty pounds—but has another fifty to go.

"I had no neck; now I have a neck," she says.

Kathy's husband seems to respect her more now that she's thinner, and she feels she has more power in their relationship, especially sexual power. Every time they make love she reminds herself, "This is good, we're burning calories." They even have what she calls their own "pleasure palace," a room her husband built in the basement with a lock on the door, where they have sex by candle-light. Still, she resents the fact that he judges her by the way her body looks, but that's another story.

In her family, Kathy always comes last. On important family holidays, for instance, her priorities don't count. Kathy's fourteen-year-old daughter believes that her "every bodily crevice has to be clean before she can leave the house." So Kathy never gets to use the family's only bathroom to take a shower before leaving the house. She's a grunge, but her kids are gorgeous.

"I run around getting everybody ready, but then I'm looking horrible. I'm running around like a chicken without a head, throwing on clothes, and everybody else looks perfect."

From New Year's to Christmas and back again, Kathy suffers from bathroom self-denial. She never shops for herself either, just for the children. Her bedroom slippers are now so ratty that her four-year-old daughter recently volunteered to buy her mom new slippers, as soon as she saves up enough nickels and dimes. She has no expensive perfume because it's, well, too expensive. And she doesn't get her nails done because that's "too much luxury," she says.

Kathy works twenty hours or so a week, but she also does all the cooking and cleaning and shopping for her family. No one offers to help, and she doesn't ask, mostly because it's easier to do it all herself, although the immense burden sometimes makes her so furious she could pop. Kathy also takes care of a friend's eight-year-old daughter every day, both before and after school, because the woman is a single mother who can't afford day care. She does this as a favor, not for pay, to offer her children an example "that you don't do everything in life just for money."

Kathy is not only a servant, she's like a human household appliance: Plug her in and she works. Just like a servant or a machine, everyone takes her for granted.

Everyone, that is, but Kathy's dog, a female Labrador retriever named Charlie. "She listens to me all the time and never asks anything in return," Kathy says, only half kidding. "If I could teach Charlie to vacuum, I'd be so happy. Sometimes, when I leave the house, I tell her, 'Just empty the dishwasher.' And she'd do it for me, if she could."

The only person in her family who respects and adores Kathy Vecchio for her sacrifices is not even a human being; she's a dog.

Showerless, in her ratty slippers, Kathy Vecchio could be a poster woman for sacrificial motherhood.

## A Loss of Self

Mothers like Kathy put themselves last nearly all the time. They weave a web of small self-denials that can, over time, trap them into a complete loss of self. As a friend says about her life as a wife and mother of three: "I haven't had a 'me' for fifteen years."

Another mother I know feels as if she's employed by her five-year-old daughter, because it's her job "to be attentive and to wait on her and that kind of stuff." The girl is her responsibility, she says, so her job isn't herself. She never has "me time" because "there is no me, only us."

In my research, most mothers with children under the age of eighteen tell me that their relationship with their children leaves them little time to fulfill their own needs and desires. And nearly all women also tell me they're convinced that "most wives sacrifice their personal pleasure for the needs of their family." But almost no one says that a husband has to give up his satisfactions.

One woman I know is firm in her belief that she can only get real pleasure by taking care of her family. She'd no sooner indulge herself for half an hour than she'd cook her pet rabbit for dinner. She lives on nine acres out in the country and spends her days raising a horse, three dogs, a cat, a rabbit, three children, and an every-other-weekend stepdaughter, while also working part time. Although her husband sometimes treats himself to a fishing or hunting trip with the guys, she doesn't leave her homestead except to go to work. As she tells it, she'd much rather muck out a stall than get a manicure.

But when women deny themselves for too long, they lose a sense of who they are as separate human beings, apart from their family. So many of them, like my horse-crazy friend, are proud when they say "My family is me." That may be true, yet it's also dangerous.

The road to sacrificial motherhood begins with this loss of self for the sake of the marital union. A great many women actually *expect* to lose themselves when they get married. Many women have told me that they believe wives "submerge a vital part of themselves in marriage."

One of my neighbors has spent so long submerging her self that it's probably sunk deeper than the *Titanic*. Married for twenty-five years, she works full time and has three teenage children. This past Thanksgiving, for the first time ever, my neighbor had the pleasure of being invited to someone else's house for the holiday. She was thrilled to be able to escape her annual toil over the turkey. But her husband was upset: He loves the smell of roasting turkey. He likes to have a turkey carcass to pick at; the man wanted his own turkey. So my neighbor spent Thanksgiving Day cooking a turkey—a turkey that her husband *could smell.*

Then the family went out to eat someone else's turkey.

An extraordinary number of wives and mothers do things like this, going out of their way to make their family happy. I find that many more women than men—mothers in particular—agree with this statement: "I take better care of my family's needs than my own needs." Women are so used to sacrificing themselves that they get into a universal nurturing habit. They begin to feel that it's their job to take care of everybody. I worry about the boy with an older man at a local bagel shop, because I notice that he flinches when the man touches him. I'm upset by the man who seems to be accompanying three children on my airplane flight, although he doesn't speak to them at all. As they leave together, I notice that he's carrying a belt, folded up, that he slaps on his palm, over and over, without saying a word. My husband doesn't notice the man at all, but I want to steal these children away; I want to make sure they're okay.

Some women fall into a habit of mothering their husbands too, taking care of the grown man who is supposed to be their partner. About half of the wives I've interviewed say they sometimes think of their husband as "just another child." Almost no men, though, think of their wives this way, probably because they don't make a practice of sacrifice.

Sometimes women are forced to think of their husband as a child because he expects to be treated like one. That's what happened to Alison Salinger, thirty-one, whose husband, Jay, can't be bothered to worry about anyone but himself. Alison earns most of the family's income; Jay is a free-lance writer who works at home. When she walks in the door every day at dinnertime, after picking up their two-year-old daughter from the baby-sitter, Jay is just beginning his workday, so he can't help prepare the meal and he can't watch his daughter.

"He's so needy," Alison says about him. "I have to remember that he's partly a child too. He's available in the house, but he's not available to help."

She resents having to take care of Jay the way she does her daughter, because the child is obviously so much more helpless than the man. But because both are so needy, Alison gives to them equally, leaving almost no time or energy for herself.

Alison is fulfilling the standard maternal formula for sacrifice, which equates being a good mother with having no time for one's self, no time to think about one's own needs. Mothers simply get out of practice in considering what they want, like a violinist who hasn't touched the fiddle for so long, she can no longer pick out a tune.

When I ask mothers what they do for just for themselves, I almost always hear the same incredulous response.

First, they usually repeat the question, wanting to make sure they've heard me correctly.

"Just for me?" they ask, with eyebrows raised, eyes crinkled in disbelief.

Then they laugh. But most of them don't really answer, because they can't. They don't do all that much just for themselves.

I posed this question to a group of about fifteen mothers I met in Los Angeles. When I ask these women how they pamper themselves, there is a stunned silence. They can't think of a thing.

Finally a mom blurts out a one-word answer, in the form of a cautious question: "Chocolate?"

A pause, then everyone laughs, embarrassed but greatly relieved. That's it! They treat themselves to chocolate!

But no one has anything else to add, anything they can think of that is important and that they do just for themselves.

Wherever I go, I speak to mothers who find it difficult to think of even one small thing they do for their own pleasure. Some consider going to *work* as something they do just for themselves. For a great many mothers, especially those who work part time, work is the only chance they have to think of themselves, the only time they consider their own. A mother of a disabled child finds her four-hour-a-day job a relief. Although all she does is heat up pork barbecue for sandwiches and mix coleslaw, she gets a brief reprieve from the intense sacrifices of her life at home. A woman who went back to school for a degree just got a part-time job as a nurse in the county jail. For the first time in her ten-year marriage, her husband has had to learn how to prepare dinner, do laundry, wash dishes, and get the children ready for bed. That's her idea of pampering herself.

Other mothers tell me that they indulge themselves by spending time in the bathroom, that being alone in a room with a toilet and a tub is their only luxury. A mother of four confesses that she sometimes sneaks away so she can sit on the toilet and read, moaning the excuse to her four children, who are usually waiting outside the door, that she's suffering from crippling stomach pains. Having a bad bellyache is the only legitimate reason she can think of for being alone in a room with a book.

Another mother says that she indulges herself by going to church every Sunday, because in those two hours she satisfies all of her social and spiritual needs for the entire week. It's the only time she sits in a room containing more adults than children and the only chance she gets to focus quietly on her deepest, inner self.

Then there are mothers who take time for themselves only because they disguise it or make it nearly invisible to their family. A mother I know gets up every day at four-thirty in the morning so that she can exercise for an hour and a half, doing her 1,000 daily sit-ups, before the sun, and her son, rises. The two-year-old boy never sees his mom on the treadmill, and she never has to tell him to leave her alone so she can exercise in peace.

Another California mother literally sneaks outside, on her apartment balcony, to eat a piece of almond roca from Trader Joe's, for a secret treat.

A mother of three in New Jersey plans what she calls a "Cinderella Liberty" trip each year. Every spring, for no more than thirty-six hours, she gets on a bus and goes somewhere, while her husband takes their children to his parents' house. The children never notice that she's gone for this day and a half of sweet freedom.

Mothers like these, who finagle their self time, seem to feel *guilty* about doing things for themselves, as if they are harming their families somehow by focusing on themselves. To them, self-indulgence feels nasty and forbidden, something they have to work hard to hide, like masturbating or eating a whole box of jelly doughnuts. They resist talking about sacrifice; the word itself offends them. Their golden rule is that family comes first, last, and always, and they act as if it would be committing a sin to think about themselves.

When I mention "sacrifice" to women like these, I sometimes sense a sharp hostility. A friend of mine who didn't have her first child until she was thirty-five bristles with irritation every time I inquire if she's doing anything for herself. She lives for her two children, so she doesn't need to do anything for herself, she tells me with great annoyance. She's just not interested in her self anymore. That's why she pretends she doesn't understand what I'm saying when I ask her about self-denial.

"Down the Nile?" she asks me in mock innocence.

My resistant friend is one of many women who insist on being defined by motherhood. Every cell in their body is focused on mothering. They believe with all their heart and soul that it's their job to sustain, guide, cherish, and sacrifice for their children every minute of every day. They don't realize that too much sacrifice can make them sick, both physically and psychologically. Even worse, too much maternal sacrifice probably does absolutely no good for the very people it's meant to help—the children.

Part of the reason that so many women are so unrelievedly stubborn about their faith in the benefits of sacrifice is that they have been targets of a public campaign for the selling of sacrifice to women for as long as they have been alive.

## Selling Sacrifice to Mothers

A wave of subtle social propaganda washes over women so that when they become mothers, they will be fit for sacrifice. It's a form of cultural coercion that rewards mothers who conform to the sacrifice norm, one that never addresses a similar lesson to fathers. Every day, in many ways, mothers receive hints that sacrifice is good, self-focus is bad.

News stories, for instance, inform them of their sacrificial duties by offering examples of women who make dramatic sacrifices, either foolish or courageous, for their children. Wanda Holloway's seedy sacrificial story made the news in the early 1990s. She was the Texas woman who tried to murder the mother of a high school cheerleader so that her own daughter would have a better chance to make the squad. She assumed that the other daughter would be bereft without her mother, not cheerful enough to cheer. Then, when the girl quit, a spot would be left for Holloway's daughter.

This ridiculous tale made many women laugh with scorn, mostly because it was so extreme, so nutty. But deep, deep down, what mother hasn't ached for her daughter to get chosen for the lead role in the school play or picked to perform the solo in the ballet recital or voted to be homecoming queen? And how many mothers would do just about anything to get the object of her desire for her?

Most mothers can understand, at least in part, the Texas mom's twisted logic, which is why the incident was so deeply disturbing. And why, ultimately, it became a long-running national news story and a book and a television movie.

It hit a sacrificial nerve.

Other kinds of sacrificial mothers make the news too. A mother in California was caught after she had set five forest fires in the Shasta Trinity National Forest. She'd become a pyromaniac to help her son's career as a seasonal firefighter. She wanted to give him a chance to fight a lot of fires and to earn some extra money, she explained.

A more honorable example, perhaps, is the doctor who spent two years in a Washington, D.C., jail rather than reveal where her daughter was hiding so the girl wouldn't have to spend time with an allegedly abusive father.

Or the federal judge who promised to give up her seat on the bench so that her son could take a similar job, one that was prohibited to him unless she resigned.

Or another Washington, D.C., woman who sacrificed her life for her unborn son, refusing aggressive chemotherapy for a metastasizing cancer so that he would be born unharmed. She died four months later.

A truly astonishing example is the mother in South Carolina who was chained to her fifteen-year-old delinquent daughter, day and night, for a month, by order of a juvenile court judge. She was attached to the girl by wrist and ankle shackles and informed that she could be sent to prison for up to a year if her *daughter* wandered free. The judge also forbade the mother to drink or smoke while in the girl's presence, or she'd be in contempt of court.

The mother, Deborah Harter, agreed to the punishment because she thought it would give her daughter "a second chance."

The judge obviously believed that sacrifice is the duty of a good mother. Why not chain mother to child? After all, the woman is already bound to the girl by sacrificial ties of duty. Apparently it never occurred to the judge that Harter had her own life to live, one in which she'd already attended the tenth grade. The judge learned how difficult it is to adjudicate sacrifice, though. After the mother and daughter had been shackled together for several weeks, the mother had to be hospitalized for an overdose of antianxiety medication.

Women receive similar, though less bizarre, sacrifice messages by reading magazine and newspaper stories about famous mothers who take time off from their successful careers for the sake of their families. They learn that even rock stars, actresses, and athletes boast about how proud they are to sacrifice for their children. If a famous mother doesn't mention how much she denies herself for her children, she'll seem like a bad mother.

When Patti Smith, the 1970s rock-and-roll musician, began to give concerts again after dropping out of the music scene for more than a decade, she was adamant about how glorious she felt to give up her career for her children. "There's no job harder than being a wife and a mother," Smith said. "It's much more demanding and required much more nobility than the other work that I did."

The once wild "rock chameleon" Annie Lennox, as *People* magazine calls her, asks now only to be a mother. After more than ten years of rock superstardom, she tells the magazine that "my children are the focus of my life." She would gladly give up all her former glamour just to paint and bake and be a mom.

Actress Susan Sarandon, a mother of three who won an Oscar for her starring role in *Dead Man Walking*, tells *Entertainment Weekly* that she's happiest just watching her children grow. "It takes so much to get me to break out of domestic paradise. There's hardly anything that interests me as much as my family."

Even athletes brag of their maternal sacrifices. Susan Butcher, the four-time winner of the Iditarod, a 1,160-mile Alaskan sled-dog race, named her first baby Tekla, after a favorite dog. But she has since put aside mushing for mothering. Interviewed by the *New York Times* in Wyoming, where she'd entered a 400-mile race just for fun, she said she didn't care if she won, because that "would have meant I was being a poor mother."

Of course, if these women just stayed at home baking and watching their children grow, they'd never make another CD or win another Oscar. So while they preach the standard sacrificial line—"I am a good mother who denies herself for her family"—they also manage to focus on their own careers and to succeed.

Famous mothers are rewarded for appearing not to want to achieve, for seeming to put themselves last. But if they don't seem to sacrifice enough, then they're punished.

When Marcia Clark was prosecuting the O. J. Simpson murder trial in 1995, her ex-husband tried to get custody of their two young sons. He claimed that her long and highly visible work hours were bad for the children. She was, he implied, too ambitious to be a good mother. (Two years later, the two boys still live with Clark, and the judge has forbidden press coverage of the custody proceedings.)

More judges in divorce cases nationwide are awarding custody to fathers when mothers work full time or attend school during the day, in part because the women do not seem to be sacrificing themselves sufficiently. In Washington, D.C., a judge took away a lawyer's two sons because she often worked late. The judge gave custody to the children's unemployed father, although he, too, sent the children to day care or hired a baby-sitter.

Mothers are sold on sacrifice in movies and on television too. Powerful images of sacrificial mothers on the big and small screen can last for decades, long after the film or show has disappeared. Movies are especially effective at touting sacrificial motherhood as a great and glorious goal. Those that sanctify mothers who suffer for their children are called "maternal melodramas." Sacrificial movie mothers are nearly always portrayed as saintly, as the epitome of motherhood. A classic of this type is the 1937 movie *Stella Dallas*, remade in 1990 as *Stella*, with Bette Midler. Audiences at the original showings wept, even during the Great Depression, at the sight of the disgraced and forgotten mother, Stella Dallas, who had to wait outside in the rain to catch a glimpse of her beloved daughter's wedding to a wealthy man. She gave up her life, and her daughter's love, so that her daughter could marry well.

More recent movies like *Terms of Endearment*, *Beaches*, *The Turning Point*, *The Joy Luck Club*, and the dark *Dolores Claiborne* all feature mothers who martyr themselves for their children. Even the violent *Terminator* movies star a muscular, selfless mother of the future. She sacrifices her freedom in the present to help save her son of the future.

On television, almost all situation-comedy mothers are sacrificial ones, even on cartoon shows like *The Simpsons*. But the most powerful and influential of all sacrificial television moms is June Cleaver, the mother on the 1950s series *Leave It to Beaver*. So many women possess a mental black-and-white image of June, in her starched dress and ironed apron, standing by the door waiting patiently for her children to come home from school. It's as if women are haunted by that vision of Mrs. Cleaver, women who weren't even born when the original series aired. So many mothers believe that they're supposed to be just like June, ready to serve their children milk and cookies every day, ready to devote themselves totally to their children's lives. She's the source of so much pain and guilt for working mothers who can never, ever achieve her level of sacrifice.

## The Biological Roots of Sacrifice

Even a century of sacrifice propaganda couldn't make women as sacrificial as they are, and so much more so than men, without some powerful support from nature. In fact, women probably have a hormonal and biological predisposition to sacrifice—one that makes them open to sacrificial sales pitches. Childbirth endows women with a hormone that encourages them to nurture and to sacrifice. In addition, they may even carry a specific gene that guides their maternal judgment and equips them with a need to sacrifice.

This potential sacrifice hormone, oxytocin, is released by the pituitary gland. It enhances a woman's ability to nurture when she gives birth and when she nurses her newborn. It also helps to induce labor in the first place, which is why doctors give its synthetic version, pitocin, to begin labor in pregnant women whose natural oxytocin level is too low.

Scientists have learned about the subtle effects of oxytocin through experiments with animals. When they inject oxytocin into female rats that have never had babies, the virgin animals suddenly begin to care for and try to nurse another female's newborn pups. It seems that it's not pregnancy itself, then, but oxytocin that transforms an ordinary female rat into one that can be a mother. The hormone probably works the same way in larger mammals. When experimenters deprive a mother sheep of oxytocin, for instance, she completely ignores her newborn lamb, forming no attachment to it at all. Unless the infant is removed from its indifferent mother, it will die.

Oxytocin is almost certainly vital to human beings, since it helps women forge a bond with their newborn infant, says zoologist C. Sue Carter of the University of Maryland. She claims that among all mammals, "positive social behavior is facilitated by oxytocin." The hormone stimulates everything a mother does to nurture and care for a helpless newborn baby. Oxytocin and other hormones that are released during childbirth, Carter says, provide mothers with just "the right cocktail" to make them proper mothers. This ambrosial concoction of hormones is what jump-starts a woman's mothering activities, the spark that ignites a sacrificial flame.

Of course, human mothers don't need oxytocin to be good mothers, the way rats do, since they can *learn* to care for babies. Without a drop of oxytocin in her blood, for instance, an adoptive mother can be as loving and nurturing to her children as a biological mother. Oxytocin may simply act as a kind of insurance policy of human motherhood. When a women gives birth, she gets a dose of hormones that will boost her tendency to be warm and supportive into a higher zone, a level for potential sacrificial motherhood.

A mother's tendency to sacrifice may even be partly genetic. Scientists have found a way to manipulate the genetic structure of female mice by removing a single gene they call fosB. When they do, a formerly normal mother mouse completely neglects the litter she's just had. A mouse without the fosB gene doesn't gather her pups in a nest to keep them warm and never nurses the infants, although she's physically capable of doing so. The mutant mother mouse simply ignores her babies to death, for lack of this single gene. Maybe abusive human mothers lack a human equivalent of this gene.

Beyond hormones and genes, mothers may also inherit a biological tendency to sacrifice, simply to ensure that their offspring will survive. Mothers in other species certainly make sacrifices for their offspring, so maybe women are born with a natural predisposition for it.

In a highly publicized case, a mother cat risked her life for her newborn babies. The Brooklyn-born animal repeatedly ran inside a burning building to save her five kittens, one at a time, from certain death, burning herself badly in the process. Not only did her feat of sacrificial motherhood make national news, but the shelter that took her in had thousands of offers from people who wanted to adopt her. She became a feline role model for sacrificial women.

Scientists who study birds observe that mother birds sometimes put themselves between their chicks and predators intent on a kill. To save her nestlings from certain death, the female North American kildeer does a "broken-wing display" to lure predators, such as foxes and coyotes, away from the nest. If the predator is concentrating on attacking the mother bird, her eggs or chicks will have a better chance to survive.

Female elephants and giraffes also defend their offspring with their lives. Mother elephants attack Land Rovers to protect calves they believe are being threatened. In *When Elephants Weep*, psychoanalyst Jeffrey Masson tells a story about an Indian elephant and her three-month-old calf who were trapped by a river flooding its banks. As the calf was about to float away in the rushing water, the mother took it and gently placed it on a ledge several feet above the water line. The mother was then swept away by the river's currents. Half an hour later the mother reappeared, having escaped the flood, trumpeting loudly while running back to reassure and calm her calf, who was still shivering on the ledge where she'd left it. The mother elephant then made her way down to the riverbank and rescued her calf from above.

A herd of giraffes in Africa were attacked by a single lion. All of the giraffes escaped, except for one slow-moving calf. The calf's mother went back to try to push the baby along faster, but she was unsuccessful. The mother then turned to face the lion, ready to sacrifice herself on her calf's behalf. As the lion circled, she wheeled around. When he moved to attack, she kicked at him with her forelegs. She defended herself for an hour, until the lion finally gave up and she, and her calf, could rejoin the herd.

My favorite example of maternal sacrifice in animals comes from under the sea. A mother octopus has the ultimate sacrificial organ, a self-destruct mechanism called an optic gland. As soon as an octopus lays her eggs, the gland releases hormones that force her to lose her appetite. Because she doesn't need to eat, she won't leave her eggs or newly hatched babies to hunt for food, but she'll die of starvation within a month. She is biologically bound to sacrifice her life so her brood can survive.

Like these animals, many human mothers feel that, if necessary, they'd give their lives to save their children. We might believe that this is because mothers feel such unfathomable love and affection for their children or because it is so unbearably painful to outlive a child. But for sociobiologists, the reason for mothers' death-defying devotion is genetic. A mother loves and sacrifices for her children, they say, mainly to help ensure that her offspring survive to adulthood and pass on her genes. In short, it's a selfish love, motivated by pure biology, an "evolutionary stratagem" that's for a mother's own good, says sociobiologist David Barash of the University of Washington in Seattle. Mother love is simply a means to a biological end, he claims.

But men need to pass on their genes too, so why don't they feel a similar overwhelming urge to sacrifice?

They don't have to, Barash says, because they can spread themselves thinner by having many more children. Women have fewer children than men, so they must invest much more time and energy in each one. In Western cultures, most mothers bear no more than 4 or 5 children, although a Russian peasant woman who lived in the mid-1700s was pregnant 27 times and had 69 children, according to the *Guinness Book of World Records*. Still, men can sire a theoretically unlimited number of offspring. One Moroccan emperor, a man who must have had a glee club–size harem of wives, had 700 sons and 342 daughters before his death in 1727.

Another crucial biological fact is that, unlike fathers, mothers always know which child is theirs. As Barash puts it: "Mommy's babies, Daddy's maybes." In almost all species, females invest more in parenting than males do and they're willing to sacrifice more because they are certain of their parenthood. Among mammals, mothers are often willing to risk their lives to save their offspring, while males almost never are. Why risk their lives for an infant that might not be theirs? Female animals sacrifice on behalf of their young, but males don't, because males have a lower "degree of devotedness," Barash says.

Older females are especially willing to sacrifice for their children, because they have fewer years left in which to get pregnant. Younger mothers, though, can always have more children if the others are lost or killed. Older gulls make more feeding trips for their young and spend more time fixing their nests and less time loafing than younger mother birds do. Females "with a low probability of breeding the next year have very little to lose by investing heavily in the current year," Barash writes.

Thus, the biology of sacrifice is a trifecta, nature's triple whammy of female hormones, genes, and natural tendencies that predict how much a mother is willing to give up for her children. And it's why she's almost always more willing to make sacrifices than her husband.

Observant mothers notice their own compulsion to sacrifice and their husbands' comparative lack of interest in self-denial. Alice Russell, a thirty-four-year-old mother of two young children and a part-time lawyer on Long Island, New York, is very quick to observe her own natural tendencies to put her children first and her husband's competing belief that he is at the top of the list.

With her hawk nose and small, shining eyes, Alice is reminiscent of a very large mother bird protecting her brood from predators. Self-denial, she says, has become her way of life.

"It's a general way of being," Alice says. "I never eat a hot meal. I often don't take a shower until the middle of the afternoon." It's second nature for her to consider her children first. But to her husband, Tommy, it's natural to consider them second or third or never. She's constantly amazed by how unresponsive and unaware he can be of their children's needs and demands.

"If he's sitting eating dinner, he won't get up for them. There's not a thing that could tear him away from his plate," she says. He tells her, in fact, that his nonchalance is biological.

"He calls it a chip or a bone that I have and he lacks. The children just don't push his buttons the way they do mine," she says. She responds to them instantly, instinctively. He can't and doesn't and won't.

"He's convinced that there is a true maternal instinct or a maternal force that mothers have with children and fathers don't. It causes us to respond to every whine and whimper. We are more in tune with the kids. I can hear my son say 'Daddy' seventeen times, and I hear the first one, but if Tommy is talking, he doesn't hear it.

"It's beyond his comprehension. To me, they are my prime concern. He adores them, but they're not the foremost thing on his mind in the morning when he wakes up or when he goes to bed at night, the way they are on mine. I'm consumed with worries. 'Are they in the right environment?' 'Is this school the right one?' 'Will camp be okay?' For my husband, it's 'Yeah, whatever, it's under control.'"

Biology makes a powerful contribution to maternal sacrifice, but so do more indirect psychological influences. If biology is the key that starts a mother's sacrifice engine, then it's her personality that puts the engine in gear and takes it for a drive.

## The Psychology of Sacrifice

Women are blessed with an aptitude for empathy, compassion, and selflessness that makes them open to sacrifice. They come by these skills naturally; they are biologically endowed to be sensitive to others' feelings. Motherhood itself even hones a woman's empathy skills. Because female mammals almost always have sole responsibility for caring for their helpless newborns, they must be sensitive to the infant's feelings. Mothers who can recognize an infant's pain, hunger, and fear will be more likely to raise that infant successfully. Most mammal mothers have evolved an ability to be especially caring and empathic for this very reason, says zoologist Frans de Waal. Mothers become attached to their offspring by what he calls "an emotional umbilical cord," a tie from which mammals are never free.

In addition to 200 million years of genetic programming, most cultures also reward women for being empathic. In many parts of the world, a woman who is empathic is not only valued, but considered feminine. Psychologists even use such phrases as "being sensitive to others' needs" and "being sympathetic" and "devoting self to others" when they measure people's beliefs and attitudes about what it means to be feminine. These key words are included in just about every standard test of femininity and masculinity. If you say others are "a lot like me," you're feminine; if not, you're masculine. This doesn't necessarily mean you aren't feminine if you're not empathic, just that most people won't think of you as being particularly feminine.

Girls first learn about empathy from their mothers, mostly by example. When I cry over a news story about a plane crash, I am showing my daughter what compassion looks like. When I scold her for teasing an unpopular boy in school, I am training her to be sensitive and sympathetic. And when I stay up all night with her sick brother, I am giving her a demonstration of devotion.

Like many mothers, I'm training my daughter to be empathic, endowing her with a capacity for this female trait. Because she identifies with me—at least so far—she aspires to be equally caring and sympathetic. Mothers pass this talent on to their daughters in a kind of emotional tradition, a psychological gift from one generation to the next. But as hard as I try to pass it on to my son, he refuses to accept this gift. When he sees me cry, he laughs. When I scold him for teasing, he thinks I'm being ridiculously sensitive. When I stay up all night with him, he doesn't notice. At the age of nine, he has already refused to learn to be empathic and caring. To him, feeling deeply for other people just isn't his job.

In her book about how women learn to be mothers, psychoanalyst Nancy Chodorow writes that girls define themselves by their ability to feel for other people in a way that boys never do. Girls view their empathy skills as proper and appropriate; they know they're *supposed* to be sympathetic and caring and nice. They're taught about sugar and spice and everything nice.

Although this description may sound out-of-date and old-fashioned, a legacy left over from the 1950s or 1960s, it's not. Women's supreme ability to be empathic and to feel sympathy for other people is alive and doing very well indeed. In my research, many more women than men agree that they find it very easy to feel sympathy for other people. But almost no women find it as easy to feel sympathy for themselves. It's ironic that women's admirable ability to feel so deeply for other people doesn't extend to themselves. It's like a hostess who serves a huge and delicious meal to her guests but doesn't save anything for herself.

Women don't feel empathy for themselves either. It's their tragic empathic flaw; they give to everyone else but the one person who sometimes needs it most. Women are great listeners; they comfort, they soothe, they care. When women or men need a shoulder to cry on or someone just to listen to their problems, research shows that they almost always seek out a woman. Women are willing and able to do this for a husband or a best friend, a neighbor or an aunt, a coworker or a child, but they almost never bother to listen to themselves.

Women's capacity for caring begins so early in life, before they even understand what empathy means, that some researchers feel that it must be partly biological. Even among two-year-old children, "girls show more empathy and sympathy than boys when they see someone in distress," says Carolyn Zahn-Waxler, a research psychologist at the National Institute of Mental Health in Baltimore, Maryland. In one of her experiments, she brings toddlers into a room with a crying baby or with their own mother, who pretends to be hurt. The two-year-old girls are much more likely than the boys to bring the baby a bottle, to try to reassure the baby, or to pat the mommy or baby on the head. These are signs that the girls are feeling sympathy, that they feel bad because *someone else* does.

"It's a pattern that we see more in girls than in boys, and it begins at a very early age," Zahn-Waxler says. Early on, "females may be more receptive to the distress of others," she explains. This is true even among infants, since baby girls react much more dramatically to the distress of other babies than do baby boys. Baby girls cry longer and louder when they hear another infant cry than when they hear another noise that's just as loud. But baby boys don't.

Not only do little girls start out in life as more sympathetic than boys, but they grow up with ongoing lessons in how important it is for them to stay that way. They learn that it's feminine to be nice and caring and to put themselves last. But their large capacity for empathy might very well be what makes women so vulnerable to feeling guilty and depressed. Feeling so deeply for other people makes it harder for women to recognize their own needs. Because they use up so much of their emotional reserve on other people, worrying about the well-being of those they love, more of them suffer from depression.

The moral: Being nice carries a price.

When women comfort others, when they help people deal with pain, they begin to take on that pain as their own, like an overly sympathetic psychiatrist or priest. In fact, by the age of thirteen or fourteen, more girls than boys are depressed. And this difference lasts throughout their lives: Twice as many grown women as men suffer from depression.

Barbara Klinger, a thirty-six-year-old teacher, has such an amazing capacity for sympathy and caring, she's like a therapist and minister and social worker all rolled into one. She is hopelessly devoted to everyone in her family, but she's often overwhelmed with sadness too.

Barbara lives in California with her husband, Mark, and their children, Ellie, six, and Jamie, two. Ellie was born with a congenital heart problem and needed open-heart surgery when she was six days old. The child has had three other major operations and suffers from language and learning problems as well as a permanent immune deficiency.

Her daughter's terrible physical traumas have left Barbara so emotionally raw that it's as if all her nerve endings are exposed, open and pulsing for the world to see. She's tremulous and vulnerable. Mention her child's name and she seems ready to burst into uncontrollable tears. As she tries to write her name, her hand trembles; she shakes.

At every single moment of the day, Barbara focuses all of her love and concentration and intelligence on how to keep her daughter healthy, how to get her son to eat more, how to make sure her husband is relaxed. But for herself, Barbara doesn't have the time of day.

When I ask about her own health, how she's feeling, she literally cannot hear what I say.

"What?" she asks me, dazed and confused by a question about her well-being.

Barbara is the kind of wife who, after realizing that her husband was seriously moody and depressed, went to get counseling for herself so that she could learn to cope with his mercurial temper. Mark is not a warm or supportive man, not particularly kind or encouraging—an insight that Barbara has had but will never allow herself to say out loud. Instead, she compromises, she makes do, she sacrifices. She is overflowing with sympathy and concern for her insecure husband and for her sick child, but she has none left over for herself.

## Learning to Be Last

Along with an innate tendency to sacrifice and to be sympathetic, many women also spend their lives learning to be last. My childhood friend has moved through life's passages accommodating everyone she ever cared for—her parents, her friends, her husband, her children. She has always put other people first, accumulating so much sacrificial baggage that I don't see how she can ever let it go.

My old friend is, I think, secretly proud of how much she gives up for her family. So are many Italian, Irish, Jewish, and other ethnic mothers who have a reputation for enjoying their martyrdom, for reveling in the sacrifices they make for their children. When a young Italian mother I know, with three children under the age of four, begins moaning that her hair's a mess, her nails are a mess, and her body's a mess, I can tell that she's not complaining. She's *bragging*. Being a mess is her proof that she's a good, sacrificial mother.

My Jewish grandmother always wanted to sit in the most uncomfortable chair and to eat only the parts of the chicken that no one else wanted, like the neck and the heart.

There are hundreds of ethnic jokes about martyred mothers who live to suffer for their families. For example: How many Jewish mothers does it take to change a lightbulb?

"None. That's okay, I'll just sit here in the dark."

But the reality is sometimes even more comical than the jokes.

I have a Jewish friend who caters not only to her husband and two children but also to their big, hairy dog. The husband, the children, and the animal all come first, before she does. When her ten-year-old son scrapes his tortilla chip on the bottom of a nearly empty jar of bean dip and asks her to go buy more, she does. When her husband expects her to prepare a massive brunch for the twelve friends he invites over at the last minute, she does. And when the dog is so scared of the invisible fence that he won't go outside unless she puts him in the car and backs up to the street, she does that too.

Although many mothers, like this friend, live a life centered on sacrifice, a few have the heartbreaking suspicion that whatever they do, it just isn't enough. They want to give more, try harder, do better. So they go to incredible extremes of sacrifice just to make sure.

Clara-Lucille Rothbart, thirty-eight, went to the outer limits of sacrifice by leading an almost inhuman double life for five years.

Working as a nurse in a local hospital from eleven at night until seven in the morning, five days a week, Clara-Lucille also stayed awake all day long and took care of her two young children. In her mind, she was the perfect stay-at-home mom, except that she also happened to work full time.

She was two mothers for the price of one.

"At the time, I felt we needed the salary, and I didn't want the children in day care. I wanted my children to have me at home. This way, I could be at home, and they would never notice I was gone," she says. "And I still took them swimming and I didn't have to change their lives, and we got my salary too."

Bringing home a respectable income by night and being with her children by day, Clara-Lucille was a Supermom with a secret, nocturnal life. She stayed awake all day, so she was there in body, though not in spirit. Because she was constantly sleep deprived, Clara-Lucille wasn't always totally lucid. She didn't finish every sentence she started, nor did she always know which way she wanted to turn when she'd come to a stop sign. But she was proud that she spent all day with her children.

Afraid to drift off to sleep with two rambunctious toddlers at her feet, Clara-Lucille never took a nap, because she wasn't sure she'd be able to wake up. Scrubbing and vacuuming all day long to stay awake, she had the most spotless house in the neighborhood. When her husband came home, she'd make dinner, clean up, and collapse into bed around 8:00 P.M., waking up two hours later so she could get to work by eleven.

It was a ridiculous and dangerous way to live, but nobody told Clara-Lucille that. Sacrificing herself for her family was a habit that came naturally, one that she accepted without question.

"It was not very healthy, not something I'd ever do again," she admits now. "Nobody asked me to do it that way. It was just easiest at the time."

Easier for her husband and children, maybe, but not for her. It took a spectacular car crash to wake Clara-Lucille out of her sacrificial stupor, and then only because she had to have surgery. Not until she was in a hospital bed, as a patient and not as a nurse, did she realize how much she needed to sleep.

Clara-Lucille indulged in her extreme sacrifice for so long because nobody noticed that she was doing it. After all, she was doing what everyone expects of a mother; she was putting herself last for the sake of her family.

How did Clara-Lucille learn to put herself last so perfectly? When does a woman's talent for this kind of self-denial begin?

It begins early, and it's sustained by great social pressure. By the age of two or three, little girls are already learning to accommodate themselves to little boys, discovering that it's best to acquiesce. Preschool girls avoid playing with boys, in part because they know they'll get bossed around and not be able to use the toys they want. Thrown together in a classroom, little boys tend to ignore the girls or else don't respond when girls try to speak up. Even when little boys do pay attention to girls, it's often just to taunt or to tease. The girls figure this out pronto. So they avoid the boys; they make it a point not to get in their way.

By the age of ten or twelve, girls are beginning to defer to every-one, not just to boys. It's a time when they may also lose their self-confidence and assertiveness, when they begin to suppress what they really think and feel, says psychologist Carol Gilligan. Just before puberty, girls lose their passion to disagree and to fight for what they believe in. These girls turn into submissive women, females who are always nice and caring and selfless. Eventually, such girls probably will become sacrificial mothers.

Another symptom of how girls lose a vital part of themselves is the way their self-esteem plummets between fourth and tenth grades. They go from being confident and cocky ten-year-olds to hesitant, self-demeaning fifteen-year-olds. Part of the reason this happens is that when they reach puberty, girls are much more nega-tive and unhappy than boys about the way their bodies are chang-ing. Teenage girls are unbearably self-conscious about their bodies, and they begin to hate the way they look. For this reason, girls invariably have lower self-esteem than boys.

Parents reinforce their daughters' insecurities by treating their teenage boys and girls very differently, by training their daughters to expect to sacrifice. Mothers and fathers are less likely to pay their daughters than their sons for doing things around the house, for example. Parents pay teenage boys to do outdoor chores such as washing cars and windows. But when girls do indoor jobs, such as cooking and washing dishes, they often work for free. The message parents send to daughters is that girls do family work for love, but sons do it for money. So while daughters have to sacrifice for family, sons don't.

In *Reviving Ophelia*, Mary Pipher writes that teenage girls suffer from a chronic inability to think well of themselves. She advises them to avoid this fate by holding on to their true self, trusting it "as the source of meaning and direction in their lives." If girls do lose their true self so young, then they are primed and ready for sacrifice when they become wives and mothers.

It's not likely, though, that every single girl loses herself on her journey to adulthood. Only some teenage girls succumb to this loss of self. These unlucky girls suffer from "false self" behavior; they pretend to be someone they're not. In her research about what happens to girls who have a false self, Susan Harter, a psychologist at the University of Denver, finds that they're the ones who really hate themselves. She asks boys and girls between the ages of twelve and fifteen if they agree with such statements as: "Some kids usually don't say what's on their mind." If they do, they probably have a false self. These girls often have another emotional handicap—they have an extremely feminine outlook on life. Feminine girls aren't necessarily the ones who wear frilly dresses or speak softly or have curly hair; it's not their physical style that matters. They do hold traditionally feminine beliefs; they have a feminine *emotional* style. These girls care about what happens to other people, they feel bad if someone else does, they always try to understand people's problems, and they see themselves as kind and caring. They are the epitome of a traditional, selfless woman, budding June Cleavers for the 2000s. Girls who are utterly feminine suffer from the curse of niceness, of trying to please everyone else all the time. They've learned the lesson that it's easier to catch flies with honey than with vinegar, so they smile when they're not happy and they laugh when they're not amused.

Add false self to feminine outlook, wait a few years, and you've got a sacrificial mother.

If a feminine girl has a highly feminine mother, then she's really in trouble. A mother who buries her true self, who has no views of her own, usually doesn't respect her daughter's right to think for herself either. This kind of mother raises her daughter to believe that what she thinks doesn't matter, that it's her role in life to be equally self-less and self-denying. So sacrificial mothers raise daughters who grow up to be sacrificial mothers, in an endless cycle of sacrifice.

A feminine mother who raises a feminine daughter produces a girl who is as self-negating as her mother. And when a girl's true self vanishes early, it will be that much harder to rescue when she grows up to become a wife and mother.

If only for their daughters' sake, then, mothers must learn to temper their impulse to sacrifice, to balance it with a robust attention to themselves and their own needs, to give their daughters a healthy example to follow.

Some mothers might argue, saying that it's not so terrible to put yourself last for the sake of your family. After all, if nature has given women a predisposition for sacrifice, it must serve a useful purpose. Surely it helped prehistoric mothers keep their infants alive. Mothers spend only fifteen or twenty years in deep sacrifice, so why not?

Because there is very little evidence that a mother's constant sacrifice does her children any good at all, and it may actually harm her daughters. Mothers who are extreme sacrificers encourage their daughters to have a false self, almost guaranteeing that the girls will suffer from low self-esteem and an inability to form opinions of their own.

Mothers who take sacrifice to the limit also hurt themselves. Years of self-denial pile up like unwashed laundry until a sacrificial mother loses her self completely. What she wants doesn't matter, what she needs doesn't count. This is a woman without a self, a woman who is not fully human. She might as well be a Stepford Wife, a robotic device built to service her family, a live-in servant.

A mother with a false self probably doesn't know that she has such a problem. She may deny it or insist that because her sacrifices help her children, her fate doesn't matter. But mothers with a false self often suffer silently and unwittingly, sinking into a quiet anger and bitterness that can fester for years.

When my children were young, I always put myself last but never admitted to myself that I was doing it. I lost confidence in myself as a competent adult. I often felt uneasy and confused. I spent those years in a slow burn of resentment that culminated in a near ulcer and waves of unpredictable and terrible headaches.

Mothers who sacrifice too much, as I did, who submerge their true selves too deeply, live a lifetime of lies. They are troubled by self-doubt and a lack of confidence; they have bouts of depression and sadness. Not only are they plagued by these serious emotional problems, but they will even suffer physically. Sacrificial mothers are likely to be bothered by headaches, weight problems, stomach ailments, and an array of other symptoms that don't trouble men nearly as often.

This is the sacrifice syndrome, and it can be extremely harmful to women.

## Two

# Making a Habit of Sacrifice

It might be one of life's great truths that mothers sacrifice more than fathers do and that these sacrifices may ultimately harm them in insidious ways. But let's not forget the other equally vital truth about motherhood: Babies bring women infinite joy.

With all this talk about self-denial and sacrifice, it's important to remember that children deliver to their mothers the purest happiness there is. The intense elation that accompanies childbirth is unmatched by any other event in a woman's life. It's better than great sex, more moving than first love, more satisfying than winning a Nobel Prize or an Academy Award.

Sacrifice becomes that much more tolerable because it's accompanied by such enormous pleasure, like lying on a bed of nails while finding out that you've won a million-dollar lottery. In case it's not obvious, my research leaves no doubt that children bring women their greatest joy in life and their deepest sense of fulfillment. Half of mothers fall in love with their baby even before it's born, and many say that the intensity of that love is absolutely overwhelming.

As the years pass, a mother's relationship with her children becomes the best part of her life, my research confirms. Mothers are almost unanimous in their view that the bond they have with their children is the most thrilling and satisfying one in life, that it's better than marriage, better than sex, better than friendship. When they are stripped bare, facing the day of judgment, women confess that they value their children more than anyone or anything else on Earth.

This is the reason that mothers are willing to give up their lives, and their selves, for the sake of their children. And it's why they do.

When I ask mothers to name the one person they need most of all, they don't hesitate to answer. Their need for their child, or children, runs deepest. Mothers need children more powerfully than they need a man or a best friend or a sister or even their own mother. It's why they're so afraid of letting go, of losing that precious child. It explains why one mother I know begs the head of her daughter's nursery school to cut back on its hours, because she can't bear to have the child out of her sight for so long. It's why a friend of mine is terrified of sending her five-year-old off into what she calls the "black hole" that is kindergarten, because she'll be uninformed about whole chunks of her child's day. And it's why another has recurring nightmares about sending her only child off to college, bad dreams in which the boy is kidnapped and she never sees him again.

Mothers admit that they devote the greatest amount of emotional energy to their children, more than they ever give to their husband or to their friends or to themselves. It's as if their heart pours out love like rays from a lighthouse beacon, focusing millions of watts of candlepower on that precious child.

I call this fervent and passionate love baby joy. Baby joy is vital, because it's what triggers decades of sacrificial motherhood. Some mothers outgrow their baby-inspired, insane levels of sacrifice, easing up on self-denial as their child grows and becomes less needy. Others, though, become addicted to it, turning themselves into sacrifice machines. These mothers crank up their sacrifice thermostat to high and keep it there, at a boil, for decades.

A boiling-point sacrificial mother is easy to recognize. She's the woman who takes all four of her children to the hairdresser every time she needs a haircut, although her husband has volunteered to watch them during the evening, because she feels guilty about doing something by herself, for herself. She's the mother who exercises only when she's pregnant, because it's for the good of her unborn child, but won't when it's just for her. She's the working mother who happily shops for groceries at ten-thirty at night, so that she can see her children for a few hours before they go to sleep.

There are lukewarm sacrificers too, loving mothers who don't make sacrifice a priority, like the friend of mine who can't wait to ship her three children off to sleepaway camp every summer, even though they beg to stay home, because she wants that month of freedom. Or another woman I know who got pregnant for the first time at the age of forty-nine, by artificial insemination with another woman's eggs, then left her very premature twins for a week, only a few months after they were born, so she could attend a professional convention in Canada.

None of these mothers is best, they're just different. The haircut mom believes that her relentless self-denial will make her children happier. My professional friend doesn't agree; she makes her career a priority. When I first heard that she'd flown off and left her babies, I admit that I instantly disapproved. After all she went through to conceive and deliver those babies, I thought, how can she just abandon them? Then I took a deep breath and stopped to think. Her ability to focus on herself and her own needs, as I know very well, will ultimately benefit her twins a lot more than her ability to sacrifice for their sake.

As we'll see, there is *no evidence* that a mother's extreme sacrifices will influence her children to grow up any healthier or wealthier or wiser. In fact, just the *opposite* may be the case. All of my research points to the conclusion that women who learn how to indulge themselves occasionally, who make a point of taking time for themselves, make better mothers and wives, and they're also happier in just about every way possible.

## Measuring Sacrifice

Other than blatantly obvious examples, such as the highly sacrificial mother who's practically surgically attached to her children and the less sacrificial one who yearns for an annual vacation from it all, how do I know for sure which mothers are most sacrificial and which are less so? I give women a test to find out, one I devised to be a simple but reliable way to measure people's attitudes to sacrifice. It includes such questions as: How often do you sacrifice your needs and desires for your children or your husband? Deep down, do you believe that sacrifice is your job? Do you get so little help from your husband that you view him as just another child? In my research, about one in three mothers turn out to be an Extreme Sacrificer who believes that her primary job in life is to sacrifice for her children.

When I give this test to parents, I find that mothers score consistently higher than fathers do. This is one of the strongest pieces of evidence to support my assumption that sacrifice is a primary "should" of motherhood, that mothers feel compelled to make sacrifices for their children in ways that fathers do not. The difference is partly biological, partly psychological, and partly social, the result of a complex conspiracy of nature and nurture.

What's also intriguing is that there aren't special demographic characteristics that distinguish the mothers who sacrifice most. Extremely sacrificial mothers are not more educated or wealthier than less sacrificial mothers. A dentist is not necessarily more sacrificial than a hairdresser. A mother who stays at home all day making brownies and play dough from scratch might not be more sacrificial than one who works twelve-hour shifts in a hospital emergency room. In other words, social and economic factors, such as education, income, work status, and marital status, don't have much effect on how much a mother sacrifices.

There is, however, one extremely reliable way to predict how much a mother will sacrifice—by knowing how old her children are. Mothers of newborns and toddlers are definitely the most sacrificing. If a woman has at least one child younger than the age of five or six, it's a fairly good bet that she'll score above a 12 or 13 on my Sacrifice Test. If her children are of school age, her score will be slightly lower, and if they're teenagers or beyond, it will be even lower. Remember, though, that even though this is true, mothers of children of all ages have higher sacrifice scores than fathers do.

Maggie Fisher, thirty-eight, is a mother with young children whose soaring sacrifice score goes well above the boiling point.

She's caught in a web of sacrifice from which she can't imagine escaping, one that her husband, Bob, has never even noticed. The couple have four children under the age of eight, including five-year-old twins. Bob's unwritten rule is this: "I never take all four." Neither does Maggie's mother or an occasional teenage baby-sitter. The only person willing to be with all four Fisher children at once, then, is their mother.

Maggie deeply envies Bob's delectable freedom.

"He gets a shower, he eats breakfast, and he leaves the house. He can just be gone. He goes out at night, to baseball games. If I want to go out, I have to make complicated arrangements, but his stuff always gets first priority," Maggie says. She even resents the fact that when he goes to the bathroom, he gets to do it alone. She never has the luxury of solitude, even in the john.

Driving her van loaded with all four children, Maggie grows teary and sentimental when she's caught in a traffic jam at a major inter-section or if she's stuck at a red light that lasts too long. She used to be a civil engineer who designed those traffic signals for the state highway department, and she loved her work. She may not have been a master of the universe, but she was definitely master of the red, yellow, and green.

Maggie's extreme sacrifices have left her with almost no life of her own. Her children need her, her husband needs her; there's no room at all for what she needs.

Like Maggie, mothers of young children often face suprising obstacles in the early stages of motherhood, struggles that are char-acterized not only by a great deal of sacrifice but also by incredible frustration and unhappiness. It's shocking for mothers of such sweet, innocent little lambs to also feel so strangely unhappy and so alienated from their husbands.

## The Baby Bomb

Babies are so heartbreakingly lovely that many first-time mothers don't realize that the cuddly darling in the damp diaper just might be what's instigating mother's misery. The mother has to spend hours doing maintenance on her baby: he needs to be fed, dressed, diapered, played with, potty-trained, put to sleep, read to, chased away from traffic, steered clear of stairways and hot stoves. A baby is like a little car that needs constant tinkering for upkeep and repairs.

Many women, in fact, don't realize just how deeply traumatic that first year or two of being a new mother really is. Motherhood deals a woman two crushing blows at once—one to her sense of self and the other to her marriage. I call it the baby bomb, because it can pack the emotional equivalent of a devastating explosive device.

An enormous number of mothers with young children are deeply troubled. They're much less happy about their lives and about being a parent than all other mothers combined, according to my research. They're also incredibly insecure about their ability as parents and believe they just aren't good enough at it, especially when compared with parents of older children. They're more miserable about their bodies and they hate the way they look. Compared with other moms, they feel ugly most often, even though they're youngest and, theoretically at least, in the best physical shape.

My research shows that when they give birth, new mothers are intimidated, terrified, frustrated, and anxious for at least a year. They also feel as if they're not using their talents to the fullest. They're subject to crushing self-doubt and are at risk for serious depression, not only right after childbirth but for two or three years afterward.

In fact, an extraordinary number of mothers are depressed and unhappy long after their baby is no longer an infant. Rates of depression for mothers of one- and two-year-olds are twice as high as for other mothers, according to a recent medical school study.

While most mothers gain a sense of meaning and purpose in life from raising small children, half also confess that the job is essentially a perplexing and irritating one. One British study finds that it makes them want to scream with frustration and pull their hair out with boredom and annoyance. Mothers invest so much of their hearts and souls into their children that they are bound to feel anguish and sorrow sometimes. Children are a mother's greatest source of stress and worry, I find, and they cause much more frustration than she ever expected.

Being so sacrificial takes a toll on new mothers' sanity, and it's probably what makes them so vulnerable to depression and despair.

I met a woman a few years ago who was suffering from a full-blown depression when her two children were three years old and eight months old. She had no self-confidence, no sense of herself as a person other than a chubby, curly-haired drudge who could recite the lyrics from Sesame Street songs backwards and forwards. She told me once that every single thing she did was for her husband and her children. She was so self-negating that if she had ever looked into a mirror, she wouldn't have seen a reflection. But her unyielding sacrifice also made her hostile and remote. She'd wake up in the morning feeling an inexplicable and towering rage. I remember her as being mean and nasty, and so does she.

Following the advice of some friends, and reacting to a fear that she might harm her children, this woman saw a counselor who put her on Prozac, a powerful antidepressant. It was only when she emerged from her depression, she tells me, that she realized it was okay to pay attention to herself. Now this mother no longer considers it her job to take care of everyone in the family every moment of every day. The last time I spoke to her, she was thrilled with herself, because she'd also lost thirty pounds.

Becoming a mother can wreak havoc on a woman's equilibrium and her sense of self, and it also can seriously disrupt her marriage. More than half of couples discover that parenthood nearly ruins their relationship, at least temporarily. New mothers complain that after their baby is born they get less attention from their husbands. They say husbands not only kiss and hug them less often, but the couples argue more. And husbands say the same about their wives. Even a full year after the birth, about half of marriages are much worse than before; barely one in five is better, according to research by psychologists Carolyn and Philip Cowan at the University of California at Berkeley. And when I compare mothers with childless wives, I find that mothers are less happy about their marriage, regardless of how long it's been since their first child was born.

If you could fly in a spaceship and randomly zoom down on any married couple on the planet, it's a safe bet that you'd find a wife who's more unhappy about the marriage than her husband is.

Maybe wives are just more in tune with how they feel when things go wrong in relationships, like being able to recognize a bad cough or a suspicious rattle in the dishwasher. I find that more wives than husbands wish their spouse appreciated them more and listened to them more. This is especially true for mothers, who yearn to be cherished by their husbands. More wives than husbands also feel *unheard*—that when they have something "really important to say," their husbands don't really listen. These women feel as if they're pleading for support and understanding from men who are standing on the wrong side of the moon.

These problems only intensify after the birth of a first child, a time when wives are most likely to feel the aftershock effects of the bomb that hit their marriage.

A baby bomb landed right on thirty-seven-year-old Wendy Kellogg, despite the fact that she'd been taking birth control pills for years. Living a smug, child-free life, she worked long hours, exercised religiously, and took expensive and eccentric self-improvement courses in beading, wine-tasting, and hand-tinted black-and-white photography. She and her husband, Gerry, indulged and pampered each other by traveling, buying fine wines, and acquiring dogs, cats, birds, fish, and even a horse.

After she announced her pharmaceutically impossible pregnancy, Gerry made it clear that his life was not going to change one bit.

"I'm not giving up my hockey league," he told her.

And he never did. For Wendy, though, this miracle baby was an invitation to sacrifice, an entry into a self-denying world she barely knew existed. After her son was born, she cut back on work and exercise, she canceled all her classes, she farmed out every one of her pets, even the fish. She started cheating on her husband too, because her son had become the new love of her life.


## Becoming Baby Obsessed

The baby bomb is especially catastrophic if a mother becomes so obsessed by her baby that she completely neglects her self and her marriage. A baby-obsessed mother seems possessed, as if her infant has somehow cast a spell over her, turning a normal female into a kind of whirling sacrificial dervish. A mother who surrenders herself to sacrifice, who loses her self in her baby's demands, seems to have slid into an unbreakable trance.

One baby-obsessed mother I know won't let anything enter her four-month-old daughter's mouth that hasn't been washed first, even Mama's fingers. Every single night she washes all the baby's toys with soap and water. This formerly clear-headed woman used to run a day-care center for a large Hollywood studio before her daughter was born. Now that she's a mother, though, she'd never send her own child there—it's too dirty. This woman also sings to the baby all day long, even though the effort exhausts her. But she only hums "Rock-a-Bye, Baby," because she doesn't want her four-month-old daughter to hear scary stories about babies who fall out of cradles.

Another baby-obsessed mother I met takes the Beverly Hills approach to child rearing—her not-quite-three-year-old son gets what he wants whenever he wants it. He is the true head of the household, a tiny tyrant in command of two cowering and submissive adults. Because he insists on drinking whatever his parents are having, for instance, this woman and her husband are allowed to drink only water for breakfast, lunch, and dinner. If they have any wine or coffee or soda or beer, he'll want some too. So they drink only water, and so does their boy.

It's easy to recognize baby-obsessed mothers like these, even ones who are slightly less fervent. They're the women who ride in the back with the baby in his car seat while their husband drives alone up front. They use a crib monitor for years, long after the newborn is no longer new. They carry special food in Ziploc bags and small juice bottles or boxes everywhere, in case he's ever hungry or thirsty. They refuse to leave the child with a baby-sitter unless it's a certified blood relative.

A mother I met in California calls herself "leery and wary" of leaving her child with a sitter—she doesn't trust any strangers, even the nannies her friends use. She says she'd insist on knowing if the woman could administer CPR; she'd want to give a potential sitter some kind of qualifying quiz. Really. She'd leave her daughter with her parents or sister, but they live 3,000 miles away, so that's out. Instead, she always asks herself if this particular movie is worth being away from her daughter for three hours; since her answer is always no, she never goes.

Extremely baby obsessed and sitter phobic, this woman hasn't been to a movie in two years—and she's in the entertainment industry!

She's not all that unusual, as it turns out. During their first year with a firstborn, most mothers are never away from their baby for a weekend, and more than half wait at least six months before going out for an evening with their husband, according to my research.

Indeed, a surprising number of new mothers become baby obsessed, superanxious about every sound and movement their infant makes. They panic at every loud burp; a sudden twitch terrifies them. More than half of mothers either worry constantly or much of the time during their child's first year of life, I find. These worrywarts call the doctor more often, feel guilty about more things, and get up more times with their baby during the night. They even change their baby's diapers more often!

Many mother's groups are chock full of these baby-obsessed mothers. The classes, for mothers of newborn babies or toddlers, are a kind of hothouse for baby-obsessed mothers, women who are attracted to such places like bees to a can of Coke on a hot day. They thrive in the company of like-minded obsessives, where new mothers can compare whose baby holds his head up best and which one turns over first. They join the group to give their six-week-old infants a chance to look at other baby faces.

In one such class, a mom and baby group held in a Los Angeles psychotherapist's suite, I met ten new mothers, at least seven of whom were baby obsessed. The group was held in a large, high-ceilinged room furnished with comfortable chairs, huge pillows, mats, and a gigantic Oriental carpet. The place was decorated in an overabundance of Klimt posters featuring voluptuous and exotic longhaired mothers holding pudgy, rosy-cheeked babies, images that bear little or no relationship to real life with a newborn. Most of these moms were in their twenties, and they entered the class carting their babies in special seats, weighted down with diaper bags, blankets, bottles, and burp cloths. Many had that recognizably stunned new-mother look, a combination of sleep deprivation and euphoria, confusion and bliss, that takes months or years to dissipate. Still, they seemed happy to be here: out of their pajamas, out of the house, out in public with other adults.

These new mothers paid for six weeks of maternal group therapy because they were desperate to find out how badly they will damage their baby when they go back to work, if other new mothers feel as disoriented and disturbed as they sometimes do, and if anybody else knows how to care for their newborn by instinct, because they surely don't.

They also love being with other new mothers who are as baby obsessed as they are.

Mothers who are baby obsessed for the long haul often enroll their toddlers in a once- or twice-a-week class for mothers and two-year-olds. These moms are often older, on the far side of thirty, and I'm struck by how incredibly anxious these gray-haired mothers are about caring for their child. They're the kind of mothers who, at snack time, crowd around the toddler-size table to choose the most pleasing combination of crackers, Cheerios, and Crispix for their child. They'll push and shove each other to get that last Ritz for the little darling. One mother addresses a question to her barely verbal two-year-old, loud enough so that all the others can hear. "We learned about syncopation last night, didn't we, Justine?"

But all this worry and overeager devotion to mothering may not be doing these babies and toddlers much good. By their own admission, baby-obsessed moms seem to have the most troublesome tots. They're most likely to describe their new baby as noisy, a poor sleeper, and cantankerous. It's not surprising, then, that they feel exhausted all the time and don't enjoy their precious one as much as other mothers do. They wear themselves out with worry.

A mother I know tells me that her child's first year was the longest of her life, stretching as if into infinity, because she was so consumed by sacrifice. She never let that baby cry for more than five seconds, she ate dinner while holding the child, she didn't breathe while the baby slept, and she carried the infant everywhere, all day long.

She made me laugh, not out of contempt but from sympathy. I was exactly the same kind of first-time mother. My daughter cried constantly when she was born, and so did I. I worried about her nonstop. I rocked her in my arms all day and all night; at three in the morning, I'd hold her in front of the television, swaying gently to MTV. I held her as I ate, dripping pizza sauce on her tiny head. The first time she had diarrhea, I was hysterical and mobilized three friends, late at night, to search the city for the special water my doctor had recommended. I once raced her to the doctor because she had a really red tongue, not remembering that she'd eaten cherry Jell-O a few hours earlier.

Many sacrificial mothers lose themselves in obsessive baby tending, as I did. In some ways, it's easier for a mother to give in to sacrifice than it is for her to try to keep a part of her self as her very own, a core identity separate from her family. That's hard work because it takes so much conscious effort to focus on one's self, especially for a new mother, for whom being self-centered is taboo.

A self-absorbed mother is a bad one, like the bad-mother cartoons that show moms who make promises they don't keep and who are so preoccupied they give their kids orange soda instead of orange juice. A bad mother doesn't go overboard for her baby, and she worries about herself way too much. If a woman is too ambitious or too successful or too self-satisfied, then she must be a bad mother.

The seeds for this idea, that a bad mother is one who is not sacrificial enough, were planted fifty years ago, when Dr. Benjamin Spock published his first advice book for new mothers. The concept was immediately accepted as gospel, as totally natural. Early in the century, good mothers had to be concerned only about their child's physical well-being, how often and what he ate, when he learned to use a toilet, how straight his spine was. But Spock advised mothers to cater to their child's emotional needs, not just physical ones. So mothers had to worry about their child's self-esteem, popularity at school, happiness. In Spock's psychologized world, a good mother became the one who sacrificed herself to her child's inner life. Since mothers were the ones with most of the responsibility for their children's welfare, they were usually to blame if things went wrong.

Spock fertilized the seedlings of maternal guilt too, implying that a good mother takes the blame. In part, that's why so many sacrificial mothers feel so guilty so often.

## The Guilt Olympics

When I talk to mothers, they almost always use the word "guilt" within the first five minutes of our discussion. It doesn't really even matter what the topic is. A mother's guilt is like an itch that can't be scratched, a nagging annoyance that refuses to go away. I don't think I've ever met one mother who didn't feel guilty about something. We all have "the guilties," as one writer puts it.

Erma Bombeck once said that "some mothers have so much guilt, they can't even eat a breath mint without sharing it." That's the problem in a nutshell: Mothers can't do anything for themselves, even if it's only having a better-tasting mouth or buying a pair of new shoes or getting a haircut.

There are as many guilt stories as there are mothers, so the list of potential guilt is just about infinite. Mothers feel guilty, of course, about what they do, especially if they're having fun by themselves. I've spoken to mothers too guilt-stricken to enjoy, say, an all-expense-paid business trip to Hawaii. One mother of a sixteen-month-old went on a five-day trip to Bermuda that her husband had arranged for her. But she felt so guilty about spending the money on herself when she should have been at home, cleaning, that her girl-friend offered to get a vacuum cleaner sent up to their hotel room.

Mothers feel guilty about what they don't do, too. One divorced mother forgot to pick up her two sons from her ex-husband's house because she was so busy at work. That was good, she told me, for several weeks of unrelenting guilt.

Mothers even feel guilty about what they think; another mother tells me that she's so guilty because, as she rocked her perpetually cranky, colicky infant daughter, she had a mental image of throwing rocks at the child.

Mothers always feel guilty about what they do wrong, of course. A well-meaning but exhausted working mother of two girls woke up at midnight when her daughter was crying about an earache. She sent the girl back to bed and fumbled in the dark for some Tylenol. After dragging herself to her daughter's bedroom, she had to shake the child awake to pour the medicine down her throat. It really annoyed the exhausted woman that the girl didn't seem to know which ear hurt. That's because it was the wrong ear, wrong daughter.

Finally, mothers even feel guilty about what they do *right*. A mother who is convinced that she's doing a pretty good job raising her three children tells me that she feels guilty about not feeling guilty!

Most of the mothers I've studied feel guilty almost as soon as their first child is born: With baby obsession comes baby guilt. During their first baby's first year, mothers feel guilty about being too tired, about not spending enough time with their husbands, about not playing with the babies enough, and about being furious at the babies. Yes, although mortified and ashamed to admit it, half of new mothers confess that they get angry at their newborn baby. One mother tells me that she screamed at her two-month-old for being so "immature." As she was yelling the word, she knew it was asinine, but she couldn't stop herself.

Unlike baby obsession, which some mothers outgrow, an extraordinary number of mothers seem to feel even more guilty as the years pass. Mothers find whole new worlds of guilt possibilities as their children grow. Working mothers, for instance, feel guilty about not being there when children come home from school, about not being able to go on class trips or to participate in school activities. And they feel just as guilty about not spending enough time with their husbands and about losing their sexual desire.

Working mothers who are especially sacrificial also feel tortured and guilty about their free time—they feel obligated to spend all of it with their children. It's as if taking time for themselves is somehow *stealing* it from the children.

A mother of two school-age children feels crushing guilt about being out of the house "for all those hours" at work, even though she's a school librarian who's home every day no later than 4:00 P.M. She can't bring herself to use any of her after-work time for herself, although her husband doesn't seem to have that problem. He runs every morning and plays basketball and volleyball after work. But, she says, it's *her* responsibility to be with the children, not his, so she feels guilty when she has to leave them. He doesn't.

The librarian's guilt arises not because she's bad or stupid, but because she feels so much tenderness and love for her children. The source of most mothers' guilt is a blinding and benevolent love that gets disastrously bent out of shape and distorted into guilt. Because women tend to be so empathic, feeling the needs and fears of loved ones as their own, they react with guilt when those desires aren't fulfilled.

If my children aren't serenely happy at school or at camp or at home, I feel twinges of guilt. When they were small, I remember feeling that it was somehow my fault when my daughter came home from kindergarten crying because her best friend had made a nasty comment to her on the bus ride home. I also felt guilty about my son one fall, because he was assigned to a soccer team with a terrible, unfriendly coach and played ten games in sheer misery. It felt like my fault that he hadn't gotten a place on a better team.

In retrospect, it's easy to see how foolish I was for feeling so responsible for every emotional injury or disappointment my children faced. But I was proud of being so in tune with them, with their defeats and sadness and with their elation and pride. Yet after a while I could no longer distinguish between my needs and those of my children. I was constantly worrying about their friends and their sports, behaving as if all their problems were mine, and I began to feel guilty and responsible for everything that happened to them. I didn't really ever worry about my friends or my husband or my life. This was not, I came to realize, a good position to be in. I had to learn to separate myself from them, to go through a kind of second, psychological childbirth, to wrench my needs from theirs. I had to find a way to give equal time to my needs, to unlearn my aptitude for guilt.

Getting rid of guilt is a personal challenge, the key to becoming less sacrificial in a way that improves a mother's feelings about herself and will ultimately benefit her children as well.

Avoiding guilt, though, is not as easy as it sounds. It's not like avoiding wet paint on the street or finding a detour around a traffic jam. As long as mothers love their children, they will find a way to channel part of that love into guilt. Mothers must tease apart these two distinct strands of feeling that bind them to their children—the love and the guilt—to try to strengthen the first while letting go of the second. They must take steps to temper that guilt, to keep it down to a level that won't be crippling.

One way to dampen guilt feelings is to step back for a moment, to get an objective view of the situation, as I do when recalling my feelings of long-ago guilt. The way to gain some objectivity about your situation is to talk about it with someone else or to write it down. When you talk about your guilt, you will gain an outsider's opinion of your position from someone who isn't as emotionally enmeshed as you are. The longer you talk about it, and the more details you disclose, the more obvious your options will become. Find an unbiased friend or a counselor, a sympathetic sister or an aunt, and unburden yourself.

If you have no one to talk to about your guilt, write it down. Make a list of everything that makes you feel guilty, then put it away for a week. When you look at it again, some of it will probably seem foolish. Examine the list carefully and make a note about who is making you feel guilty. Feeling guilty for not being there when your children get home from school gets a C, for child-induced guilt. Feeling guilty about having a dirty house or being out of shape is personal guilt; mark it M, for me. Feeling guilty for not going out often enough with your husband is spouse guilt, so give it an H, for husband.

Which person is the source of most of your guilt—your children, you, or your husband? Figure out where you need to focus your guilt-destroying energy and what you can actually change to get rid of the guilt. You may not be able to be there after school, but you can be there before school or at bedtime. That will have to do; it's good enough.

If your personal guilt count is high, do whatever you can about it. Take a walk every day to get in shape, assign cleaning chores to your family so the house is neater. Or give up the idea that a spotless house is best; admit right now that you don't have a clean house and probably never will.

If your marital guilt is high, set a date once a week or once a month that you spend only with your husband, either out in public or in the living room, all alone. Do what you can to assuage your guilt about him.

Change what is changeable and learn to let go of the rest.

If feeling guilty were productive, schools would teach it and pediatricians would prescribe it. But a mother's guilt doesn't help anyone—certainly not her children—and it makes her much less effective as a mother and as a person.

## Work as Sacrifice

Mothers have an ongoing and intimate dance with guilt, and now that so many of them are working, they have a whole new arena in which to practice it, a Madison Square Garden for waltzing with work guilt.

Here's how the new work-and-guilt equation operates. Mothers feel they *should* stay at home with their babies, because children *need* a full-time mother. They feel that women have a responsibility to take care of their family. But mothers also want to work, because women have a responsibility to earn a living.

When I ask women what they think of a mother who stays at home and takes care of the children while her husband works, a majority say they respect her *more* for living her life this way. Women believe, then, that motherhood should be a full-time job for women. But when I ask the same women how fulfilling it is to stay at home with children, most say that although it's rewarding, it's not enough to "keep most women satisfied." In addition, a majority of wives feel that it's their responsibility to support their family, just as men do. So they believe women should work too.

Holding these two contradictory views at once—that it's best to stay at home but also not—is driving mothers crazy. If women have to work to provide for their family, then they feel guilty about not being full-time mothers. And if they don't have a paying job, they feel guilty about not working. It's a lose-lose trap; no matter which solution mothers choose, they lose.

Mothers are often torn between two sacrifices: sacrificing family for work or sacrificing work for family. Either choice hurts.

When Christine Laughlin gave up her career to stay home with her daughter, she thought she was doing what was best for her child. But what she didn't realize was that she had sacrificed her soul, the best part of her self, and it was probably doing more harm than good for her little girl.

Christine gave up an unusual job: She was a spy.

Right after graduating from college with a dual major in Russian and international relations, Christine got a job with an intelligence agency at the Department of Defense in Washington, D.C. She informed them that she wanted to go "into the field," spy lingo for being an overseas agent, as long as she could have running water and an absence of insect life. Unfortunately, in the former Soviet Union, generally speaking, inadequate plumbing and small, scurrying pests were quite normal. So, instead of going undercover, Christine got a plum job at agency headquarters as a project manager who analyzed what-if disaster scenarios.

Christine knew she had grabbed a brass ring on the career carousel, and she loved every minute of it. She was constantly challenged and excited about her work, waking up every day so eager to get going that she arrived at the office two hours before everybody else.

But when Christine got pregnant, she felt it was her duty to her baby to give up her career and stay home. She moved out of Washington, to a small town several hundred miles away, so that her husband could join the family business. It wasn't long before she became bored, fidgety, and frustrated. She was angry at herself, angry at her baby girl, and angry at her husband, resenting them for the misery she'd brought on herself. She'd given up thinking for a living—the worst thing that could have happened to her, she says. The woman who was so self-assured that she turned down a fabulous job offer because she doesn't like bugs now had no self-confidence at all.

Christine spent a long time mourning the loss of her spy self. It had been stolen from her, but she herself was the thief. All that unnecessary sacrifice had been *her choice*.

Two years after she quit the job of a lifetime, Christine decided that she had to find some kind of work, something that would require mental effort. But she'd moved too far away to go back to her old job, and in her new town, there wasn't appropriate work for an overeducated, Russian-speaking oddball like Christine. So she found a part-time job at a low-cost furniture store in a local mall. Instead of planning the defense of the free world, she now sells bunk beds and wall units. Believe it or not, she's better off than she was before she got this job.

Christine is convinced that she's a better mother when she works, because she's happier, her husband's happier, and so is her daughter. They spend their free time together, and she's no longer furious and frustrated all the time.

But for every mother like Christine, for whom it was a sacrifice not to work, there's another who'd give her front teeth to be able to stay at home. These mothers work full-time because they must, but every time they have to leave their children to go to work, it's a sacrifice. One of these moms tells me that her four-year-old daughter asks her, every day, why she has to go to work. Another says that the last sounds she hears as she leaves her two-year-old at day care are his cries. A third had to leave her seriously ill fourteen-year-old daughter alone during the day for three weeks and was grief-stricken because she could only check the child's temperature by telephone.

The irony is that work was supposed to take the sacrifice out of mothering; at least that's how Betty Friedan saw it thirty-five years ago when she wrote *The Feminine Mystique*. A satisfying career would provide mothers with an escape route from the mindless housewifery that trapped so many of them, Friedan believed. It was in work that mothers would derive their sense of purpose; it was how they would forge lives of their own.

A majority of wives and mothers do work outside the home now, but more in response to financial necessity than as an answer to Friedan's feminist dream. Half of married women even earn as much as their husbands do, which means that they contribute at least half of the household income. The economic result of this phenomenon is that women have become the new providers. Unfortunately, they have also been given the burden of twice as much responsibility, twice as much guilt, and twice as much sacrifice.

And twice as much work. Mothers now do a second shift of chores at home after a full day on the job. Maybe these mothers feel guilty about leaving their children every day, so they compensate by doing everything at home too. The woman who worked all night as a nurse and all day as a mom is someone who took the second shift to its hellish extreme. While most working mothers don't have a second shift that lasts eight or ten or twelve hours, they still do an enormous amount of what has to be done around the house. A great deal of research shows just how much more wives do than husbands. You probably don't need a Gallup poll to convince you that mothers do more laundry and cooking and vacuuming and grocery shopping and children's shoe-buying and birthday-party arranging than their husbands. It's just a fact of life.

Among mothers who work full time, my research shows that fewer than one in ten have husbands who share child care and household jobs. Instead, most mothers say that their husband does nothing or less than a quarter of what needs to be done around the house.

Working mothers can try their best to be Supermoms, racing home to serve nutritious meals, to help children with homework, to do laundry, to make Halloween costumes from scratch. But most of us know that this is an impossible dream, beyond the reach of mortal females who can't afford to hire a domestic staff. How can mothers reconcile their need to work with their compunction to do everything at home too, without getting sick or losing their minds?

Either they can find a husband who will eagerly do at least half of the chores without being told and without complaining, or they can cut back on their work, freeing up some time to do things at home. Either option will do, but the latter is almost always easier to arrange than the former. A major problem for women is that they don't learn to train their men to sacrifice.

A mother who finds part-time work can indulge her need to be at home and her need to be at work with the smallest possible doses of sacrifice and guilt. She can spend time with her children, run the household, and also earn an income. For families who can afford it, a part-time job is a mother's work solution for the millennium.

More and more mothers are sensing the inherent advantages that part-time work offers. Eager to find a part-time job, they are jealous of those who do. Most mothers now say that if they had a choice, they'd work part time. In my research, about half the women who work full time would really prefer to be working part time, and nearly as many at-home moms even wish they could find part-time employment too.

One mother with a part-time job as a YMCA lifeguard says she has the best of both worlds, because she gets to be at home and she also gets out of the house. Stuffing herself into a swimsuit for a few hours every day is her only form of self-indulgence. A pediatric nurse who works three days a week says that her life is so perfect that she's afraid it's all a dream that will end when she wakes up. She loves being a mom and she loves her part-time work, precisely because the dual responsibilities don't overwhelm her.

"I don't feel I'm missing out by not working full time or being home full time. My daughter goes out and catches frogs and salamanders and I get to be there, to hear her excitement," she says, "and I get to be a professional, with grown-ups who care about what they do."

It's clear to me that mothers who work part time are in better emotional health than both mothers who don't work and those who work full time. My research shows that the mothers who work part time, for example, are happiest about their work, their marriage, and how their lives are going.

A disadvantage of part-time work is that it's less engaging. Women who work part time are less likely to call it a career, referring to it as "just a job." Maybe it's this very *distancing* from their work that helps to keep them balanced. By not investing so much of themselves in their jobs, they don't have to sacrifice too much.

The flip side of a job that doesn't require sacrifice, of course, is that employers tend not to take part-time workers seriously, because they're not around all the time. Part-time workers are usually paid less than full-timers, they're promoted less often, and they rarely receive benefits of any kind. They're an exploitative boss's dream.

Then there's the biggest difficulty of all—finding decent part-time work. If you're lucky, like the pediatric nurse, you'll find an employer who's in the vanguard of hiring part-timers. She works in a pediatric practice in Philadelphia that consists only of part-timers, even the doctors, all of whom are mothers. You could be fortunate enough to strike a part-time deal with a former employer, but more likely you'll have to quit and start your own business. Doing so takes not only courage but also a bit of a financial cushion to soften the blows of lean times.

## The Procrastination Generation

As I've said, the majority of mothers raising children today work outside the home. All mothers these days belong to a baby-boom tribe of sacrificers. But what about the next generation, the girls who are now teenagers and young women in their twenties? Isn't it possible that they will be relatively free of the social constraints and psychological traits that encourage self-denial and sacrifice?

Not at all. I believe they are just as likely to become sacrificial mothers. It's clear that many of them have already taken a first step on the road to sacrifice by having problems with a false self. This early inability to express an authentic opinion or belief, combined with a strong empathic tendency, will lead them to sacrificial motherhood as surely as it did those of us who are already mothers.

The only way that young women can avoid sacrifice is by avoiding motherhood and marriage altogether. And they seem to be doing an excellent job of that. Young women now defer getting married and having children longer than ever before, according to Census Bureau statistics. Half of American women don't marry until after their twenty-fourth or twenty-fifth birthday, and one in five women in their early thirties has *never* married. A rather large group of adult women, slightly more than two in five, has not yet had children.

This is a generation of young people with a theme song right out of Peter Pan: "I won't grow up." They aren't compelled to mature in a hurry because they've had no great wars or terrible economic depressions to hurl them into adulthood. Many receive years of financial support and coddling from their parents, who pay for their college educations, for the security deposit on their first apartments, for the down payment on their first cars. I have neighbors, women in their mid-twenties, who still live at home with their parents and who look upon sacrifice as their mother's province. Both work full time, but they don't pay rent or grocery bills, and their parents subsidize their month-long vacation abroad every summer.

My neighbors are living a prolonged childhood, a deferral of adult responsibility. A fairly large group of women in their twenties tell me that they don't feel grown up yet. They want to finish school and begin a career at the age of twenty-two, but that's not a prerequisite for maturity. They intend to wait a long time before they get married or have a baby, until the age of twenty-eight at least. Becoming a wife and mother, they suspect, will initiate them into official adulthood, but they aren't so eager for that to happen; in fact, they absolutely dread it.

Young women avoid motherhood for two reasons: a deep fear of sacrifice and an addiction to self-centered pleasure. They are truly afraid of how much they will have to sacrifice when they marry and become mothers. They've seen how much their own mothers and aunts and grandmothers have sacrificed, and they don't want any part of it.

A twenty-four-year-old woman in medical school tells me that she's much more afraid of how much she'll have to give up to be a mother than she is of the sacrifices she's making to become a doctor. When she has a baby, she'll be committed to that child for as long as she's alive, even after he's grown. She'll have to put his well-being and happiness above her own, she says, and she's not ready to do that. Right now, she works a twenty-hour shift at the hospital and then stays awake even longer to study the next day, but this sacrifice is for her. She doesn't want to give up a part of her self to a baby, and she can't imagine that she ever will.

I remember feeling the same way at that age, when I was totally uninterested in children, creatures who seemed to inhabit a different planet from the one I knew. I lived on my own after graduating from college and married at twenty-seven, but I would have planned a trip to the North Pole in winter before I would have considered having a baby. Having seen how much my mother sacrificed for me, I wasn't ready to give up that much of my self and my life for anyone. Nor could I imagine ever wanting to. This terror of sacrifice, hovering over me like a blimp over a football game, kept me oblivious to the charms of motherhood until I turned thirty. (And then I had a serious infertility problem to overcome first.)

A young friend of mine who is a professional singer feels the same way. She's so focused on her career and on her fantasy of becoming the new Barbra or the next Liza that she refuses to think about sacrificing any of it for a baby. Only when she's had the thrill of superstardom will she lose her fear of sacrificial motherhood, because then she won't have to sacrifice. After she's performed at Carnegie Hall, she'll be so successful that a baby won't cramp her style. At least that's what she thinks now.

Not only are young women terrified of sacrifice, they're also in love with fun. Men used to brag about wanting to sow their wild oats; now young women want a chance to do the same. They've got just as many of those oats as their brothers do, and they intend to plant them. Young women want to worry about only one person—themselves. They look to the twenties as ten years of fun, a kind of self-centered Decade of Me.

A twenty-year-old tells me that being a grown-up means having no fun and no freedom. So she wants to have years to be responsible just for herself and no one else, to savor her life "as an independent person." Other young women tell me that they want to live a bohemian student life for as long as possible. They want to have fun before they have to settle down and become obedient, sacrificial mothers, human beings who never have fun. So they party, drink, go to clubs, travel, spend weekends at rental houses with groups of other single people.

Once they get over their queasiness about sacrifice and have babies, twenty-something mothers are not much different from other mothers. In fact, most of them become just as sacrificial as older moms. When I compare mothers in their twenties with those in their thirties, I find that the younger ones actually score higher on the Sacrifice Test. They make even more sacrifices for their children, such as not reading as often as they'd like, not watching television shows they'd like to see, and not getting together with friends. Young mothers also feel more guilty about not spending enough time with their children, and they rarely take a moment to do things just for themselves.

After a few years of hard drinking, motorcycle ganging, and some light drug-taking, Donna Casey had her first baby when she was twenty-six. She's completely devoted to motherhood now and has willingly abandoned her old self to her little Ricky. Her only goal, every day, is to make Ricky happy.

Dressed in black leather, a six-foot-tall redhead with slightly off-kilter eyes, Donna doesn't look much like a sacrificial mother. But she's the one who teased her husband into drinking massive quantities of beer and tequila on New Year's Eve and deliberately jumped him before he could manage to put on a condom. Ricky, the fruit of that seduction, is her new love, a boy she can't imagine letting out of the house to go to kindergarten.

Donna has become the kind of mother who's smug about the fact that she does nothing for herself. For her, sacrifice is a kind of maternal badge of courage; it feels like a privilege to deny herself.

But the consequences of self-denial for younger mothers can be just as detrimental as they are for older mothers. Mothers in their twenties are much more unhappy about their lives than older mothers are, and they're much less satisfied with their accomplishments in life. It seems as if the more they sacrifice, the more uneasy and disturbed they are about themselves.

Even more upsetting, though, is the fact that younger mothers simply don't like themselves as much as older mothers do. When I ask them questions about how often they feel disgusted with themselves—a test of what I call self-loathing—they feel it even more often than older moms do. They also say they haven't been successful as a human being, and they're less satisfied with their lives.

These signals of personal misery and unhappiness are hints of what I believe to be the true and devastating consequences of too much self-denial. It's when mothers sacrifice too much that their devotion to family backfires, that they can literally make themselves sick from a lack of self-respect, from a failure of personal dignity.

This is what I call the sacrifice syndrome, and it's a problem that can be hazardous to women's health. It also can threaten their emotional and spiritual well-being.

# The Sacrifice Syndrome

The best reason to avoid sacrifice is that it's bad for you.

When mothers sacrifice too much, they get sick. Sick at heart, sick in spirit, sick in body.

Sacrifice is not as devastating as smoking or drinking or taking drugs, because it's not an addiction. But sacrifice is a nasty habit that becomes increasingly difficult to break the longer it lasts. A mother who nurtures others while forgetting to nurture herself, a mother who denies her own needs, a woman who always puts everyone else first has a serious and potentially disastrous sacrifice problem.

The cyclone of sacrifice leaves a trail of emotional debris that includes personal vulnerability, emotional instability, and physical illness. Mothers who indulge in excessive sacrifice have a distorted and very negative image of themselves. They have little self-confidence and often loathe who they are and how they look. They feel sad or depressed, anxious or angry. They lose interest in sex, contracting a bad case of the sexual blahs. And they suffer from a range of troublesome physical ailments, such as headaches, stomach problems, insomnia, and muscle aches and pains.

I think many mothers sense that too much sacrifice isn't healthy. But they do it anyway, hoping and praying that if they sacrifice enough, they will be transformed into that enviable and elusive object of desire, the perfect wife and mother. Sadly, though, they're mistaken. Sacrificial mothers make all that effort in vain, because they turn out to be worse wives and mothers than those who don't sacrifice as much. These women are like students who stay up all night to study for an important exam, then get only a C, and whose friends, who hardly studied at all, get A's. It doesn't seem fair, but that's life: To the victor belong the spoils, and the victor is not always the one who sacrifices the most.

Sacrificial mothers are their own harshest judges. Maybe that's why they feel so much less successful as wives and mothers than those who don't sacrifice as much. Their standards are so impossibly high that they can never reach the top. When I ask them to rate themselves, sacrificial mothers say they fail at being the best wife and lover and mother possible. They aim for a fantasy life, but they get reality instead. The dream is an attentive, affectionate husband who plays with his children without being asked; real life is a man who parks himself in front of the television and needs a written invitation to spend time with his children. The dream is an amiable, loving child who does what his mother says; real life is a toddler who throws tantrums at the mall.

In their own eyes, then, sacrificial mothers can't do anything right. They spend their lives sacrificing for their family, but they don't feel gratified by their marriage or their love life. They compromise a lot for their husband, mostly because he depends on them so much. They feel they put so much more effort into their marriage than other wives do. But all of this hard work and sacrifice doesn't pay off, because their husband doesn't even appreciate their struggles.

Sacrificial mothers do more for their husbands than other wives, but they enjoy it less. They buy his shirts and underwear, they fold his socks, they pay his bills, they serve his meals. But he doesn't acknowledge their exertion and they don't respect him because of it. In fact, they feel more resentment than love. They expend so much energy taking care of him, yet they never feel cared for by him. They come to begrudge the fact that he never gives as much as he gets. Of course, they're giving so much that he'd have to be Superman, or a saint, to be able to reciprocate in kind. They're like a millionaire who's annoyed because her poor relations never give her birthday presents as fancy as the ones she gives them.

A woman I know sacrifices just about everything for her husband and four children, but she's always complaining that her husband never cares for her enough. When she was pregnant with twins, she asked him to keep her van filled with gas, because when she went to the gas station, the fumes from the pumps made her nauseous. He didn't, and she ran out of gas twice. She was more upset about not feeling cared for than about standing by the side of the road, big belly and all, waiting for a tow truck. She cried with disappointment then. When he didn't give her a Christmas present because he said their new house was her gift, she cried again. She didn't really need anything, she told me, but she needed to know that he cared enough to buy her *something*.

What this woman doesn't understand is that her husband will probably never be able to sacrifice as much as she does, that she's setting unrealistic standards for him, almost like asking him to pole-vault at a world's record height. She needs to clarify what she expects from him and why; she needs to tell him that she wants a present for what it represents, not for how much it costs. The sad fact is that her supreme sacrifices undermine her effectiveness as a wife and as a mother. Her husband doesn't really understand her; the children take her for granted. She sacrifices everything to win their love and devotion, but all she gets is their laundry and complaints.

One of the most sacrificial mothers I've ever met, Maria Podlaski, also suffers for her children's sake because she tries so desperately to please them. That's why she has birthday parties for the entire class that last twenty-four hours; it's why she drives her two oldest children to every soccer game and ice-skating class they want; and it's why she lets her six-year-old with Down syndrome wander the house during the night, even though she has to get up and put the girl back to bed each time. Maria's children aren't reaping many benefits from their mother's enormous sacrifices. Instead, they are living with a stressed, overburdened woman who is as emotionally needy as they are. Because she denies herself so much, she's anxious and depressed. She's got a chronic upset stomach and recurring chest pains. She feels lonely and irritable, and she's often angry for no apparent reason. She has crying spells and she's fed up with sex.

Maria sacrifices so relentlessly, in fact, that her doctor advised her to get a part-time job, just so she could escape from her family for a few hours a day. This was, in fact, a *prescription for selfism*, a female doctor's unusually insightful effort to force Maria to become less sacrificial. But it didn't work. Maria just squeezes in more sacrifice to make up for the time she spends on the job.

Any confidence that Maria ever had, any ability to look at herself as a vibrant, intelligent woman with a sexual twinkle in her eye, has vanished. She's like a lovely piece of silk fabric left out in the sun and wind too long: Her self has faded so completely that she has become a tattered version of who she used to be.

This personal vanishing act happens to many mothers who sacrifice too much. They lose the ability to care about and for themselves, and it's one of the reasons that their self-esteem plummets so precipitously.

## At Times I Think I'm No Good at All

One of the most obvious consequences of sacrifice is a simple and overwhelming loss of self and self-esteem. Over time, sacrifice can corrode the foundation of a woman's ego, the secret place that protects her finest self. Just as termites infest and then weaken a house, sacrifice eats away at a woman's sense of confidence and pride. Sacrifice diminishes a mother's self-respect by forcing her to always think of herself last, or not at all, as the woman who tells me she feels nonexistent does. If a mother doesn't believe she's worthy of respect, then who will?

At my sacrificial peak, I never gave my self a thought. I felt I simply didn't matter. I was in such bad shape that I didn't bother to figure out what I thought about anything. I'd start an argument with my husband but be unable to articulate why he was wrong and I was right. I'd show up to vote in a local election and discover that I didn't have an opinion either way. I was sleepwalking through my life for what I thought was the sake of my children.

At the time, I didn't connect my sacrificial tendencies with my inability to focus on myself or on my gnawing stomach pains, my recurring headaches, my vague feelings of sadness and uneasiness. I had all the signs of the sacrifice syndrome but never once acknowledged its presence; it was like ignoring a full-grown hippopotamus sitting in my living room.

If I'd bothered to measure my own self-esteem at that point, I'm sure it would have been at rock bottom, as low as it could go. I've come to believe that I am not an exception: I'm the rule in sacrificial low self-esteem. I believe it's because the sacrifice problem is so common that so many women suffer from a similar lack of self-regard. When I compare women and men, I find that women always score lower on tests of self-esteem. And when I separate the extremely sacrificial mothers from others, I find that their self-esteem is lowest of all. It's virtually impossible to think well of yourself when you spend days and weeks and months thinking only of other people.

With this lack of self-respect comes a creeping self-doubt, a suspicion that nothing you do or say is all that important. It's easy to recognize self-doubt in a sacrificial mother. It's what makes her add an "I think" to every definitive statement she makes and what allows her to listen quietly when someone contradicts something she knows is right. At the peak of my self-doubt, I'd ask my husband if I was serving the right amount of food for our dinner guests, even though I knew he didn't have a clue.

When a mother doubts herself long enough, she'll also begin to criticize and deprecate herself, as if to prove she was right to have so much doubt, as if it's completely natural to see only what's bad, never what's good. This practice is certainly not natural for men. Ask any woman, and she'll probably admit that sometimes she just doesn't like herself. Ask any man, though, and he probably won't understand what you're talking about.

Every other woman—one in every two, I find—confesses outright that she often feels disgusted with herself. So many women indulge themselves in this kind of orgy of self-recrimination and self-loathing that it's virtually an epidemic. The nastier and more disagreeably they can insult themselves, the more satisfied they are. Some women, for instance, get into a habit of calling themselves names, such as sloppy, fatso, and stupid.

Sacrificial mothers are most self-loathing of all. These martyrs are the most scornful and self-despising, seeing themselves as ignorant, ugly, and undeserving of praise in the deepest part of their soul. But they don't merit this kind of self-revulsion. To the contrary, their self-denial and sacrifice should make them seem saintly, or at the very least, heroic. It takes great heart to be able to give so faithfully, with such single-minded determination. At least they could respect themselves for being so self-denying.

When I first met Ellen Brown, I assumed she'd be extremely self-congratulatory about her self-denial. After all, she's a super-sacrificer who spends her days driving her children wherever they need to go and waiting for her husband, an FBI agent, to get home, either at two in the morning or two in the afternoon. So I was dumbfounded to discover just how vehemently self-loathing she is. A petite and expensively dressed woman with a superchic haircut and understated gold jewelry, Ellen is gorgeous. She's also a first-class self-denigrator, a woman so expert at mental self-abuse that she could legitimately seek help at a shelter for abused wives. Only her husband doesn't do the abusing, she does!

Ellen's self-loathing is an unconscious response to her life of sacrifice. For the sake of her family, she has no work of her own, because she quit her law enforcement job to stay home with the children. She has no life of her own, either, because she's moved for her husband's work so often that she has no roots in any community. All she does is give to her family, but she doesn't value her contributions, so nobody else does either. She doesn't feel she deserves respect, so her family offers her none.

As I listen to Ellen speak, her voice a monotone of sadness and resignation, I sense that she feels as if she's sinking in sacrificial quicksand, without a branch or a hand to grab. And there's nothing I can do to save her.

"My entire life is ferrying my children from here to there," she tells me. "I kind of feel I'm one of those women saying, 'There should be something more to my life than being Mom's Taxi.' In the back of my mind, I miss having an outside identity and purpose, being someone other than a wife and a mother."

## Body Wars

It's almost a universal female rule that a woman can't like herself if she doesn't like the way she looks; a rule that has fueled many scientific studies and been the focus of dozens of popular books. A woman who views herself with disgust tends to dislike her body, and a woman who dislikes her body also views herself with disgust. These two subjects—self-esteem and body image—are so closely linked, they're like psychological Siamese twins. You can't talk about one without also talking about the other.

Sacrificial mothers tend not to like themselves very much, so it's no wonder that they don't much like the way they look either. They're like grown-up versons of adolescent girls with a false self problem, except that their problem is *no* self.

As teenagers, many girls are frightened and repelled by the way their body changes during puberty. Because they are already unsure of themselves and lacking in confidence, this new insecurity about their looks damages their self-image even more. As I mentioned earlier, from the age of twelve or thirteen on, girls are more negative than boys about their appearance. And grown women are also more negative than men about their appearance.

Women's magazines take advantage of this widespread female body anxiety by publishing an avalanche of articles about thigh shapers and tummy tighteners and butt molders and breast enhancers and makeup tricks that will make noses seem smaller, cheeks higher, chins less prominent. I myself have participated in the magazine-sponsored body-trashing orgy by asking women to rate their various body parts and sections of their anatomy to see which ones they love and which ones they hate. Women express a lot more negative feelings than positive ones about nearly every inch of their body. Once, because I wanted to avoid getting too many pessimistic answers, I decided to ask women about their bodily features only from the neck up. The trick worked, because women are much more content—or at least a lot less negative— about their eyes and hair than they are about their hips and thighs.

When I compare mothers' opinions of their looks with how childless women see themselves, I find that mothers are least happy about their physical appearance. And sacrificial mothers are the most distressed of all about their looks, in part because they rarely take time to make any improvements. Sacrificial mothers focus on their children with such ferocity and resolve, they have little time or energy to pay attention to their image. By ignoring something they consider so very crucial, mothers entangle themselves even more in a knot of self-disgust.

Mothers spend less time than other women on their appearance. When I ask them to tell me exactly how many minutes they take grooming themselves every morning and evening, I learn that mothers use less time every day to shower, do their hair, brush their teeth, and put on makeup. This is true despite the fact that mothers are most likely to admit to feeling completely naked without makeup. So even though they realize they need it desperately, sacrificial mothers don't bother putting on a finished face to face the world.

That's the least of their worries, it seems. Many of them are pleased if they can leave the house, fully dressed, by eight or nine in the morning. A few sacrificial mothers tell me, only half joking, that they're grateful if they can escape wearing clean underwear and a fresh tampon, with one contact lens in each eye.

Because sacrificial mothers have so much trouble paying attention to how they look, they struggle with dramatic weight gain after giving birth. It's not unusual for them to gain twenty or thirty or forty pounds after having a baby and to keep it on because they neglect to make self-improvement a priority. When sacrificial mothers forget to pay attention to their own needs, the pounds pile up and up and up. That postpregnancy weight gain can loom as large as Mount Everest—and be just as difficult to conquer.

A sacrificial mother in Indiana tells me that after having three children, she simply forgot to concentrate on whether she looked decent or not. It was seven years until she could focus on herself for the first time. And then it came as a revelation to her that she had the right to try to lose weight.

It took Joy Stevens eight years to come to a similar conclusion, but only because she was horrified by the idea that she'd have to buy a new size 20 dress to wear to her son's first Holy Communion. Joy had gained ten or fifteen pounds with each of her five pregnancies, but she couldn't afford a packaged weight-loss program, such as Weight Watchers, or membership in a gym. So instead she used enormous determination and willpower, packed into a hidden, very early hour before her children woke up.

Every morning at six, Joy went out for a walk. Even on the bleakest, darkest January morning, when it was so cold that it hurt to inhale, Joy forced herself to go. At first it took her an entire hour to walk a mile. Gradually, little by little, she worked her way up to six very fast miles in the same amount of time. That hour of exercise became the only one in twenty-four that belonged just to Joy, the only sixty minutes that she used for her own benefit and nobody else's. It took her years to feel that she had a right even to this sliver of secret time for herself—and she did it mostly for her son, so that he wouldn't be embarrassed by a mother who had to sit in church wearing a dress the size of a tent.

## Feeling Bad

The psychological troubles associated with being sacrificial add up to a mountain of melancholy. Extremely sacrificial mothers have *twice as many* psychological problems as other women. Twice as many of them feel irritable, have trouble sleeping, and have difficulty concentrating; twice as many often feel guilty, twice as many feel terribly lonely. They also have more headaches and stomach problems and muscle aches too. They feel less successful in life than other mothers, and they're much more unhappy with their friendships and with their work and with the way their lives are going.

Don't sacrificial mothers deserve better? What is it about sacrifice that floods women with a sea of emotional sorrow?

It isn't necessarily being sacrificial that causes so many woes; it's the three key traits that accompany it. Sacrificial mothers almost always have an excess of empathy, an overload of worry, and the primary responsibility for taking care of their children.

Almost every sacrificial mother alive comes equipped with an overabundance of empathy. She believes that it's her duty to be as sympathetic and caring as possible. She feels that she must take on and share in her child's unhappiness. She suffers with him and for him. Every moment of grief or disappointment or fear that her child feels, she feels too. She feels it not just for two years or twelve, but *always*—for as long as she is alive.

To have this talent for empathy is a gift, often an admirable one. Priests, ministers, and rabbis have it; so do psychotherapists and some doctors. Feeling deep empathy for their children is what makes mothers believe that they are doing a good job. A mom I know in Arizona claims that she can tell when her four-year-old is depressed, and that makes her depressed too.

But overly empathic mothers pay a price for their great emotional investment in their children. Empathic mothers tend to be depressed mothers. This doesn't mean that every single empathic mother is guaranteed to suffer from depression, just that she's more prone to it than a mother who is not quite so gung-ho about empathy.

Another reason that empathy and depression are so strongly linked is because empathy is a highly feminine quality. Women who are traditionally feminine, who are "other-focused," give most of their attention to other people, and they too are most often depressed. As psychologist Susan Harter describes them, feminine women of this type put their partner's needs ahead of their own, because they automatically consider everybody else first. They are very sensitive to their partner's feelings, but ignore or dismiss what they themselves feel. They let their partner take the lead, and he makes most of the important decisions as well. Put these phrases into a computer, and it would spit out the perfect profile of a sacrificial mother.

These empathic, "other-focused" women suffer from the same problems as sacrificial mothers. They have low self-esteem, they're often depressed, and they lack energy. As Harter puts it, they have little zest for life. It's tough to be perky if you're always preoccupied with feeling others' pain and trying to figure out what they want before they know they want it.

With empathy comes worry. Mothers who feel for their children so deeply, who care about them so profoundly, are also guaranteed to worry.

The kinds of things mothers worry about range from the absurd to the truly heartbreaking. I worry about my son's bad dreams and why he yells and screams in his sleep. I worry about the huge wart on the bottom of his foot. I have a friend who worries that her baby's one tooth is coming in crooked and another who worries because her daughter hasn't been invited to one birthday party in their new neighborhood. A mother I know in California worries because she knows she shouldn't tie her four-year-old's shoes all the time, but she does it anyway. I know a mother who worries, with good reason, about her teenager's suicidal depression, and another who worries about whether her seriously ill thirteen-year-old child will live to be an adult. A woman I met in Chicago worries that her daughter with Down syndrome may never manage to live alone, that the girl will never learn to speak so that people can understand her.

Whether their worries are silly or sad, sacrificial mothers are crazy with love for their children and also a bit terrified of the responsibility of caring for these little human beings. These mothers, I find, are especially anxious; they seem to experience motherhood as a lifelong lesson in worry. They're incredibly nervous about everything related to taking care of their baby, from accidentally dropping him, to watching him begin school and having teen sex and getting AIDS.

Maternal worry can result in stomach-churning, teeth-grinding, nail-biting anxiety, for a newborn baby who's not nursing properly or a first grader who's having trouble learning to read or a teenager who's not home by midnight. The point is that sacrificial mothers never, ever outgrow worrying about their children. To paraphrase an old saying: little babies, little worries; big children, big worries.

All of this worry can only worsen emotional troubles such as depression. Worry is a kind of anxiety with a purpose, and it can lead to headaches, digestive troubles, and other stress-related psychological problems.

Having the main responsibility for caregiving is a third aspect of sacrifice that also causes similar troubles. Sacrificial mothers who make extraordinary efforts for ill children or those with disabilities are most obviously at risk. But so are mothers who are dedicated to taking care of their healthy children and who get very little help in doing so.

Just being the one who cares for a child's health and well-being can put sacrificial mothers in harm's way. Too much nurturing responsibility can be so emotionally burdensome that it may begin to affect a sacrificial mother's immune system. Adults who take care of a senile spouse, for instance, are likely to be more depressed and to get sick more often than adults who don't have such a burden.

Single mothers and women whose husbands don't participate in everyday child-rearing chores are just as vulnerable to becoming depressed and physically ill. A single mother I know just recovered from a six-week bout of anemia and jaundice because she was so wrapped up in caring for her two-year-old that she literally forgot to eat. She tells me that she's often moody and has trouble falling asleep, although she can't figure out why. She's not depressed yet, but I think she's teetering on the edge.

Another sacrificial friend of mine is married, but her husband spends so little time with their son that she might as well be single. Pale and haggard, she admits that she's bone-weary, struggling with a fatigue that she can't seem to shake. Her face is frozen into a mask of despondency, as if her depression has slowly chilled her from the inside out. She had her first child at the age of thirty-nine, and the effort of caring for him makes her feel more like a grandmother than a mother.

It's not just extremely sacrificial mothers who suffer, though. *All* women have more emotional and physical problems than men do, according to social scientist Walter Gove, who points out that he and his colleagues have been trying to explain the phenomenon for more than fifty years. In all my studies, for example, more women than men complain about an almost-unbelievable variety of symptoms: frequent headaches, indigestion, muscle aches, back pain, allergies, dizzy spells, insomnia, fatigue, trouble concentrating, feelings of guilt and loneliness, irritability and anger, sadness or depression, crying spells, irrational fears.

There are two possible reasons for this vast gender gap in emotional health. First, it's possible that because women are such masters of complaint, so ready and able to share their burdens, they only *seem* more distressed than men. Because many men value stoicism and hate to voice their feelings nearly as much as they hate asking for directions or giving up the television remote, they keep their problems to themselves. If this is true, men have just as many complaints as women, but they just don't express or confess to them. I don't think this is the correct explanation, however.

Here's a better one: Women suffer more than men do.

Women's lives are more difficult than men's, in part because they are more likely to be sacrificial. This disparity makes women more susceptible than men to both emotional and physical ailments.

It's also true that while parenthood is difficult for both partners, it's most distressing and painful for mothers. It costs more, socially and emotionally and physically, for a woman to be a mother than for a man to be a father. She goes through pregnancy and childbirth. And she takes more direct responsibility for the children's welfare, and she makes more sacrifices. As a result, mothers are more worried, more anxious, and more depressed than fathers are. Mothers are even more *angry* than fathers, because they feel more economic pressure to make ends meet and because they have to do so much more of the child care, one study shows. There appears to be a simple formula for figuring out just how irate a mother will be, a kind of Angrier-by-the-Dozen Rule: The more children a mother has, the angrier she gets and the more often she yells. When sociologists Catherine Ross and Marieke Van Willigen of Ohio State University studied a random group of adults, they found that women were angrier than men and that each additional child cranked up the mothers' anger level even higher.

Part of what makes a sacrificial mother so angry is that she gives and gives and gives and comes to feel trapped by the should-bes, all the things she should be doing for her children and family. She should be playing more and reading more and cleaning more and cooking more and spending more time; the list of should-bes is nearly infinite. But she forgets what is equally important, all the things she should be doing for herself. She should be eating well and exercising and getting enough sleep. She should be mining nuggets of time to do whatever she likes to do—gardening or reading or renting a movie to watch with friends. Just as she makes sure to read to her preschooler at bedtime and to do a load of laundry, she should also make it a rule to add herself to her to-do list. She should begin by staking a claim to twenty or thirty minutes every day as her own. That time should be hers, sacred and inviolable. She can't count time at work, and she can't count sleep either.

A sacrificial mother should be spending time with her husband, too, and nurturing her sensuality. Just because it seems not humanly possible to find the time and energy to make love doesn't mean that her sexual needs have to be obliterated.

## Sacrificing Sex

Unfortunately, many sacrificial mothers do consign their sensuality to oblivion and beyond.

It's a great tragedy that so many sacrificial mothers completely lose interest in anything sexual. Depriving themselves of sensual pleasure is an odd form of self-denial, similar to rejecting an offer of ice cream and cookies for dessert or refusing to go for a swim in a chilly lake on a hot summer day. Their warped logic goes like this: If it feels good, I don't deserve it, so I won't do it and you can't make me. On top of all this, they're almost too tired to breathe, let alone to think sexy thoughts.

Maybe that's why so many sacrificial mothers are sexually frustrated. They feel least successful as lovers, and they're less satisfied with their sex lives than other mothers. Fewer of them say they're in passionate love with their husband. It's as if all their sexual fervor and lust have been sucked out and the energy's been redirected to their children. They funnel that libido like a tornado and aim it right at the kids.

One mother I met spends every night reading bedtime stories and singing lullabies to her two adopted boys, while her husband tinkers with junk in the garage until midnight. They've become more like friends than lovers, she tells me. It's as if they've made an unspoken antisex pact so that they can both point their passion in other directions. He picks old coffee tables and water beds out of the trash and takes the useful bits to build huge shelves and storage systems. She spends every free minute until she falls asleep with her kids.

But sacrificial mothers like this woman suffer for their sexual self-denial, because they're cutting off a rich segment of their adult lives. When you think about it, sex is one of the few simple sources of mutual comfort, tenderness, and enjoyment that a couple has, and it's real cheap too. Why look a gift horse in the mouth?

All too often, this sexual lull begins just after the birth of a first child. It's during that super-sacrificial era of motherhood that women begin to develop a severe case of sexual amnesia. It's as if they can't remember what sex is for, why it's fun, how it can be good, when to do it. Most obstetricians warn mothers not to have sex for the first six weeks after having a baby, but that's a kind of joke. I remember thinking to myself after my daughter was born, "Did he say six weeks? Oops, I though he said six years!" I don't think I've ever met a mother who felt her sexual appetite return only six weeks after having a baby. Many mothers say it takes more like six months, sixteen months, or even sixty months.

A woman I know swears that her sexual recess has hit the thirty-months-and-counting mark. Her sexuality is missing in action, mostly because baby passion has replaced her sexual passion. Being obsessed with her now two-and-a-half-year-old makes paying atten-tion to orgasm and birth control and erogenous zones seem beside the point and way too sticky and sweaty. She can't quite figure out where her sexual desire went, how it disappeared so thoroughly, but it's as gone as Jimmy Hoffa. And she has no intention of doing any-thing about it. When she talks about this with other moms, she tells me they all feel the same way, that sex is passé, like discotheques and polyester pants suits.

"No one's interested in sex anymore, we're more interested in our children," she tells me. It makes her sad, and she knows that it's wrong and off-kilter, but she figures it will straighten itself out after a few more years. She's apparently never heard the expression "Use it or lose it."

But another mother of a two-year-old has. She's only half joking when she tells me that it's been so long since she's had sex, she doesn't know if she remembers how to do it.

Most new mothers agree that their sexual-desire temperature gauge often hits zero, and they're almost unanimous in their antipathy to sex, in their revulsion at the idea of coitus. Making love, they'd say, is about number 857 on their list of life priorities. New mothers are physically drained, they're sleep-deprived, and they're so touched out from holding their baby all day that they don't want to be fondled by anyone else. They have stitches that are healing, a baby that needs nursing, a lot of sleep to catch up on. They don't remember themselves as sexual beings, and until they get some sleep, they don't want to, either.

This sexual lapse is quite normal. In fact, a brand-new mother with a ravenous sexual craving would be such a rarity that she'd probably make headline news: "New Mother Wants Sex! (Husband Dies of Shock)!"

Six months to a year after the birth, some mothers renew their sexual vows. Sometimes, though, when sacrificial mothers try to rejuvenate their sexuality, they can face an uphill battle with fatigue and lethargy and lack of opportunity. A woman I know with a five-year-old tells me that she and her husband put a lock on their bedroom door, to prevent their wandering daughter from causing an embarrassing case of coitus interruptus. But it's a lock that doesn't get much practice, and neither do they. This working mother is so tired so often that she just can't get into a sexual rhythm, like trying to jump rope but not being able to hop in at the right time.

An extraordinary number of mothers, in fact, don't recover their sexual joy for years after their first child is born. About one in three mothers suffers from an ongoing and persistent loss of interest in sex, I find. But only about one in ten fathers has the same problem. As you'd expect, this mismatch in sexual zeal causes a lot of marital tension.

Husbands married to sacrificial mothers always have their own answer ready when I ask their wife what she's given up for the children. Usually the men yell a one-word answer: "Sex!" They resent her loss of libido, and they take it personally too. After all, she's not doing it for a good cause, like ending war or world hunger. So why the sexual malaise?

Many sacrificial mothers balk at giving so much all day long, then giving in bed too. Their sexual restraint becomes a way to exert control over their lives and their bodies. It's just about the only time they ever say no. A very sacrificial friend tells me that she gives her whole self in service of everyone in her family, so she's determined to keep her body to herself. Every day she's torn between her four children's demands pulling one way and her husband's needs yanking her the other. When she's finally escaped her clinging children every night, she has to listen to her husband's whimpers, his singsong pleas for sex. She wants to tell him to go away, to leave her alone, to let her be. She itches to scream at him: "Sorry, I'm closed!"

I think my friend has sacrificed her sexuality on the altar of motherhood. Deep down, she feels that being a mother and being sexual don't mix. Trying to be a good mother and a sexy woman makes her feel sick, as if she had to drink a milk shake made of ice cream and kerosene.

By exercising her right to refuse sex, she proves to her husband that she has some power in their relationship. But she hurts him, and she hurts herself as well. When sacrificial mothers turn away from their sexuality, they scorn their only chance to be cared for and nourished in an intimate way. They deny their husbands the same chance.

Sacrificial mothers tell me that they have to be in the mood to make love. So they wait—for romance and candlelight, soft music, and endless free time for foreplay. They're waiting for the life they had before children. They might as well be waiting for Godot, because those days are gone. The reality of sexuality as a mother is that they were tired before, they are tired now, and they will be tired in the future. Their back hurts and there's a load of wet laundry on the floor. There's a giant stain, maybe spitup, all over the sheets. It's true that none of this is sexy; it won't ever make a scene in an X-rated movie. But that's still no excuse not to have sex. Do it anyway; do it now.

Couples should never wait to be in the mood, because they'll never get there.

Just do it.

Once you begin to make love, you'll get in the mood, even if you're almost done and you're half asleep. Anyway, being in the mood isn't the real goal. You want to try a little tenderness, to feel some intimacy, to relax and feel grateful to be alive.

A very close friend of mine has three young children and is deep into a sacrificial stage of motherhood. She tells me that she and her husband are never in the mood. Two months ago, partly because they're having sex so rarely, he developed a prostate problem. The man's doctor advised him to have sex often, every night if possible. She was horrified when she told me that she was supposed to get in the mood every day.

Still, being a good wife, one who worries about her husband's health, she complied. She joked to me that she worried that they'd both die of exhaustion before the man's prostate was cured. He's almost recovered now, so they don't make love daily anymore, but she tells me she misses the closeness and consideration that their randy sex life used to inspire.

Although most sex therapists wouldn't have the nerve to tell couples to have sex every day, they often suggest that parents make a sexual schedule. Designate one evening a week as sex night, they advise. The problem with this plan is that it's almost a sure thing that your special night will be the one when your three-year-old has a terrifying nightmare or your seven-year-old is vomiting every twenty minutes all night long or you have an incredible headache (no, really). Or, after a while, you may feel you can do it *only* on that night, but no other one, that you *have* to do it then or you're a bad person. Sex becomes just another obligation, a duty, like mowing the lawn or doing the dishes. So forget about it. Just do it when you can do it.

Remember too that the longer you don't, the longer you won't. Make it a policy to make love. Avoid entering the sexual freeze of sacrificial motherhood. If you do, you might not thaw out until it's too late, and you'll find yourself in middle age, with your marriage sabotaged and your sensuality ruined.

## Getting Sick

Over time, too much sacrifice leads to poor physical health.

Sacrificial mothers are sick mothers. I'm no longer amazed when they whisper their confessions to me about headaches and allergies, stomach pains and backaches, colds and fevers. Sacrificial mothers have more psychological symptoms and physical problems than other women and men, I find. They also visit the doctor most often, at least five times a year.

Sacrifice can make a mother sick, but her habit of neglecting herself and her health also contributes to her troubles. A mother is chief cook and bottle-washer and nurturer; her job is to take care of everybody else. She tends to children when they are feverish and to hubby when he is injured; she cures the cat of fleas and cleans the hamster's smelly cage. But she often forgets to nurture herself, especially when she gets sick.

When I got a cold not long ago, both of my children had the flu, so I didn't pay much attention to my own sneezes. After a while I noticed that I had a wicked, rasping cough, but I figured it would go away. It didn't. I hacked and heaved for eight weeks before I made time to see a doctor. I'd become sicker than my children, and needed antibiotics and an inhaler for my bronchitis.

Nobody in my family even noticed that I was sick until my coughing became so loud that my husband couldn't hear the television. This is par for a sacrificial mother's course. When my husband is sick, I take care of him, but when I'm sick, the only one who takes care of me is me. (Once, when I had strep with a high fever, though, my mother volunteered to cross two state lines to come and take care of me.) Most families are like mine: The wives take care of sick husbands, but no one takes care of sick wives.

It's because women neglect their own health that they get sick more often than men do, according to scientists who probe health statistics. This research, like mine, reveals that more wives than husbands suffer from minor health problems such as colds and coughs, sore throats, stomach woes, muscle aches, and headaches. They also find that women visit doctors more often, probably because the only way they can get someone else to focus on their health problems is to pay for it.

It could be that women have a weaker, more fragile constitution than men, so they're more vulnerable to picking up viruses and germs. That's possible, but an analysis of health figures for single men and women refutes that theory. Single women, it turns out, are just as healthy as bachelors; it's only wives who suffer from more physical ailments than husbands. When a woman has a man to care for and worry about, she gets sick. But if she has no one else to worry about or to sacrifice for, she's just as healthy as a man in the same situation.

A woman I'm fond of is not only a sacrificial mother now, but she grew up as a sacrificial child. And she's suffering for it too. When she was only nine, her father deserted the family and her mother had to take three jobs to support the family. So it was up to my friend to raise her four younger brothers, help them with homework, cook their dinner, give them baths, put them to bed. She did this every day, all year, every year, until she graduated from high school and got married. To this day, all four of her brothers send her a Mother's Day card every year.

My friend also had her own children at the age of nineteen. She lives for her two girls now and insists that it's her duty to see that they have a better childhood than she did. Her husband doesn't feel any obligation toward his daughters one way or another. As far as he's concerned, going to work every day is the only sacrifice he should have to make. So my friend, who also works nearly full time, does everything around the house that needs to be done: all the cooking, cleaning, grocery shopping, laundry, and homework-helping.

She's the kind of mother who does the laundry at one in the morning so that she can spend time with her children when they're awake.

She's the kind of mother who, when the girls want their nails painted red, white, and blue for a neighborhood Fourth of July party, does it instantly, dropping her plans to curl her own hair.

She's the kind of mother who goes out on a Saturday afternoon to buy herself a summer dress and comes home instead with jeans, shorts and sandals for her daughters and a pair of work pants for her husband.

She's the kind of mother who resigns herself to watching the cartoon network, because she wants to spend time with her girls and they won't tune into something she prefers to watch.

I once asked this woman if she ever did anything just for herself. In her thirty-one years on this planet, she has: once. Last year she took a four-day trip to a big city with some friends. Before she left, she cooked and froze meals for every day she was going to be gone and prepared a three-page list of instructions for her husband about how to defrost all the food and what to do with the children, the house, and the car.

But this wonderful mother pays for her ultra-sacrifices with a vengeance. She's got nearly every psychological and physical health problem you can think of, including a daily headache. Some days they're mild, but other times they're so bad she hallucinates hazy images of flames and fire, then passes out. Nobody takes care of her when this happens: Her children and husband have learned to avoid her during these episodes.

I always feel that she should be walking around with a big sandwich board hanging from her neck, painted in red, telling the world: "HI, I'M HERE TO GIVE. WHAT WOULD YOU LIKE ME TO DO FOR YOU?"

Sacrificing everything for the sake of the children can seem to be the honorable and virtuous choice. But what if it devastates a mother's sense of well-being? What if it destroys her health?

So many sacrificial mothers like this woman make the mistake of assuming that focusing on themselves will harm their families, when just the opposite is true. Focusing on themselves will help their families, because it will keep them healthier and happier and put them in better psychological shape to be successful wives and mothers. Taking time for herself is emotional exercise, like a treadmill for a mother's soul.

Mothers must avoid the sacrifice syndrome by learning to do things for themselves, by redirecting some of their overabundance of empathy and worry and caregiving onto themselves.

# Four

# How Sacrifice Helps Men

If sacrifice makes a woman sick, it keeps a man healthy. If sacrifice overburdens her with chores and child care duties, it lightens his load. And if sacrifice threatens her emotional well-being and happiness, it strengthens his feelings of contentment and connectedness. In nearly every way that sacrifice hurts a wife, it favors her husband; her disadvantages often reflect his blessings.

Many husbands have trouble viewing their wives' devotion and self-denial as sacrifice, because it seems to be so natural, so effortless, so simple. They think it's something wives choose to do; therefore, it can't be that much of a sacrifice. My husband never thought of what I did as sacrifice, exactly. To him, I was simply doing my job as a mother and wife. But I felt that I had no option but sacrifice, and because I did, I kept my husband permanently off the hook. I was the one who took care of everybody when they were sick; I was the one who took the children to buy school supplies, to check out library books, to friends' houses to play; as a result, he didn't have to do any of the inconvenient chores. I was the one who worried about and agonized over teachers and teams, teeth and scars, not him. I almost never had the luxury, as he did, to contribute to the family at his discretion, deciding what to do and when to do it.

After four or five years of our life as parents, it was clear that I had become the family nurse and maidservant and nanny, giving my husband a life of relative luxury. He was like the Rockefeller; I was like the help.

But my husband didn't see it that way. Because he earned more money than I did and commuted a long distance to work every day, he felt justified reaping the rewards of my sacrifice. And I didn't feel I had the right to complain; I felt humbled into a sacrificial stance.

Sacrificial mothers rarely rebel against their lot in life; they're short on imagination when it comes to being in control and taking charge of their lives. A sacrificial mother doesn't pick up and decide to run off to Tahiti with the plumber or to join a country and western band or even to sleep really late on a Sunday morning. Part of what it means to be sacrificial is to be utterly reliable and steady, a rock of maternal Gibraltar. A sacrificial mother is so boring in her dependability that you can set your clock by her: Monday at 9:00 A.M., she's at toddler gym class; Tuesday at 10:00 A.M. she's at work; Saturday at 11:00 A.M. she's doing the laundry, mopping the bathroom floor, and collecting coupons for her biweekly trip to the grocery store.

This doesn't mean that sacrificial mothers can't dream, of course. They imagine what it feels like to be the one who is coddled and pampered. In Japan, the culture that invented the geisha, there are now "host clubs" for women who eagerly switch roles for a few hours. Female customers book the services of a man who will serve *them*, please *them*, and offer *them* warmth and sympathy. This isn't a reverse brothel either. They're not paying for sex, they're paying for *attention*. Maybe this is the only way a modern woman can find a sacrificial mate—she's got to rent one!

And perhaps the only way to find a man willing to sacrifice as much as a woman is to bribe him to do it. If every sacrificial mother paid her husband to walk in her shoes for a day or a week, men would begin to understand how it feels to sacrifice. Maybe then they wouldn't be so blind to how much their wives give up—or to how much they benefit by it.

The fact is that men are blessed by marriage, and the more sacrificial their wives, the better off they tend to be. Being married to a sacrificial woman provides men with physical, emotional, and practical rewards that they rarely comprehend or appreciate. Men are oblivious to the ways in which marriage plugs them into a vibrant world of human attachment and passion. It gives them a sense of meaning in life, a capacity for tenderness, a feeling of obligation to another person that only fatherhood can rival. While some men may suspect in their hearts that single life is preferable—better sex, more beer, faster cars, louder stereo speakers—they're dead wrong. Married men are actually healthier, happier, and even more sexually satisfied than single guys, and not just by a little but by a lot, according to sociologist David Popenoe of Rutgers University. Living with a supportive, nurturing, slightly sacrificial woman gives a significant lift to a man's spirit and improves both his health and his psychological well-being.

A man I know used to be the worst-nightmare-come-true for a blind date: a goofy-looking single guy whose life revolved around his job as a live-in landlord. He devoted his days and nights to his tenants' complaints—leaky toilets, sticky locks, increased rent payments. This fellow was so compulsive that he kept his shoes arranged in perfectly parallel pairs at the bottom of his closet; he was so full of bitterness and resentment that he would sputter with rage when overcharged by a few cents on a restaurant check. The man was an unredeemable nerd who didn't even have the genius or wealth of so many computer-software nerds. And he was miserable as a bachelor, with no real friends and no close family, no hobbies and no fun.

But a kindhearted, loving woman rescued him from a gloomy sentence of permanent bachelorhood by marrying him before his thirty-fifth birthday. In the past seven years, she's humanized him, transforming this aloof and bumbling Clark Kent into an almost compassionate Superman. Drawing him out of his self-serving shell, teaching him how to care for other people, she's become his Pygmalion, the man's personal sacrificial miracle worker. She devotes so much time to taking care of him and their two children that she never has time for herself. She gives up her own desires and dreams to focus on his happiness. Her sacrifices are providing him with a free ride through life: She is pulling the family rickshaw, while he sits and enjoys the trip.

Unlike many men who are too dumb to realize how much their wives do for them, this man knows how lucky he is. He admits to me that he's become totally and desperately dependent on her. He's even a bit ashamed, because he gets so much more than he gives and sometimes he can't help being moody and testy. But his wife never, ever complains.

That's because she accepts selflessness as part of her job. So many sacrificial mothers like her have grown accustomed to settling for what they've got in marriage, instead of fighting for what they deserve. They sense that their husbands give them less intimacy and caring and respect and understanding than they would like, but they feel helpless to change the situation. When I ask, they tell me that they view their husband as not very successful, as either a husband or a parent, a lover or a person. But they seem to accept his minor failings as just another part of their sacrificial fate.

Sacrificial mothers are often disappointed by their marriage, in part because they never bother to rearrange things to suit themselves. By insisting on giving and giving, never receiving, they demand less of their husbands than other wives do. And they get what they ask for: less. Meanwhile, though, their husbands get more.

## Healthy, Happy Husbands

Husbands are healthier and happier than unattached men, in part because they have wives willing to sacrifice for them, just as their own mothers did for them when they were little boys.

Social scientists pick up some fairly obvious clues that having a wife is good for men's health. The most convincing hint is that husbands live a lot longer than single men do. Married men are just much less likely to die prematurely than bachelors are. It's certainly possible that women pick only the healthiest men when they're shopping around for a mate, so husbands are already healthier than men who never marry. But this explanation doesn't hold true statistically. Men who used to be married but who lost a wife to divorce or death, for example, also die sooner than men who are still married. Researchers find that divorced men are especially likely to succumb before their time to cancer and widowers tend to keel over from heart disease. It's as if these men lose the power of wifely protection as soon as she's gone. Maybe a warning should appear on every divorce attorney's contract: Lose your wife, lose a piece of your life.

It's not that wives have any special voodoo or magical powers of healing or warding off evil spirits. It's just that they seem to have more common sense than men do when it comes to keeping safe and being healthy. Many wives protect men from themselves, by preventing their husbands from doing the impulsive and dangerous things they'd be tempted to do if they were on their own. Sometimes wives have to insist that their husbands cease and desist in foolish behavior before it's too late.

A friend of mine told me a while ago that she was worried about her husband, because he was drinking at least six or eight cans of beer every night. He was so full of beer that he could barely eat dinner, and by the end of every evening, his alcohol intake made him mean and nasty. By his seventh beer, he'd be snapping at her and screaming at the kids. When she confronted him, he claimed he didn't notice that he was drinking that much, and anyway it quenched his thirst and relaxed him. Basically, he told her to lay off. Then he'd pop another beer. So she went on strike, refusing to buy beer or even food for the house until he got some help or cut back on the six-packs. After enough prodding and a seconding of her opinion by a friend, he did, going whole hog to the other extreme. Now he's a teetotaler who drinks only alcohol-free beer and diet soda. But if it hadn't been for her caring and persistence, he might have become an alcoholic, drowning his anxiety in a sea of beer suds and foam.

Some wives don't have to go to these lengths to protect their husbands, because they can use more subtle management systems. When another friend found out that her relatively young husband's cholesterol level was like that of a 300-pound senior citizen, she was terrified. But instead of nagging him about the hot dogs he downed at lunch or the potato chips he hogged on weekends, she stopped making fried eggs and pancakes on Sundays and cut out ice cream and bacon and chips from her weekly grocery trip. With gentle persuasion and subversive shopping, she knocked his cholesterol level down by fifty points.

As a result of direct wifely influence or more stealthy methods of control, husbands don't engage in as much of what researchers call "risky behavior" and some of us would call just plain stupid. Husbands don't drive under the influence as often as single men do. They don't drink as much hard liquor, nor do they take as many drugs. Husbands don't have as many household or automobile accidents, and they don't get into as many fistfights or violent arguments as single men do. Wives' constraint keeps husbands from living a wild and crazy life, but it also keeps them alive and well. It's as if wives force their mates to be mature, ensuring that husbands behave like grown-ups and not like the rowdy frat boys many seem to prefer to be.

Women are as vigilant about their husband's health as about his safety, and many view protecting his physical well-being as part of their duty, just as it's part of their maternal responsibility for children. It's very much like the wife in a *New Yorker* cartoon who is shown carefully watering all of her large living room plants, including her husband, patiently standing in the largest pot of all. Single men just don't have somebody to water them, unless they still live with Mom, and they aren't nearly as effective at monitoring their own health as women are at keeping track of everybody else's.

Wives do things like making sure their husbands take the right dose of prescription medication. They offer him orange juice for a cold and rice for an upset stomach. When my husband has a fever, I bring him hot soup and glasses of V-8 and keep the children quiet so he can rest. When my neighbor's husband is sick, she massages his feet and rubs his forehead and brings him tea in bed.

While men love to complain about their nagging wives, and some comedians make a career out of it, they are actually incredibly lucky to have their own personal nag at home. Often it's that annoying and persistent badgering that keeps men healthy.

There's something about being married that keeps men happy too. Deep down, most men seem to know this. Men are not at all embarrassed to admit, for instance, that for a man to be truly happy, he needs to have a woman around. We know from a great deal of social scientific evidence that this piercing male insight is, in fact, quite true. Taken as a group, husbands are significantly happier and more satisified with their lives than bachelors are.

But the same can't be said for women. When I ask them if they agree with the sentiment that a woman needs a man to be truly happy, they laugh in my face; they're adamant in their disbelief. They must sense, somehow, that as soon as a woman signs on the dotted line to take a husband and life partner, she's offering a promissory note for sacrifice. Sooner or later it will come due, and that means that an intimidating, and potentially harmful, sacrificial motherhood looms on the horizon.

Women's hesitation about marriage and motherhood is justified, if only because women don't gain quite the same dramatic benefits from marriage that men do. Women move up the financial ladder when they marry, because they've linked their economic fate to a man's ability to earn a living, which is usually better than their own. But men gain something more intangible and ultimately more precious when they marry: a sense of emotional well-being. Marriage is men's guarantee of love and friendship, support and comfort. Women certainly get these blessings when they marry, but they don't need to be married to find them, as so many men do. Women are better than men at finding other sources of affection and kindness—in their close friendships with other women, for example, or in their network of friends at work. When I ask mothers to tell me whom they consider close, somebody with whom they can speak from the heart, they usually have no trouble coming up with at least two or three names. But when I ask their husbands, the men pause and sputter with confusion, because after naming their wives, they can't think of anybody else.

Because they have a woman to look after them, husbands are also insulated from a great many psychological troubles in a way that bachelors are not. Married men are depressed less often than single men, and they're happier with everything from their work and their friends to their body and the way they look. It's as if being married offers men a protective "happy bubble" to live in, a good-health sphere that surrounds and shelters them with contentment and warmth. These conclusions are based on averages, so, of course, some husbands will be depressed, miserable, or unhappy. It's not as if these statistics guarantee a "happily ever after" for every man who ever gets married. Nevertheless, when social scientists compare husbands against bachelors, the psychological advantages of being a husband stand out quite dramatically.

The nucleus of men's happy bubble is, not surprisingly, at home. Husbands feel best when they're snug at home, not when they're out drinking with the guys or off alone at work. It's clear that home is the only place in which men feel truly loved, and this sensation gives them the ability to relax and be themselves. They don't have to impress anybody at home, they don't have to compete with anybody, and they don't have to do what the boss says. A man is in control at home, especially if he's married to a sacrificial wife who makes sure he feels this way.

A man I met in Illinois loves to be at home, because he has a sacrificial wife who makes sure he feels like the king of his castle every day of the year. He brags that she gets up at four in the morning to pack his lunch and to have some private time for chatting over coffee before he leaves for work. When he had an accident on the job, she drove him home and put him in bed. For the next week, she changed his bandages, gave him massages, and served him meals in bed. He met this woman, his second wife, at a bar, and when she agreed to dance with him, he felt deliriously happy. She's made him feel that way ever since, he tells me. He's a huge bear of a man—"wide, not fat," as he puts it—who pours concrete for a living. The man is a member of a rare and endangered species, a construction worker who's eager to tell his wife how grateful he is for her love and devotion to him. The big guy chokes back tears as he explains to me that his wife has made his life worth living.

The woman has also rescued this man's sex life in a way he never thought possible. The tenderness they share, he says bashfully, is unlike any he's ever had before. He refuses to be more specific, but it's clear that they're on the same sexual wavelength. Aside from the promise of a more or less regular sex partner, husbands reap a sexual bonanza from marriage. Married men have sex more often than single men do—twice as often, in fact. Not only that, but they say that it's better sex. Husbands get more physical pleasure in making love with their wives than bachelors get making love with girl-friends. Married men also assert that they get more emotional satis-faction out of sex, that they feel closer to their wives, with a deeper sense of intimate connection, than bachelors do.

Husbands may not be having wilder, more adventurous sexual escapades than single guys are, but they're certainly having gentler, more loving ones. By investing time and caring and affection in their relationship, husbands learn how to please and satisfy their wives, which is probably why married men are more sexually ful-filled than bachelors are. It's a matter of skill and technique; hus-bands take the time to learn it, single guys don't.

An active sex life is a clear sign of a healthy marriage—couples who get along tend to have regular sex. One of the most well-matched, happiest couples I know has been married for nearly fif-teen years, but they still do kinky sex more typical of singles and newlyweds than of middle-aged parents. Whenever they're hiking in the woods, for instance, they sneak off the trail and do it right there, an au naturel quickie.

It's also true that having sex once or twice a week helps couples learn to get along. It's the same principle of psychology that shows that smiling makes people feel happy; if they're smiling, then they must be happy. Well, the same is true for married sex: If we're hav-ing sex, we must be in love. That's why couples with new babies, who feel too tired to kiss, let alone to make love, would do best to just do it once a week, for marital medicinal purposes.

More sex means a better marriage; a better marriage means more sex.

Better marital sex begins with the sharing of sacrifice. Couples who learn to balance their sacrifices, who don't automatically assign all of it to the wife and mother, have the most vigorous and active sex lives. But marriages that include an extremely sacrifical woman almost always produce a doomed or dying sex life. This is the only instance in which a wife's sacrifices can harm her husband instead of helping him. An overly sacrificial woman often ignores her sexual needs, and her husband suffers accordingly, unless he's preoccupied with an affair or enjoying a private fondness for his own hand.

In general, though, marriage is an all-around bargain for men.

They get armloads of positive emotional merchandise for rock-bottom prices. And they often get a whole lot more than they give. Few are as openly appreciative of how much their wives do for them as is the Illinois construction worker. Few offer their wives explicit gratitude or special attention for their efforts, and sacrificial women come to expect little or none of it. That's what makes them sacrificial, and it's how they let their husbands coast through marriage, simply taking what's offered.

Sacrificial mothers must learn to transform their marriages into equal partnerships in which both members divvy up the sacrifice. Contrary to their intuition that everybody's better off if Mom is the sole sacrificer, it's better for families when couples share the work. And women who have learned to share the sacrifice are better off in every way as well. They're happier with themselves, with their children, and with their marriage. And their husbands are just as content, if not more so, than other husbands.

There's no question that raising children requires self-denial and sacrifice, but there's no social rule or federal law requiring Mother to be the one who makes all the sacrificial investments. It may seem overly simplistic, but the truth is that the more often a husband does housework without being asked, the more often he worries about the children, the more often he feels guilty about not spending enough time with his wife, the more sexually receptive she'll be.

It's a marital equation made easy: more dishes = more sex.

## Beneficiaries of the Second Shift

Perhaps the dishes-to-sex equation is too complex for men to solve, because most husbands don't seem to have figured it out. Men take full advantage of the reprieve they get from doing household chores. By having a wife who is willing to do most of the cooking and cleaning and shopping, they don't have to do that dirty work. But then their sex lives suffer, and they don't have a clue as to why their wives are never in the mood. Still, men accept this domestic bonus, not realizing that they've traded off sex for chores. Because the wife feels obligated to do most of the domestic chores and child care, even if she works for pay, her husband has that much less to do when he's home. So instead of scrubbing scum off the stovetop, he can read the paper; rather than volunteering to do the food shopping, he can watch television. It's a simple precept: When she does more, he does less. But then she spends her evening hours doing a slow burn of resentment. So it's no wonder that when she falls into bed, she wants sleep and not sex.

Not long ago I did all the chores at home. My more was my husband's less. He only had to take out the garbage and recycle the newspapers. Not a bad deal—for him, that is. Being saddled with this work had become my mindless, sacrificial tradition, one that I never challenged. Although my husband and I viewed ourselves as a modern, egalitarian couple—I kept my name and had my own credit cards—we fell into this unliberated traditional pattern as easily as a toddler jumps into a mud puddle.

This was our nightly scenario: After we finished dinner, my husband and children would bring their dishes to the sink and drift away. I'd be left alone, facing a kitchen full of dishes to wash, counters to clean, leftovers to put away. I'd feel sorry for myself, miserable and put upon. Then I'd pull myself up by my martyred bootstraps and do what so many other sacrificial mothers do. I'd heave a loud, pitiful sigh, put on my yellow rubber gloves, and finish all the dirty work alone. This happened almost every evening, unless I had to rush out for a meeting or I was sick with a fever of, let's say, at least 101 degrees. And even then I'd feel a stab of guilt for not being able to clean up.

My husband never swam against my sacrificial tide. He certainly wasn't going to beg me to let him wash the socks or cook the meals. Why should he? My sacrificial leanings, my insistence on doing this second shift of work at home, meant that he had more free time to do as he pleased. A friend jokes that she realized only recently that her husband of ten years, a very short man, could actually reach the kitchen sink; since she'd never seen him use it, she didn't know he was able.

An enormous number of couples do exactly the same thing, automatically allowing the mother to assume responsibility for chores and children until she becomes the household servant. Some sacrificial mothers even enjoy their burden, in a masochistic sort of way, feeling smug about doing it all and having no help. They view their home and family as a reflection of themselves, and they judge their worth by how clean the sinks are or how well their children behave. They invest themselves in their domestic life in a way that their husbands don't. They fool themselves into believing they are in control because they have final say about how the children are dressed, what the family eats for dinner, or when a sick child stays home from school. Being in control, though, just means that they end up doing most of the work.

Apparently, there are women like this all over the world. A Russian cosmonaut said that being in orbit for 169 days was like a vacation from "home work," mostly because she didn't have to do any cooking or cleaning in space. Shannon Lucid, the American astronaut who broke the Russian's record by orbiting the Earth for 188 days, feels the same way. She loved floating around in space, she says, because she didn't ever have to worry about going to the grocery store.

Maybe this is what every sacrificial mother needs—to get blasted into orbit for a while!

Many sacrificial mothers find that getting help with chores every night seems more difficult than just doing the work alone and getting it over with. Trying to convince their husbands to cooperate can be so futile, time-consuming, and irritating that it seems not worth the effort. They rationalize that the household runs smoothly when they're in charge, so why rock the boat? They treasure being in control and having things done their way, as in the right way. The forks have to go in the dishwasher tines down, the soccer shirts have to be washed in cold water, the tuna salad has to be made without celery or the kids won't eat it. Sacrificial mothers pride themselves on mastering these details and informing their husbands exactly what to do and when. But when husbands do want to help, they resent being told how to do it. Sharing the chores can become a tug-of-domestic-war, not only over who does what but also over how it gets done.

Sacrificial mothers who work for pay consider doing household chores a matter of honor, sensing that they should not only bring home the bacon but fry it up in the microwave. But by taking on that second shift of work, sacrificial mothers unwittingly turn their husbands into men with no shift at home. In this way, they relieve husbands from doing the most tedious tasks but also rob them of the precious ones too, such as bathing their babies and feeling the satisfaction of cooking a family meal.

More than ever before, husbands believe they should be doing more at home. It's just that when crunch time comes, they *don't* do much more at home than their fathers did. The only real difference between them and their fathers, in fact, is that they've got a modern sensibility that makes them feel bad about not doing more. Men with sacrificial wives are understandably reluctant to give up the luxury of having so much free time at home, to be able to choose what they will do and when they will do it. This is probably why researchers find that men are so much happier at home than women are—they've got the freedom of choice. At home, a sacrificial mother is always on duty, like an emergency-room doctor, but her husband is a man at leisure.

Husbands are not totally to blame for being reluctant household contributors. My husband never offered to help out in a substantial way, but I never insisted that he should. Years and years passed before I realized how much harm I was doing myself by not asking him to share. And the painful irony is that he would have done it if only I'd been confident enough to insist.

Sacrificial wives like me are co-conspirators, because we allow men to get away with not doing a fair share. There's an unspoken collusion between husbands, who benefit by doing less, and their sacrificial wives, who believe they benefit from being sacrificial. Sacrificial mothers feel almost noble about the inequitable nature of their household duties. They take a kind of masochistic pride in how much more they do, believing that it makes them better mothers and wives and superior women. But they're wrong.

The reality is that sacrificial mothers do not benefit by doing the second shift at home; in fact, they're actually hurting themselves and their families. When sacrificial mothers do too much at home, their family begins to view them as slightly inferior, as a subservient member of the tribe. By doing too much, they teach their children to denigrate them as well. Sacrificial mothers end up with three-year-olds who order them around the house, demanding to be read books and refusing to take naps. And their husband demeans their expertise at home, downplaying their contributions and trumpeting the fact of his income or his occasional plumbing repairs or lawn maintenance work. He falsifies the argument by trying to equate fixing a leaky toilet twice a year to washing the dishes every night.

Sacrificial mothers have to learn to think of doing their second shift as a big mistake, as a terrible habit that robs their husband of the chance to participate fully in family life. It's like dropping him off at a golf course with no clubs or at the tennis court with no racquet. A husband isn't part of a family unless he does not only fun things, such as playing ball and picking up pizza, but also the routine dirty work, such as weekly loads of laundry and staying up all night with a delirious, vomiting child.

When I first decided to limit my sacrificing, I did it for my sake, not for my husband's. After ten years of nonstop sacrifice, I'd reached a point of no return. I just couldn't take it anymore. All that sacrifice had left me empty; I had no core; I felt myself slipping away. I was scared that if I wanted to talk to myself, I wouldn't find anyone there.

At first, my husband was confused and upset when I renounced my sacrificial state. He'd been comfortable with our arrangement, if only because it was familiar. The first few months of our trial period of shared sacrifice disoriented both of us. Eventually, though, he became much more accepting and understanding of my point of view than I had ever thought possible. Like so many women, I'd underestimated my husband's willingness and ability to share.

Sacrificial mothers may find it hard to believe, but husbands who do household chores and child care actually benefit from marriage too. Married men will still be healthier and live longer than bachelors if they take on a second shift of their own. These husbands will have a new appreciation for the meaning of "family values," because the most successful families are those in which both partners share the responsibilities.

A mother in Minnesota tells me that although she worked part time as a private-duty nurse for handicapped children, she also used to do all the chores at home. Partly because she had a three-year-old and a nine-month-old baby, she always felt frazzled and distracted, and sometimes, uncontrollably angry. She also resented her husband's demand for sex every day. She got into the habit, she told me, "of treating everyone like garbage," including her stoic but unhelpful husband. When she went back to school for an advanced nursing degree, though, she had no choice but to reach out and beg him for help. Her husband, who'd attributed her three-times-a-week rages to female moodiness, was used to pulling himself into his shell until the storm passed. He was also used to being served a cold drink and a hot meal every night. But he astonished and impressed her by rolling up his sleeves and pitching in when she asked. Now he does laundry and cooks dinner a few times a week, and she's the one who organizes their half hour of privacy for daytime lovemaking on weekends. They're equally thrilled with their new domestic arrangements—she gets help around the house, and he gets a no-longer-angry wife who's eager for a roll in the hay.

An important step in creating an equal opportunity family is for a sacrificial mother to learn to let go. She has to relax her standards for how the chores are done and how the children are cared for. Her husband won't fold the sheets the way she wants, nor will he cook a delicious, healthy meal every chance he gets. He won't dress the children the way she does, and he won't floss their teeth every night. It's almost a certainty that her husband will not have the same expectations of cleanliness that she does either. While she may want a kitchen floor to be clean enough to eat off of, he may expect to be able to eat off it too—because there are so many crumbs and chunks of food still sitting there.

To become less sacrificing, a woman must come to accept her husband's different standards, or at least to learn to live with them. If she jumps up to redo everything he's done, he won't want to try again, and she's throwing away her chance for equality. To shed some of the work, a woman has to bite her tongue, button her lip, and let him do it his way.

It's possible that some husbands are oblivious to how much extra work their wives really do. If so, a wife has to make sure her husband learns about the reality of her days. In the best marriages, experts say, husbands make a mental "love map" of their wife's day, an imagined schedule to help them know what she's doing and where she is. This isn't so they can control her movements or keep track of her spending. It simply helps husbands empathize with her, and figure out her highs and lows, so they can both talk about it later. Husbands can prove their love by taking the initiative and showing an interest in their wife's life.

Without such a map, a husband doesn't have a clue about how much extra work his wife does at home, especially if she's doing it while he's asleep or out of the house. Sacrificial mothers are adept at doing laundry at midnight or five in the morning, so they don't have to take time away from their family. But this superhuman consideration keeps their work invisible to everyone in the family. A friend used to do all her family's laundry early Friday morning, after her husband and children had left for the day. They'd leave a house full of dirty clothes and come home to find everything clean and folded and put back in the drawers, as if an industrious, thoughtful elf had visited. Now that she works full time, the whole family does laundry on Saturdays. The best part, she tells me, is that it's no longer her job, it's a family job.

## The Paternal Plus

Many men love competition, but there's no Heisman Trophy for fatherhood, no Most Valuable Father Award. That's a shame, because men don't seem to realize just how valuable being a father really is— for *them*. In advertisements for the United States Army, the army claims that it can help a person "be all that you can be," but it's really fatherhood that inspires the best in men.

Men approach a kind of personal best as they climb the ladder of family relationships, as University of Chicago demographer Linda Waite points out. Single men, those with no family ties, are on the lowest rung, since they are in the worst shape, both physically and emotionally. Married men, those with a wife but no children, are halfway up, because having that one intimate relationship makes them better off than single men. Finally, being married and having children puts men on the very top rung of the ladder, because having close ties to both a woman and a child makes men healthiest and happiest of all.

Men who are fathers are simply more satisfied human beings than men who are not, says David Popenoe, author of *Life Without Father*. Being a dad gives men an array of subtle psychological benefits. When I compare fathers to husbands without children, I find that fathers are happier about themselves and their lives. They're more satisfied with their marriage, with their work, and with what they've done with their lives so far. Fathers even feel better about the amount of respect they get from women, and they feel more masculine than other men do.

Not all men are liberated and enhanced by fatherhood, of course. Some fathers are hateful, self-centered, or nasty, never reaping the psychological bounty that fatherhood offers. Others never even acknowledge the fact that they are fathers, abandoning their infants before they have a chance to achieve fatherhood. In a sense, though, these men aren't really fathers, because the advantages of fatherhood come not just with paternity but with the day-to-day practice of fatherly duties.

What is it about fatherhood that's so good for men? There are obvious factors, such as learning responsibility, providing for and protecting a child, and being a role model. Becoming a father also may unlock a tightly closed inner door in men, liberating them emotionally. Fatherhood can free men from the constricting, inhibiting role that traditional manhood requires. It's like a "Get Out of Jail Free" card in a Monopoly game, only this is a "Get Out of Overly Macho Manhood" card, and it's good for as long as a man dotes on his children.

Men who would normally fall into the traditional masculine role by being unemotional, overly analytical, or extremely aggressive are allowed to relax when it comes to their children. Fathers have social permission to be wildly impassioned, irrational, and weak at the knees with love for their children. Being a dad gives a man license to gush: He can brag and coo over his baby in a way that he can't for just about any other reason. A construction worker told me that he wept when his son was hospitalized for minor surgery, sobbing silently as the boy slept under anesthesia. Two of the cynical, seen-it-all nurses in the pediatric ward thought that his emotional display was so touching that they both developed a crush on the man in the hard hat who wasn't afraid to express his fear and love for his child. To them, his crying was incredibly sexy, though he admits he rarely lets go like that over anything or anyone other than his children.

When a child evokes all of the nurturing, loving, and protective impulses that many men try so hard to suppress, it's considered okay, especially if that child is a baby or toddler. Men are "forgiven," even indulged, for their displays of emotion and bursts of pride over their children. That's why a news item appeared in the *New York Times*, describing a burly Manhattan bus driver who pulled over in the middle of the street to telephone his little girl and ask about her first day of school. You can almost hear women as they coo, "Isn't that sweet?" (Employed mothers, of course, make loving gestures like this nearly every day.)

Being a father also takes men out of themselves, forcing them to make sacrifices they might never dream of doing for anyone else. Becoming a father gives them permission to be sacrificial, at least up to a point. Most men won't sacrifice beyond what they deem an acceptable level.

A paraplegic in Michigan was forced to go way beyond his normal sacrifice level when his wife left him and he had to care for his nine-month-old daughter by himself. For the first time since his cripping car accident, he had to stop worrying about himself and start paying attention to his child. The responsibilities of fatherhood rejuvenated and rehabilitated him in ways that no hospital ever could, he says. When people see him, a ponytailed, tattooed man in a wheelchair holding his daughter in his lap, they refuse to believe he could be a good-enough parent. They don't realize, he says, that fatherhood has saved his life.

Fatherhood is indeed a terrific boon for most men. In fact, parenthood may actually be more beneficial for men than it is for women.

Having children certainly enlarges and enriches the lives of both fathers and mothers. But because men and women bring very different approaches to the job of parenting, they have very different expectations of it and they're affected by it in very different ways.

For many of the fathers I've interviewed, parenthood is a delightful hobby; for mothers, it's a lifelong vocation.

Such fathers get much joy from their children, just as they get pleasure from playing a great game of touch football or driving a fast car. Their breezy attitude toward paternity may explain why fathers spend so much less time with their children than mothers do, even when both work outside the home. This is true, by the way, all over the world. In eleven very different countries, from Belgium to Thailand to Italy, fathers spend less than an hour a day alone with their four-year-old child, according to an international study sponsored by the High/Scope Educational Research Foundation in Ypsilanti, Michigan. The research shows that fathers in Hong Kong spend about six minutes alone with their child in a sixteen-hour day. Meanwhile, mothers in the United States, Germany, and Nigeria spend the most time with their preschooler, some as much as ten hours a day. Even in families in which the mother works outside the home, fathers don't spend much more time with the child. In China, where nearly all mothers work outside the home, research reveals that mothers spend almost seven hours a day alone with their child, but Chinese fathers spend just fifty-four minutes a day.

The time that fathers do spend with children is more leisurely and relaxed than the time mothers spend with children. Fathers tend to have quality time; they use it to play and mess around, because they don't have to do the parental grunt work. Fathers bounce and jiggle, tickle and toss their babies; mothers bathe and feed, dress and discipline them. Fathers entertain older children by taking them to ball games, watching television with them, and coaching their soccer teams. Meanwhile, mothers are washing the filthy towels and supervising the homework and driving the car pools to team practices.

Most children find out that fathers are for fun, mothers are for work.

Because fathers tend to worry less about getting the chores done, they enjoy parenthood more. As a result, they don't tend to worry about their paternal performance as much, either. It seems quite likely that fatherhood is not as central to men's identity as motherhood is to women's. The proof is that when men want to give up on marriage, many are also willing to quit being fathers. An extraordinary number of fathers simply leave their children behind when they want to escape a failing marriage, according to sociologist Popenoe. In reviewing a massive amount of data, he finds that one in five fathers hasn't seen his children for at least a year after the divorce. In addition, fewer than half of divorced fathers see their children more often than just a few times a year, he says.

Many fewer mothers would ever consider running away from motherhood, in part because they're so much more personally invested in the role. Mothers, especially sacrificial mothers, often judge themselves and their own worth by how successful they are at motherhood. A woman with well-adjusted and happy children will view herself as valuable, someone who's competent and secure. But a woman who believes that she has failed her children somehow will feel inadequate and unworthy. These feelings of incompetence can last not just a few years, but for decades.

It's no wonder, then, that fathers feel so much less parental stress and strain than mothers do. For many mothers, a bad day of mothering is a tragedy; for fathers, it's no big deal, there's always tomorrow. Fathers feel much less debilitating everyday tension than mothers do. Being a parent doesn't make men feel as rushed or as overwhelmed by problems as it does women. It doesn't make them feel too tired to cope or unable to think straight either, according to survey research conducted by Duane Alwin, a sociologist at the University of Michigan.

Because sacrificial mothers take their job so seriously, they're not surprised if they suffer—nor are they deterred by that suffering. What's more, they're certain that their problems are worth it, because their children will prosper and thrive as a result.

It's too bad that they're so very wrong.

# Five

# Children Don't Need
# a Sacrificial Mother

Like a mother octopus, she's quite willing to hover and starve, as long as it will help her children.

She goes without sleep in order to spend time with her children; she gives up the last chocolate chip cookie, she denies herself small pleasures such as hot baths and long walks, or she quits her job to stay home, because she knows in her heart that it will be better for her children.

A sacrificial mother believes that there's a grand maternal balance, one that measures her present sacrifices against her children's future gains. If she sacrifices, they benefit; she gives so they may get. In her mind, her sacrifices make her children stronger, happier, smarter, better. It is through her efforts that they will become the most well-adjusted, most self-confident, most popular children around.

But her great passion for her children makes her blind to everything around her. She's like a carriage horse that wears blinders, unable to see anything on either side, only what's straight ahead. A sacrificial mother has eyes only for her children, so she ignores her own desires and passions. Yet she senses something's gone wrong, that there's a part of life she isn't seeing—any part that doesn't include her children. Sacrificial mothers tell me that they feel a gnawing inner absence, a troubling lack of purpose in their lives. They long to have more of their own passions, but it's as if they've used up every bit of their supply on their children, and trying to find more is like trying to pound more ketchup out of an empty bottle. So they lock up their personal passion deep inside, keeping it alive but invisible to their family. Sacrificial mothers tend their secret garden of fantasies in private, in a hidden hothouse for passion. They nurture these personal fantasies like precious orchids, tending them with great care but never letting anyone share in the scent. Mothers tell me that they dream of building their own house from the cellar up. They yearn to be a restaurant-owning bartender or to be an astronaut traveling far into space or to be a spy in Europe, one who's fluent in every language. They even harbor kinky fantasies, such as becoming a dominant mistress with a submissive man as their slave.

In real, everyday life, though, most mothers don't have time for any passion that doesn't involve their children. A Catholic woman I know would consider it a mortal sin to fantasize about any child-free passion. She works twenty hours a week as a computer programmer and puts in another twenty hours a week volunteering at her children's school. She spends her evenings driving her four children to Scouts, swim meets, ice-skating lessons, and speech-therapy classes. She's the only mother in her modest Chicago neighborhood to invite nineteen third-grade boys for a birthday sleep-over party and then, only a week later, seventeen first-grade girls for another. She prays that her single-minded passion for her children will prevent them from accusing her, some time in the future, of not doing enough, not caring enough, or not being sacrificial enough. Such imaginary recriminations, based on anxiety and guilt run amok, are a recurring nightmare for women like her.

I have a friend who tortures herself by picturing her daughters, ten years from now, lying on a messy bed in a dormitory somewhere and smoking cigarettes. They're complaining bitterly about their mother to a roomful of other girls, all of whom hate their moms. This prophetic image fans her passion for her children, making her even more determined to sacrifice enough now so that her daughters won't ever be able to remember one thing she did wrong.

Mothers like these don't realize that trying to keep children from complaining about Mom is like trying to prevent skin from sagging or wrinkling. You can ignore it or postpone it or cover it up, but you can't stop it from happening. Mothers will mother and children will blame and complain, a fact of life long before the first psychoanalyst put the first patient on a couch.

Because they hope to avoid this future blame, sacrificial mothers are most vulnerable to all kinds of imaginary fears about what they're doing wrong. They want desperately to believe that they control their children's destiny, because it's too frightening to sense that their love and devotion might have almost no effect on how their children turn out. So they develop superstitions and vague theories to justify their belief that what they give up now will benefit their children someday.

Sacrificial mothers love to assume, for instance, that "No pain, no gain" can be applied to motherhood. If sit-ups have to hurt before they can tighten abdominal muscles, then maybe a mother's sacrifices have to hurt before her children can benefit. A woman I know in Florida used to have great faith in this cod-liver oil logic, the feeling that if something tastes bad, it must do good. So she used to deprive herself of her beloved cappuccino and she refused to listen to music or to watch television, all so that her children would be better off. If she deliberately forbade herself the things she loved, she figured, her children would blossom because she'd sacrificed so much. Also, never doing anything for herself gave her that much more time to spend with them. She thought it was her duty to give them every single moment of every day, except when she was at work. Eventually, though, she realized that she was resenting every self-denying second of every day and that her children couldn't possibly benefit from her teeth-gritting, fist-clenching, suffering in silence.

So she flipped her life upside down and inside out. Now this Florida mom drinks the special coffee she loves two or three times a week. She sits and listens to music that she wants to hear, and she watches her favorite television shows every so often. Not only is she happier about being less sacrificial, but she claims that her children are more relaxed too.

Sacrificial mothers also secretly believe that *more* is *better*. The more a sacrificial mother does, the better off her children will be. That's why she doesn't just enroll them in soccer, but she signs them up for music and skating and ballet too. That's why she invites nineteen of their friends to sleep over instead of only four or five. She feels she has to spend more money, if she has it, and, sometimes, even if she doesn't have it. She senses she should give up more as well—more time, more privacy, more of her personal life.

But, in truth, more is not always better. The *New York Times* reports that a Georgia mother of twins decided right from the start that she wouldn't sacrifice her life to enrich her children's. And her less-is-more theory of motherhood became national news. She thought that her twins should just learn to get by on their own, to relax and enjoy being children. So she never drove them to piano lessons or soccer games, she never bought them computers or video games. She probably never gave them the last pickle either. Despite her refusal to be overly sacrificial—or because of it—her twins were the first ever to score a perfect 1600 on the SAT, the college entrance exam.

Another unspoken rule that sacrificial mothers hold dear is that anxiety is good, because being anxious and worried means that you care. That's why my friend in Texas is proud that she worries so compulsively about her children's education. She wakes up at three in the morning, in a panic, agonizing about whether they're learning enough at school, if the teacher can control the class, if they're happy about where they live. She loves being distressed, so if she hasn't worried herself into a frenzy about her children, she's sure she's not doing her job properly. But it seems fairly obvious to me that my friend's anxieties probably make her children more nervous and uneasy, not calmer and more carefree.

Likewise, many sacrificial mothers seem to feel they have proprietary rights over their children, that these small human beings belong to them. Fathers are essential, they feel, but not part of the maternal main event. If Dad is like a circus sideshow in parenthood, the dancing poodle act, then Mom is the star, the tiger tamer in the center ring. Perhaps this is why some sacrificial mothers unconsciously ease their husbands out of being responsible for much of the child care. By forcing him to be peripheral, they make sure they're in charge. Even more often, though, sacrificial mothers discover that their husband willingly and gladly gives up his paternal responsibility, because it's less work, and less worry, for him.

A mother I know found herself handling all of the care, and feeling all of the heartache, for her deaf son, when her husband shrugged off his share of parenthood as soon as the boy was born. Instead of taking his son to doctor's appointments or helping the boy learn to speak, this man spends all his free time racing stock cars. He contributes two-thirds of the family's income but absolutely none of its emotional support or comfort. His wife stoically accepts her sacrificial lot in life as a given, in part because she feels at fault for having given birth to such a seriously damaged child.

But the most fundamental assumption of all, the one that motivates and guides a sacrificial mother's every word and gesture, is that hers is the true sacrifice, the only one that really matters. In what may be her sole self-aggrandizing thought, she considers herself to be the *only* one who counts when it comes to her children's growth and ultimate happiness. With this attitude, of course, she sets herself up for terrible blame ten or fifteen years down the road. By the time her baby has become an unhappy teenager who's flunking English or using drugs, she's the only one who's at fault. And she accepts that blame wholeheartedly. Her first thought when anything goes badly for her child—from a broken arm to a lousy report card—will always be "What did I do wrong?"

By this logic, then, Mother is the one who *has* to sacrifice the most.

Our culture sincerely encourages mothers to believe that they matter most. After all, nearly everybody has faith in the sacred mother-infant bond, the attachment that babies form to Mother in the first year of life. Most of us assume that the nature of this bond, whether it's good or bad, will set a course for the child's emotional well-being for the rest of his life. It will determine how anxious he is in school, how confident he feels about himself, how easily he makes friends, even how he'll fall in love as adult.

Researchers claim that babies become attached to their mother in three ways, only one of which is healthy. To find out how well attached each baby is, they use a rather bizarre method called the "Strange Situation Test." Psychologists put a toddler into a room with his mother and observe them together, then they ask the mother to leave and send in a stranger for a while. They observe how the child reacts to the stranger and how he behaves when his mother comes back. If the child seems glad to see his mother, or if he seems upset but she comforts him easily, he's what they call securely attached. That's the good kind of attachment.

If he can't be comforted and seems confused when she reappears, he's got an anxious or insecure attachment. And if he deliberately stays away from his mom when he sees her again, he's what they term "avoidant." These two are the bad kinds of attachment. Nobody is quite sure that this technique is a reliable way to tell what kind of a relationship a two-year-old has with his mother, but almost every researcher who wants to study attachment uses it anyway.

No wonder sacrificial mothers are so consumed by viewing themselves as the source of all of their child's strengths and all his troubles too. They've been told that this bond is their responsibility and that their child's success or failure in life rests on their ability to be completely loving and dependable during these first crucial nine or twelve or eighteen months. That's why mothers quit their jobs to stay at home, and it's why they feel so horribly guilty if they can't. It's also why hundreds of researchers have spent decades trying to prove that these kinds of attachments are real and that the bond makes a difference to a child's ultimate well-being.

But psychology's dirty little secret is that *there is no real proof that such a crucial bond exists*, or if it does, if it has anything at all to do with how sociable or well-adjusted children become later in life. Because there haven't been any long-term studies using this method, we just don't know if attachment types matter in the long run. Can an insecurely attached baby grow up to be a loving, successful man, or will he be forever handicapped by an inability to love? Nobody knows. After doing this research for several decades, for example, psychologists are still running around in circles trying to figure out if infant day care alters a child's attachment type. But after spending millions of dollars, and many years, they don't have a clue.

The truth is that the mother-infant bond is a relatively new invention, one that might be nothing more than the creative longing of a society that has little left to worship, nothing else that seems as deep and full of meaning as the link between a mother and her baby. So we imbue that relationship with great magic, with awesome power and reverence, because it's one of the few human mysteries still unsolved. When a woman puts her baby in day care or allows her husband or mother to help raise her children, it's as if she doesn't care about the sanctity of that bond, as if she's become a traitor to true motherhood.

Almost all sacrificial mothers swear by this bond, though. They need to believe that their sacrifices make a difference, because they're certain that "Men are what their mothers made them," as the essayist Ralph Waldo Emerson wrote.

But can a mother's sacrifices really change her children's lives for the better? Will her self-denial make them happier as children and more well adjusted and successful as adults?

As my daughter's Magic 8-Ball says, "Don't count on it."

A mother's sacrifices play little, if any, part in her children's overall development. It's much more likely that the genes a child is born with will have the greatest influence over his future personality. While a mother's sacrifices may not be so important, the social circumstances into which her child is born could be crucial. Growing up very poor, for example, or experiencing a number of divorces and frequent moves tends to be much more detrimental for a child than is any lack of sacrifice on his mother's part.

## What Matters More than Sacrifice

A friend confides that she thought her new baby would be a blank book, one whose pages she could fill. As the years pass, though, she sees that she's been wrong. A child is a book already written, she realizes, and all we can do is read it and try to figure out what it means.

She's more right than she knows.

As I pore over the latest studies that focus on identical and fraternal twins, I find that much of this very convincing research stresses the importance of genes in determining how a child grows and develops. A child's personality and temperament has little to do with his mother or her sacrifices and a great deal to do with what she has passed on to him genetically. These studies reveal that a child inherits a disposition that determines how he sees the world, how he reacts to it, how he experiences it, and even how the world treats him. So a mother can only react to who her child already is— she can't shape that child into who and what she wants him to become.

Behavioral geneticists have reached this conclusion by studying identical twins. Because they are born of a single egg, identical twins are twice as similar genetically as fraternal twins. Scientists observe how identical twins develop when the children grow up in different families. If parents and family life are crucial, and how children are nurtured is what matters most, then these twins should become quite different people over time. But if babies are born with traits that determine their personalities, then it won't matter if one twin is raised on Mars and the other on Venus, because their nearly identical genetic constitutions will emerge anyway.

And, in fact, that's just what happens. Identical twins grow up to be unbelievably similar, no matter who raises them.

In a story reported by Lawrence Wright in *The New Yorker*, twin girls were adopted at birth and then studied by researchers for more than ten years. The experts noticed that the first adoptive mother was cold and aloof and seemed intimidated by her daughter's good looks. This family clearly favored its biological son over the adopted daughter, whom they viewed as a disappointment. The second mother, though, adored her twin daughter, dyed her own hair to match the girl's, and sacrificed for the child often. This second family doted on the girl more than on its biological child, also a son. Yet both twins turned out to be identically shy, anxious, neurotic, and insecure. For years both girls sucked their thumbs, bit their nails, and wet their beds. Even later in childhood, both twins were hypochondriacs, afraid of the dark and afraid to be left alone.

It's as if the families that raised them and the mothers who either resented or sacrificed for them had almost no effect on the girls' personalities at all.

Indeed, when a team of researchers led by psychologist Robert Plomin asked hundreds of sixty-year-old twins to recall their family life of five decades earlier, they found that identical twins had nearly identical memories—even those raised by completely different families! It's as if, as twin researcher Thomas Bouchard writes, "the genes sing a prehistoric song," a melody that lures us along a predestined psychological and biological path. At least half of the differences in human personality—how sociable, aggressive, optimistic, and impulsive people are, how sensitive, tolerant, neurotic, and anxious they tend to be—are due to genes and not to family, these researchers find. The other half of personality is a mixture of normal everyday ups and downs in mood as well as the combined influences of father and mother and brothers and sisters and teachers and friends and social class and race and religion and nationality and family stability and anything else under the sun.

Because most psychologists rarely bother to study more than one child in a family or to compare adopted with biological siblings or twins raised apart, they can't untangle the complicated effects of genes and what mothers do. So if they find that toddlers of working mothers are more hyperactive than toddlers of mothers who stay at home, for instance, they don't know if it's because of something the mother does or, say, because working mothers have higher energy levels that they pass on to their children. And researchers almost never bother to find out if the toddler's sister or brother is as hyperactive, a fact that almost guarantees that their results will not be completely reliable.

In fact, it's almost always true that brothers and sisters raised in the same family are amazingly different, an observation that most mothers who have more than one child make all the time. The twin researchers like to say that two boys raised in the same upper-middle-class family, by a mother who takes them to the same classes, activities, and parties and who sacrifices in precisely the same ways for each, will grow up to be as different in personality as two boys plucked at random from two other families thousands of miles away.

Unless children share nearly identical genes, as identical twins do, no two siblings will grow up alike, no matter how often or how rarely their mother sacrifices for them. In part, this is because each child relates to Mother in his own way. He creates his own subjective world, in which she is a creation of his own way of looking at life. While one boy might bask in the glow of what he views as his mother's constant love and attention, the boy's brother may burn with resentment at what he perceives to be her constant nagging and crankiness. Likewise, each child may view his mother's sacrifices in very different ways. The first boy feels special because she helps him do his homework every night, even though she spends all day at work. But his brother holds a permanent grudge, since she can't be a chaperone on class trips, because she works all day. Clearly, then, children raised in the same house by the same parents can look at the same family life, and the same maternal sacrifices, in totally different ways.

Because each child has his own personal style, mothers also respond in a unique way to each child. From the day of their births, I've known that I treat each of my two children very differently. During her first year of life, I coddled and cajoled my daughter, trying to keep her happy and calm. I devoted myself to being her perpetual rocker and jiggler. This was partly because she was such a tough baby, one who screamed so loudly that the doorman in our Manhattan apartment used to call her "the Voice," because he could hear her from sixteen stories up as we descended in the elevator. It was also because I had no other children to distract me. My son, born nearly two years later, was also cranky. But because I had two little ones to deal with, I wasn't nearly as indulgent or as patient with him.

Today my children still have very different temperaments, and I still treat them very differently. My son believes that his life would be greatly improved if he hadn't been blessed with an older sister. He keeps track of how many minutes I take to say good night to her and then demands equal time for himself. He also complains that she doesn't get punished nearly as often as he does. And when I think about it, I realize that he's right.

But it doesn't matter if he thinks I'm too strict or if she feels privileged to be coddled. The way my children are now, and who they will be as adults, I believe, has very little to do with how I treated them as infants and even less to do with how much I deny myself for their sake.

I say this with great conviction. Still, the knowledge that few, if any, of my sacrifices will have a profound effect on my children's ultimate well-being is as frightening to me as it is to any mother who cares. The insight makes me feel that being a good mother is like being told to drive on a highway, without hands and blindfolded, and to get home safely. It's just not possible.

The idea that what mothers do for their children, and what they give up, may not matter at all goes against our dearest beliefs and our most profound wishes. If we don't have that much influence over how our children turn out or how happy they are, then who does?

Perhaps no one.

A child's happiness could, in fact, be biologically predetermined. Identical twins, for example, have nearly identical feelings of contentment, no matter how much money they earn, what kind of job they have, how many years they went to school, or what kind of family raised them. If people have a preset happiness level, something like a natural weight, around which they hover from infancy to old age, then there's not much a mother can do to change that level, no matter what or how much she sacrifices. A naturally happy boy may feel sad for a few months when his best friend moves, but he's going to be happy most of the time, whether his mother lets him have the last chocolate chip cookie or not. A morose girl will perk up for a while when her mother buys her a new pair of roller skates, but soon after she'll settle down to her usual, not-so-happy mood.

Having a seriously abusive or neglectful parent will, of course, alter a child's degree of happiness, but even that terrible experience doesn't necessarily leave permanent scars. About one in three children is incredibly resilient, researchers say, bouncing back from the very worst childhood experiences to become a confident and caring adult. Even if the child's parents are illiterate and unloving, or abusive and mentally ill, a child like this overcomes the odds. The secret is having an innate feeling of optimism and control. As babies, they're easygoing and sociable. Later on they almost always feel sure that they will survive, that they'll be able to surmount whatever difficulties they face in life. Growing up with a completely unsupportive mother, they find other sources of strength, through friends or neighbors or mentors at school. They learn to take affection and attention wherever and whenever they can find it.

This certainly doesn't mean that abuse is acceptable or that mothers can justify ignoring their children completely. Many children, in fact, don't ever completely overcome terrible deprivation or great poverty. Growing up very poor, with a single mother, tends to cause children to suffer from serious economic troubles as young adults, research shows. They're more likely to drop out of high school, to get pregnant out of wedlock, and to be unemployed as young adults. Even when single mothers remarry, their children aren't necessarily better off, especially if the family moves a lot. When children move, they lose valuable ties with close friends and teachers and neighbors, people who really care about what happens to them.

In itself, divorce may appear to be a more selfish act than a sacrificial one. After all, it seems that a woman who ends her marriage is thinking more about her own happiness than about her children's. But, in fact, when a mother divorces, her life becomes more sacrificial, not less so. Her standard of living, for example, drops substantially, especially if her ex-husband fails to pay child support. And the odds are good that he won't pay what he owes; at least half of fathers pay little or nothing to their families after a divorce. So a single mother works harder, for less money than she had before, but she has more day-to-day worries and anxiety about her financial situation. Even worse, she may find herself not just a single parent, but an *only* parent. After a divorce, about half of fathers end up seeing their children only a few times a year, if at all. The longer the couple has been divorced, the less likely Dad is to have contact with his children, especially if he remarries.

While it may seem that getting married again is a single mother's dream come true, that's not necessarily so. Having a new husband will certainly improve her financial situation—two incomes are better than one, especially if one of them is a man's, since men often earn more than women for the same work. But it may not help her children, because remarriage usually involves moving, and, as I said, frequent moves under these circumstances are difficult and stressful for children. If a single mother wants to remarry, it's best for her children—and probably for her as well—not to move out of her community.

Realizing this, a woman in my neighborhood didn't want to leave the place that she and her two daughters had called home for fifteen years, even after a bitter divorce. Since she couldn't afford to keep her home, she sold it and moved to an apartment in our town, so her daughters could stay in the same school and keep the same friends. As a result, after an initial blip of family trauma, both she and her girls are thriving.

But I have another divorced friend who isn't doing nearly as well, mostly because she hasn't stopped hopping from place to place since her divorce. In the first five years after her breakup, she and her two sons lived in four different apartments, all in different neighborhoods in New York City. Then, a few years ago, she moved across the country, to San Francisco. She and her boys have moved seven times in eight years, in a restless search for a better life. They have enough money but no stability, no real community or place that feels like home. As a result, the boys are having trouble at school, they have few friends, and they almost never see their father. My friend thought that she was escaping sacrifice by moving wherever her whims took her, but instead she's forsaken her own peace of mind as well as her children's.

Having a sense of community is vital for newly divorced mothers and children. When they live in one place for a while, they build an elaborate network of friends and neighbors and colleagues and soulmates. It's usually not until those connections are broken that they notice the invisible threads that tie them to their community. Only when a mother doesn't have a neighbor to help out while she races to the emergency room with a bleeding child does she realize how isolated she is. Only when a child has nobody who knew him as the funny first grader who played the mailman in the class play does he feel lonely and friendless.

That's why a newly divorced mother should step back and take a deep breath before she decides to "wipe the slate clean" and make a fresh start by moving far away. Sometimes a better choice is to make a fresh start but in the same place; to focus on those changes that occur on the inside rather than on the outside. You don't need to be living in a different apartment in a strange town to discover new inner strengths. After a divorce, many women discover that their most positive and dramatic changes are emotional ones. They learn about a true self they never knew they had. They find a sudden, overpowering resolve to be stronger or thinner or smarter than they were before, and they follow it through. This kind of dramatic inner metamorphosis is probably easier to achieve in a place where you already feel comfortable and relaxed, not somewhere new, where everything is strange and unfamiliar.

Because children tend to be frightened by change, they might be alarmed by mother's postdivorce transformation. During and after a divorce, then, is the right time to speak to children about logistical details, such as who is moving where and when they're going. You also should explain some of your feelings, about how you are changing and about how they are too. Keep them informed about the new kinds of sacrifices you'll be making, and tell them about the sacrifices you expect them to make. Remember, though, that too much sacrifice, even after a divorce, doesn't really help children.

## When Sacrifice Hurts Children, and What to Do About It

If too much sacrifice doesn't help children, at least it can't hurt them, right?

Wrong.

When a mother sacrifices too much, too often, she teaches her children not autonomy, but dependence; not consideration, but contempt. Although she may be truly dedicated to being a good mother, her good intentions backfire. It's as if instead of fertilizing her garden with mulch and manure, she covers it with bleach and laundry detergent. She assumes that she's doing her children good, but she may actually be doing them harm.

Susannah Fox, a thirty-five-year-old woman I interviewed, grew up with a very loving, very sacrificial mother. An only child, her parents divorced when she was seven, and the girl became the center of her mother's existence. Her mother worked during the day, so Susannah came home to an empty house; television was her only afternoon companion. Susannah's mom felt so guilty about this arrangement that she dedicated every nonworking minute to the girl. As a result, the mom never socialized or went anywhere without Susannah; the two were so close, they could have been joined at the hip. In retrospect, Susannah feels terrible that her mother chose to give up so much for her sake. Today she feels that her mom made the wrong choice.

In a bizarre postscript to this story, Susannah's mother remarried her father ten years after the divorce. They're still together, although her father had a stroke eight years ago that left him unable to move or speak. Susannah's mother has to care for him as if he were a newborn baby, lifting him in and out of his wheelchair, bathing him, feeding him, and putting him on the toilet.

"She's sacrificing all over again," Susannah says with a resigned sigh. She admires her mother's willingness to sacrifice, but she finds it pitiful too.

By sacrificing too much, a mother also fosters dependency in her children. They never have to load the washing machine or cook the macaroni and cheese, because they know that Mom will do it. They never have to give up something they want, either, because Mom makes sure they'll get it, no matter what. By always putting her children's needs first, a sacrificial mother leads them to believe they have a right to rule the family and everyone in it. They feel princely because Mom feels servile.

A friend tells me that her twelve-year-old daughter can't manage to open a can of soup and heat it in the microwave. The girl has never rinsed off a plate or washed a sock; she doesn't know how to take a kettle of boiling water off the stove. But my friend is perversely proud of how little her daughter does for herself. My friend works full time, and she bends over backward to make sure that her daughter will never be inconvenienced because of that. Although many children with working mothers learn self-sufficiency at an early age, my friend's daughter would starve if she were left alone for a weekend. My friend boasts that she still packs the girl lunch, braids her hair, and stitches her ballet slippers. But she's completely blind to how overindulgent she is and to how her sacrifices have spoiled her preadolescent daughter.

I once asked my friend's daughter how she feels about everything her mom does for her. The girl lowered her eyes, flashed me a guilt-filled glance, and started to cry. "I'd do more if she'd just show me how," she told me. She confessed that she can't figure out why her mom does things for her that she can do for herself. But she also admitted that she never protests against her mother's overwhelming need to sacrifice. The girl has grown up expecting her mom to sacrifice—it's all she knows. So as long as her mom is willing to give, give, give, she'll be willing to take, take, take.

Women like my friend assume that with their sacrifices, they are giving their children a wonderful example of consideration and caring. They expect this generosity of spirit to rub off so that their children will learn to perform acts of kindness for other people—holding open a door, say, or giving up a seat on the bus.

But with little or no explanation of what she's doing and why, a sacrificial mother raises children who are actually less likely to be polite and thoughtful and more likely to expect servitude as their rightful due. They learn that Mother is a second-class citizen, one who seems to have no wishes or dreams of her own but who lives to service their desires. It's as if they're permanent customers in a fancy café, waiting for coffee and dessert to be served. And Mom's the waitress.

Over the years, children with a sacrificial mother learn not to respect her. Because she allows herself to be treated like the household bath mat, that's how they come to view her: damp and scruffy, a thing they need only once a day, to step on when they get out of the shower. You can hear the lack of respect in the way children speak to their sacrificial mothers, with a mix of disdain and impatience, as if she's too slow and ignorant to understand what they're trying to tell her. And that disregard can last a long time. A grown woman whose mother sacrificed everything for her children admits that she loves her mom, but she doesn't really respect her, even now. In her heart, she feels that her mother was a bit of a sucker for giving up so much for so long. And now this woman is constantly trying to prevent herself from becoming the very same kind of mother.

It's a telling sign that a mother is sacrificial if her children are often rude, nasty, and ungrateful. I hear it as I listen to a six-year-old at the party store, berating his mother for her ignorance of cartoon heroes, while she's trying to choose the most perfect plates and napkins for his birthday celebration. I recognize it as I listen to a third grader scolding his mother for picking him up at soccer practice at the wrong time and for bringing the wrong bottled drink. And I notice it as I listen to a ten-year-old, whining and complaining because his mother didn't buy his favorite fruit roll-ups.

If it weren't so absurd, this massive ingratitude would be heartbreaking.

To prevent these kinds of scenes, it's vital for mothers to explain to children the logic and reasoning behind their sacrifices. If children don't understand that their mother is indulging them while denying herself, then they can't possibly appreciate her efforts or show her any consideration.

It was my children's obvious lack of gratitude that convinced me that my sacrifices weren't helping them at all. Just as I had to open my husband's eyes to the need to share, I had to enlighten my little darlings on the subject as well. But they adjusted rather quickly to our new, less-sacrificial-Mom regime. At first, they were confused when I wouldn't put down my work to serve them dessert or change the television channel to a show they wanted to watch. But they got the hang of it pretty fast, as if a news flash appeared before their eyes, blaring the message: "Mom is a person too." Now my son bargains with me to watch sports, and if my daughter wants to eat the last banana, she always asks me if I want half.

In the long run, I'm sure that this new strategy will be better for all of us than the old one. If I ever doubt, I consider my neighbor Sue and her mom. Now thirty-two, Sue has a husband and two babies of her own. She grew up in California with a loving single mother, a woman who never went overboard on sacrifice. Her mom made it quite clear that her needs and interests were most important. In fact, Sue's mother had a successful career as a fabric designer and interior decorator, and to this day, her mom oversees the decor on every wall and floor and stairway in Sue's house. When her mother comes to visit, she doesn't stay for a week, she settles in for five months! And what's most amazing is that Sue is delighted to welcome her mother for as long as possible. "We get along really well," she tells me. "Mom is my best friend."

If a sacrificial mother wants to teach her children lifelong respect like this, she must tell them what she's doing and why. You obviously can't discuss why you gave up a law practice to stay at home and play Candy Land and make Jell-O jigglers with your three-year-old. But you can, and should, point out to an eight- or twelve-year-old child why chauffeuring him to an after-school class means you'll have to leave work early or rearrange your trip to the grocery store. You aren't trying to make the child feel guilty or to rub in how incredibly noble and sacrificial you are, but simply to let him know that you are going out of your way to fulfill his demands.

Let your children know that you are sacrificing because you hope to make them happy and to make their lives easier. Initiating this kind of discussion with your children may be much more enlightening than you can imagine.

First, your children may be totally unaware that you're sacrificing. It may come as a complete revelation to them that what they expect as a given happens only because you sacrifice. Children are experts at being oblivious, especially if they've never heard Mom mention the fact that she has her own wishes and desires, a few of which have nothing whatever to do with her family. Making children aware that Mother pays a price for their pleasure and comfort and well-being, even willingly, will not only enlighten them, but it may inspire them to be sympathetic and grateful. It feels so much better to go out of your way to do something for a child who thanks you for it than for one who doesn't even notice that you did it.

Second, you may discover that your children really don't want you to sacrifice so much, that they don't want to take the class or go to the party or join the team as badly as you thought. So you may find that many of your sacrifices aren't necessary in the first place. That's why you should learn to haggle over your sacrifices.

That's just what my friend did with her helpless twelve-year-old daughter. One day, overwhelmed by stress at work and her chores at home, she refused to sew the elastics on her daughter's ballet slippers. Apologizing profusely, she explained to the girl that she had a terrible headache and just couldn't do it. Expecting to face a wall of sullen resentment from her daughter, instead she met a tidal wave of delight. Her daughter was tickled to be able to learn to sew all by herself. Watching her daughter mutter as she pricked her finger with a needle, then correct her backward stitches and uneven elastic pieces, my friend realized she'd done the girl a disservice by not forcing her to do more. Now the girl sews all her own ballet equipment and has mastered soup out of a can. She and her mother have come to a more equitable arrangement of sacrifices. Every time my friend goes out of her way to do something for the girl, she receives a thank-you from her daughter or an agreement to do a favor in return.

Sacrificial mothers have to get over their illusion that only they can care for their baby properly. Mothers do not retain sole ownership of their children, and they are not the only ones who can love and care for their infant. For thousands of years grandmothers and aunts and older sisters and brothers have cared for babies while mothers did essential chores, such as gathering food. The mother gave birth to and nursed the child; but afterward, the child belonged to everyone. If modern sacrificial mothers could find other people to rely on for help with the children, above and beyond their husbands, they'd reduce their burden of sacrifice substantially.

In trying to invent this kind of communal approach to child rearing, three women and two men began a Children's Collective in Amsterdam in the early 1970s. They bought an apartment for their six children, ages one to nine, a place where the children lived together during the week. Every day, for twenty-four hours at a time, one adult moved in and took care of all six children and did the shopping, cooking, and light housekeeping. Then that parent was off duty for the rest of the week. On weekends each child went to stay in his parent's nearby apartment. This cooperative, parenting by shift, lasted for seven years.

As a very small experiment in nonsacrificial motherhood, no one knows for sure if growing up in the collective was good for the children. But Ruth De Kanter, a Dutch psychologist, observed that the girls seem to have benefited most from the arrangement, in part because they were exposed to several different examples of mother-hood—none of which was sacrificial.

For most of us, of course, this kind of solution to the sacrifice dilemma is not only impractical, it also seems a bit ridiculous. But there are more realistic, and easier, ways to create your own child-rearing community, wherever and however you live.

A woman I interviewed in Florida lives near three other families, a total of eight adults, all of whom take turns caring for their ten children. They live on a cul-de-sac in a tiny town, one so small that people living in the next city over have never heard of it. They rely on each other completely. When a hurricane is coming, they help each other put up storm shutters and make pitchers of lemonade for the children to share. The grown-ups don't make plans for summer camp without consulting each other, so they can share car-pool duties. When one mom wants to get a manicure, she's got three others willing to pitch in and watch the kids. They consider nail appointments and all other forms of mother-pampering to be vital errands, supremely worthy of child-swapping for an hour or two. They've created a tribal village right in the middle of a modern suburb, one that ensures that every mom sacrifices a lot less than she would if she were on her own.

A California mother I spoke with had a slightly different variation on a solution to her overload of sacrifice. She and her husband bought a duplex apartment with her sister and brother-in-law; she lives downstairs, they live up. In essence, the families are raising their five children with two mothers and two fathers. When one mom can't be there for a child's nursery school concert, the other one is. When one dad can't drive to gymnastics class on Saturday, the other one does.

Some mothers use their own extended family to take on some of the child care, by living close to their own mother or mother-in-law. A few others, with no willing relatives nearby, simply hire an extended family. In what I call the Manhattan solution to the problem of sacrificial motherhood, a very wealthy couple I know with three young children has hired round-the-clock nannies, both of whom live in. The day-shift nanny starts at about 9:00 A.M. and works until 8:00 or 9:00 P.M. Then the other nanny takes over for the all-night shift. This young, rich-beyond-belief mother sacrifices very little for her children; she's like the Princess of the Upper East Side. She never has to give up her season tickets to the Knicks or to the Metropolitan Opera, or her twice-a-week, two-hour massage and hair-care appointments.

Unfortunately, most mothers can't rely on infinite money to cure their sacrificial tendencies. But they can depend on their husbands more than they do now. Their husband's role should be as a built-in sacrifice-sharer. In the happiest marriages, husbands willingly share the sacrifices with their wives, because they don't assume that a woman has a monopoly on sacrifice. In these marriages, husbands become as self-denying as their wives. A balding, bearded man I met in Kansas tells me that when he and his wife had their first baby, he fought with her to see who would be able to take on the *most* responsibility, not the least. He was terribly worried that she'd be overburdened, and he felt that it was his obligation to make sure that she wasn't. Being a father has made this gentle man even more sensitive and caring. He's the kind of guy who proposed to his wife by hiding a diamond ring in a pizza box and, armed with a dozen roses, made a point to propose to her on the very spot where they first met. Now he's painfully aware of how much his wife sacrifices, by exercising at nine at night, for example, after a full day of work, so she won't have to give up play time with her children. And he's the one who feels guilty about putting his two children in day care, because he's the one who drops them off there every morning.

If a husband doesn't know how to sacrifice, it's his wife's job to teach him. Teaching doesn't mean forcing, either; instead, it means gentle persuasion. Speak your husband's language by explaining that a family is like a team, and everyone in it has to work together to win. When I told my husband that I felt as if I were the only one on the field with the children, because he always seemed to be watching from the sidelines, he got my point. I might have been wrong, but it helped him understand my point of view.

Soon after this discussion, my husband started to share some of my responsibilities at home. Without really noticing, I began to take on some of his. Every so often I'd change the oil and the oil filter in the car: okay, I'd take the car to a guy I paid to do it for me. But now it's an extra errand that he doesn't have to do. The lesson, for both of us, is that sharing is a two-way street.

A mother I interviewed in Texas told me that she's always shared the sacrifices with her husband, ever since her children were born, because neither one pretended to be a child-rearing expert. Never once has she tried to change the way he treats the children. She accepts his flaws without complaint, and he accepts hers. "I don't knock him for what he doesn't do," she says. "I love him for what he is."

Take on this calming tao of sacrifice, and teach your husband and your children to share. Point out to everyone exactly what you give up and how often you do it; that way you can take stock of exactly how much sacrifice there is to go around. At the same time, you can make a point to teach your daughters and sons how important it is for a woman to have her own goals and ideals, how vital it is that she form a vision or a dream for herself in life. You have to set an example for them by learning to think of yourself, to make your own needs a priority. In doing so, you'll give your children an example of a woman who believes that she can make a contribution to the world, one that is independent of her family. You have to learn to be selfist, to consider yourself just as important as everyone else in your family. When you do, you'll be better off. And so will your children.

## Six

# Be Good to Yourself

You know you can't lock your kids in a closet, throw in some healthy snacks and a television set, and get on with your life. Taking good care of babies and children will always require an enormous amount of selflessness and devotion. And sacrifice isn't a matter of choice, despite the fact that it doesn't help mothers or their children. Because sacrifice may be the result of a female biological urge, it probably can't, and shouldn't, be eradicated. But that doesn't mean that mothers have to be the only ones who sacrifice all the time, the only ones who give up their self for the sake of the children.

Women have to learn to let go of some sacrifice and grab hold of self.

I call this talent selfism, or the art of learning to be selfist.

To be able to care for others well, a woman needs to learn to be able to love herself. To give to others, she has to learn how to take for herself. If mothers could show themselves only a fraction of the affection and attention they give to their children, they'd be so much better off. They need to reserve some emotional energy for themselves, make some room for their own needs and desires and dreams.

A woman is a selfist if she can honestly say that she feels very comfortable making herself happy and if she usually takes an hour a day to do something for herself. Using this definition, my research shows that only about one in three mothers is selfist.

Although you wouldn't think it to meet her, a mother of six whom I met in California is a quiet and surreptitious selfist. A religious Catholic who lives for her family, she gathers them together at evening meals, makes sure that they go to church together, hosts family camping trips, and arranges family videotape-viewing parties. She's very big on family togetherness. But she's just as religious about taking care of herself as she is about taking care of her family. She works out at a gym with a friend five days a week, and she makes sure to do what she calls "one nice thing" for herself each day. She also makes a weekly plan to go out to lunch or shopping or to the movies with a friend, and she has a regular, Friday-night date with her husband. She's learned that if she gets too busy to nurture herself, she'll be incredibly grumpy and then take it out on her family. So it's partly for her family's sake that she never forgets herself.

Many mothers mistakenly believe that by sacrificing their selves, they will serve their children better. So they end up living their lives for and through their children. At first, this kind of vicarious, substitute living can be thrilling, a way to redo your childhood without all the bad parts, trying not to make the same mistakes twice. But ultimately, it's a terribly damaging habit—it's stealing your child's soul to suit your pleasure. The Irish writer Oscar Wilde actually thought that this kind of self-sacrifice should be outlawed, because "it is so demoralizing to the people for whom one sacrifices oneself." The children of sacrificial mothers probably would agree.

Certainly the mothers who live through their children don't benefit either. Many of them lose their own sense of worth, because the children's successes and failures become theirs. A woman I know lives for her daughter's ballet career, so she was ecstatic when the girl won the role of Clara in a local Christmas production of *The Nutcracker.* She was walking on a cloud that whole winter. The next spring, though, the girl didn't win first place in a dance competition, and the woman was heartbroken, tumbling into a blue funk that lasted for months. It's as if she can feel extreme exhilaration and terrible disappointment, but only through her daughter, never for herself. What a terrible burden it is for her daughter too. The woman has become like a crazed ventriloquist, one who can talk through the puppet on her lap but is completely unable to speak in her own voice.

It takes mothers like this a long time, ten or twenty or thirty years, in which they give and do only for their children, before they feel the deep and inevitable frustration and depression and anger about the life they haven't lived. This is exactly how a mother in Vermont feels as she sits by and watches her two teenage daughters ruin their lives with too much beer, too many boys, and too few good grades. After seventeen years of sacrificing and living through her girls, she tells me, she's frozen with horror and great sadness, realizing that she now views her daughters as "the enemy." Her nearly grown babies have not only stolen her true self, but she's got nothing at all to show for those years of love and devotion.

Because her children have failed, so has she.

I've heard so many stories like this one, from mothers who are overwhelmed by regret and a desire to turn back the clock—to do everything again, only this time paying more attention to themselves. If they could, these mothers say, they'd insist on pursuing their own passions instead of only that lone dedication to children and family. If they could do it all again, they tell me, they'd focus more on themselves.

Another mother I spoke to in Kentucky would give anything to be able to rewind her life and play it back in a more selfist way. She wishes now that she'd continued to work as a nurse instead of quitting to stay at home. She wishes now that she'd joined the local theater group to nourish her love of acting. She wishes now that she'd learned to fly a plane, a never-fulfilled, lifelong fantasy. But all those wishes are gone with the wind, and the only thing she has to show for a lifetime of sacrifice is a loveless marriage to a man who won't sleep in her bed and four grown children whose drug addictions and multiple divorces have become abhorrent to her.

If mothers want to avoid living a life of should-haves, they have to learn to share their sacrifices and to moderate that sacrifice with a healthy dose of self-love. They have to learn to balance their need to sacrifice with an equally robust urge to pay attention to themselves.

The ability to be selfist is not at all the same as being selfish. A woman who is selfish has a concern for herself at the *expense* of others. She doesn't know how to compromise; she considers herself first, last, and always. Mothers who are crack addicts are generally selfish; so are movie-star mothers whose children are raised at a distance, by a series of nannies; so are mothers who marry and divorce and move four or five or six times while their children are young.

A woman I spoke to in Nevada admits that she used to be a fiercely selfish mother, and she's been racked with guilt about it for decades. When her children were only six and four years old, she got fed up with being a wife and mother and left home to do her own thing, as she puts it, "to live life with me at the center." She was nursing a passion for adventure as well as a passion for a young Argentinian man she'd just met. So she ran off with her South American lover, never writing or calling her children, because she was so determined to do her own thing. She thought it was "cool" that their dad was the one who was raising them. Like a modern Moll Flanders, she abandoned her children to satisfy her wanderlust and old-fashioned lust. But her husband went on to father seven children by five different wives, her children never felt loved or safe, and they never got over the feeling that they had been betrayed and orphaned by their mother.

At the age of fifty-five, she believes that she destroyed a piece of her now-grown children, and she's ashamed of her hurtful and malicious behavior of long ago. She also knows that her sorrow over her selfishness comes a lifetime too late.

But she was a selfish mother, not a selfist one.

A selfist mother is one who can devote herself both to her children and to herself; she respects her children's wishes as well as her own. She can think of children *first*, without thinking of children *only*. She can love her children with wild abandon and joy. She can care for them when they're sick, help them with their math, and save her money to be able to buy them sneakers and video games. But as a selfist, she feels that she has a right to her own happiness too. So she takes the trouble to be good to herself, by coddling herself when she's sick, setting aside time to read books and magazines that she likes, and saving money to be able to get her hair cut or to have coffee with friends. She knows that to function as a wife and a mother and a decent human being, she needs to recharge her own batteries nearly every day.

So many mothers make the mistake of confusing selfism with selfishness. They assume that anything they do just for themselves has got to be selfish. This concept terrifies them, because a good mother can't be a selfish one. So they run from any kind of self-indulgence, fleeing in panic at the idea of pampering themselves. But, in the end, their reluctance to be selfist does them more harm than they know.

While it may come as a terrible shock to sacrificial mothers who are afraid of selfishness, women who can focus on themselves are much better off than those who can't. Selfist mothers are happier and healthier than sacrificial mothers. They even view themselves as more successful wives, mothers, and lovers. Women who are self-ist get immediate benefits, such as being in good physical shape because they take time to exercise, or being well-informed because they take time to read newspapers and books, or being more relaxed because they find time to meditate or do yoga. But they also get permanent, lifelong blessings, because it's easier for them to live their lives well.

It's possible that happy, confident women are the ones who are naturally more capable of paying attention to their own needs. If that's true, then maybe it's not selfism that makes them happy but their innate happiness that makes them selfist. This is definitely a chicken-and-egg question, because we don't know which comes first, the self-confidence or the selfism. But in a way, it almost doesn't matter, because it's clear that the two are vitally and closely linked.

Being emotionally healthy makes it easier for women to be selfist, and learning how to focus on themselves clearly improves women's emotional well-being.

## Selfism Works

Women who are self-sacrificers are "always a drag, a responsibility, a reproach, an everlasting and unnatural trouble with whom no really strong soul can live."

I didn't say that, George Bernard Shaw did. The eminent British playwright and author believed that "only those who have helped themselves know how to help others, and to respect their right to help themselves." That's why women who are "self-helpers" are so much better off, he said.

It's true that selfist women get much more out of life than sacrificial ones. In my research, it's clear that mothers who feel comfortable doing things for their own pleasure and taking time just for themselves reap tangible rewards.

When I compare selfist mothers to others, the differences between the two groups are striking and dramatic. Selfist mothers are happier with just about every aspect of their lives: with their marriages, their work, their intellectual abilities, their friends, their bodies, the way they look, and how their lives are going. Because they're able to treat themselves well, they have an optimistic outlook about everything that counts. They feel as if they're in charge; they feel competent. Selfist mothers are less likely, in fact, to feel depressed or angry, but they also feel a greater ability to express their emotions. They avoid becoming emotionally constipated, because they're never blocked by the unspoken resentment and frustration that troubles so many sacrificial mothers.

It shouldn't come as too much of a surprise, then, that selfist mothers also have the highest self-esteem and the greatest amount of self-confidence. They even think of themselves as being more intelligent and more attractive than other mothers. They like themselves more, so they treat themselves better. And the better they treat themselves, the more pride they feel. It's a self-fulfilling prophecy, one that enables selfist women to deal with the world on their own terms.

Once this selfist cycle starts spinning, there's no stopping it. Self-confidence breeds selfism, which breeds more self-assurance. Mothers who are selfist also feel more control over their lives, and they feel a greater sense of power, not just at home but at work and in the world too.

The positive mindset that accompanies selfism also keeps selfist mothers healthy. They don't have nearly as many psychological problems or physical troubles as the more sacrificial mothers do. Selfism seems to function like a magic charm, one that keeps mothers hale and hearty and happy.

How do mothers become selfist?

A few women are lucky enough to have been born that way, but the rest of us have to nurture a knack for it.

The fortunate few, those who have a built-in talent for self-focus, have a natural ability to bathe themselves in attention and love, before and after they have children. An Oregon woman has a passion for planes that she's turned into a career in aviation. She can't believe how lucky she is to be doing exactly what she loves all the time. Now a mother of two, she's also a pilot of a Boeing 747; she deftly combines her love for flying with her devotion to her family. As a result, she overflows with self-confidence. Because she flies to the Orient every month, she has no choice but to sleep in teak-paneled, silk-lined hotel rooms and to call room service every day for a week. Then it's three weeks at home, being a down-to-earth mom, driving to ball games, washing dirty sheets, stirring pudding. After that, it's back to the Far East and compulsory room service again.

The vast majority of mothers, though, have to work hard to develop and maintain their aptitude for selfism. And sometimes that's a herculean effort. The voyage can be a nearly insurmountable one for mothers who are trapped by circumstances beyond their control, such as having a stubborn or uncooperative husband or a seriously ill child or a more-than-full-time job they can't afford to quit.

One thirty-seven-year-old mother of preschool twins I interviewed is trying to focus on her own needs, but she's fighting a losing battle with her husband every step of the way. Although she gets a deep sense of accomplishment from taking classes to finish her B.A., her husband won't support her, emotionally or financially. Going to school is the only thing she does for herself, but her well-to-do husband refuses to pay her tuition. As a result, she has to take out loans to pay for each class, rationing her education one course at a time. That hurts, because she gets such enormous satisfaction from doing well in school, a kind of gratification she never gets from her duties at home.

There is hope for mothers like her, though, because just about all of us tend to get better at looking out for our own interests as we age. Many women don't even begin to appreciate or to understand the value of selfism until they reach the age forty crossroads. It's the opposite of what happens with your vision: Hit forty, and you can't focus on the fine print anymore, but at that age, you become better able to see the usefulness of being selfist.

Older women are almost always more selfist than younger women are, according to my research. One of the reasons this happens, of course, is that older women often have older children, who are less demanding and needy. It's a lot easier to take time for yourself if you have a fourteen-year-old and a twelve-year-old than if you have a four-year-old and a two-year-old.

Even more important than children's ages, though, is that women begin to feel less pressure to fulfill other people's needs all the time as they grow older. Slowly but surely, they relax their sense of duty and self-negation, as if in reaction to having lived a selfless, sacrificial life for so long. There is something about being in midlife, around the age of forty or fifty, that makes women pause, take a step back, and examine their lives.

It's this mysterious impulse, almost an inner compulsion, that forces women to open up and search for their true self, the one that has been buried under family responsibility for so long. It's at this time of life that they decide to learn yoga or to exercise regularly, to find a new job or to go back to school, to reinvigorate a stale marriage or to end a failing one. It's a time of life when women want to see themselves clearly. For the first time ever, perhaps, they begin to view themselves as separate beings, as women apart, not as wives or mothers or daughters. With this new sensibility comes a different outlook on life, a desire to have a unique voice, to become a competent human being who knows what she wants and how she hopes to get it.

It wasn't until I approached my forties that I began to think of myself as a me again, not as part of an us. This odd sensation made me feel the way I did when I was in high school, the first time it dawned on me that I was more than just a daughter or a sister. Back then, all I had to do to assert my independence was to leave home and go away to college. But this time the solution wasn't as simple. For the second time in my life, I was beginning to see myself as my own woman, as someone who deserved respect. Now that I was an adult, though, I had to solve my crisis in a way that would allow me to include my family, instead of rejecting them, as I did the first time around.

Some women might try to solve their identity problem by throwing money at it. But that method usually doesn't work, because self-ism isn't a matter of money. My research shows that women's income doesn't seem to make a difference in how selfist they are. Being able to take care of oneself is not, then, a matter of how much money a woman has to spend. You aren't automatically a self-ist if you can afford a weekly appointment at the hairdresser or sessions with a personal trainer or a dinner out every week. You *are* a selfist if you are convinced that you deserve respect and attention and loving care.

This is probably why selfist women tend to have better marriages—because they won't put up with a man who doesn't appreciate or respect them. Selfist wives are almost always aware of what they need, and they know if those needs are being met. If not, they insist—either quietly or loudly—enough to change what has to be changed. Just the reverse is true too. Women who aren't selfist put up with a great deal of marital misery, in part because they feel it's their duty to sacrifice their happiness for the sake of the family. They expect suffering, so that's what they get.

Almost half of mothers are in a marriage that is either unsatisfying or deeply unhappy, according to my research. They tell me that their husband hardly ever shows them simple signs of affection, such as hugging or holding hands. They're not talking about the kind of touching that leads to passionate lovemaking, just tenderness for its own sake. The same number of wives confess that they almost never have intimate conversations with their husband, so when they need to confide in someone or to share their deepest fears, they can't turn to him. It's no wonder, then, that they also describe their marriages as either "difficult" or "bad."

But just because these wives aren't selfist doesn't mean they're blind to their own needs. They're all too keenly and painfully aware of what their marriages don't provide. One woman gives me a list of what she desperately wants but doesn't get from her husband: passionate, moonlit nights on the terrace; love notes tucked under her pillow; sensual foot and back massages. Another laments that "an arm around my shoulder, a squeeze, a tender kiss, would mean the world to me."

The longing and frustration I hear from wives like these is touching and terrible. But because so many women are unable to be selfist, they simply don't bother to try to improve their marriages. Instead, they live as if in a state of psychological divorce—two people occupying the same house, sharing the same children and bank accounts and holiday meals, but little more. After existing like this for a few months or a year or a decade, eventually some women snap. They've had enough of no hugs and no respect and no intimacy. When that happens, it's often the last straw, the motivation they need to begin to learn how to take care of themselves.

A wife who suffered in silence for fifteen years, living with an asexual, uncaring husband, was catapulted into selfism by an unexpected telephone call from a former high school boyfriend. He'd tracked her down in Seattle from clear across the country. He confessed that he'd always loved her, that he'd spent the last twenty years fantasizing about her. She too had pined for him for years. The ultra-romanticism of the call, too Hollywood for Hollywood, galvanized and electrified her as nothing else had in decades. She began to live for his every-other-day phone calls. She started to walk and to swim and to lift weights. After years of a kind of sad resignation to selflessness, she came alive. With her new determination, and gallons of liquid diet shakes, she lost 122 pounds. Once she was back into her senior-year, size 8 dress, she was ready to meet her once-and-future lover. He sent her dozens of roses and arranged to fly in to see her for three days. As soon as they saw each other at the airport, they wept. For a magical weekend, they grew to know each other; yes, even in the biblical sense of the word.

When it was over, she dyed her hair blond, lost her constant plague of panic attacks, and vowed never to forget herself again. She confronted her husband, accusing him of denying her the love and affection she deserved. And then she divorced him.

Meanwhile, her long-lost lover turned into a cad. He called again and told her he was sorry, but that he'd changed his mind. She had a good, long cry, then began to build a whole new life for herself.

Many affairs, like this one, are only a symptom of a deeply troubled marriage. But an affair can also be a sign of selfism, a frustrated attempt to find better sex, deeper intimacy, or greater meaning in life. My research indicates that nearly three in ten mothers are having an affair at any given moment. That's a lot of straying moms. Some of their marriages will end in divorce, with little or no attempt to try to fix what went wrong or to learn to share sacrifice in a fair and just way. That's a shame, because for many troubled or adulterous wives, even a small amount of help and attention from their husbands would improve matters immensely.

## Six Steps to Selfism

There is a much more effective, and much less painful, way to go about becoming selfist than having an affair or getting a divorce. All you have to do is to learn how to act and think like a selfist person. Once you have a plan, becoming a selfist will begin to feel as natural as taking a shower or brushing your hair.

The first step can be the most intimidating one. It's like taking that first fall off the tower while attached to a bungee cord or singing that first song in front of an audience. Still, that first step is essential for any woman who wants to learn the art of selfism.

Sacrificial mothers have to practice selfism every day until it becomes habitual. Ideally, mothers should exercise selfism at least as often as they engage in sacrifice and self-denial. If it's reasonable to indulge children and husbands every single day, then why shouldn't it be just as acceptable for mothers to comfort themselves as often?

This sounds good, in theory, but most sacrificial mothers have no concept of how to go about behaving or feeling like selfists. Once they've gotten into the rut of habitual sacrifice, it's very difficult for them to jump the track. It's also a bit scary, because it may seem as if embracing selfism means that you have to completely discard the idea of sacrificing for your family ever again. But that assumption is dead wrong. Achieving self-love does not preclude sacrifice. In fact, children will always need an adult who is willing to make sacrifices on their behalf. It just doesn't always have to be the same adult, every single time, every single day.

Here, then, is a six-step plan for achieving selfism:

1. *Do one small thing just for you.*

2. *Set up a pampering program.*

3. *Share the sacrifices.*

4. *Respect your self.*

5. *Find a dream.*

6. *Establish your true self.*

These suggestions are not set in stone, of course. If you skip one or two of them, you might very well change your life in ways that suit your needs perfectly. The key is simply to begin, to force yourself to take the plunge.

If the process feels forced or artificial at first, don't give up. After all, that's the whole point. You're supposed to be persuading yourself to engage in behavior that's highly unnatural and very uncomfortable for you. So when you try it for the first time, you probably will feel strange. But if you keep on pushing yourself, in the right way and at the right time, you'll become a mother who makes some sacrifices for her children but who is also able to take care of herself.

The first step to selfism is to do *one small thing just for you*.

Think of something you like to do, alone and just for you, and then do it.

You will feel a bit anxious, perhaps, or you might have trouble thinking of something at first. Don't let that deter you. Force yourself. Pretend that you have to do it for your child. Think of it as homework, as an assignment from your child's teacher that you have to complete.

When I decided I had to make my first plunge into selfism, I was even more nervous than when I went into labor for the first time. I knew that I must do one thing just for me, or my soul would keep slipping away until it disappeared completely. Still, I was having trouble feeling that I had a right to do such a daring thing, especially if it involved spending money on myself.

After a few weeks of careful thought and many telephone calls to check out the possibilities, I decided that I would try to learn something new. I figured that if I took some kind of cooking class, it would be partly for me, but my family would also benefit, so I wouldn't have to feel quite so guilty about the whole thing. Since I'm a dreadful cook, with absolutely no common sense about what to put into which pot and when to put it there, everybody in my family would be better off if I learned how to cook. But I didn't want to take gourmet lessons at a glamorous school, because that would cost a fortune, and I'd be using ingredients I'd never heard of, working with utensils I don't own, and learning to make meals my children would never agree to eat. The fancy French cuisine route to culinary self-improvement, I knew, was not for me.

So, instead, I found an Italian cooking class, "Pizza and Pasta," that met once a week for eight weeks at a local community college. It was relatively inexpensive, and it gave me a good reason to leave the house. I was thrilled, giddy with the anticipation of my emancipation.

On my first night, after feeding my children a guilt-inducing meal of hot dogs and baked beans, I dashed out my front door and arrived at the class, eager but hungry, because I hadn't eaten yet. Three hours later I'd learned to cook pasta primavera and stuffed pizza, Palermo style, and had my portion of each carefully wrapped to take home and share with my family. Famished to near fainting, I ate half of it with my fingers as I drove home in the dark.

Going to a cooking class for a few weeks may not seem like such a big deal. But for me, the experience was an epiphany. It opened my eyes to the possibilities of what I could do for me. Just being with people who didn't know my husband or my children, who saw me as me, made me feel like an independent adult again, like a person with her own private life.

By doing this one small thing for me, I was forcing myself to act like a selfist, even though I was a long way from feeling as if I deserved to be one. I felt funny about spending the money and about leaving my family in the lurch at dinnertime once a week. But

I noticed that my children accepted the new status quo almost instantly: If it's Monday night, Mom must be leaving to go to cooking class. They didn't seem to have any problem adjusting to the idea that I had a right to do this or to feel that I was inconveniencing them in any way. They liked having their dad in charge, and they appreciated me more when I was around. They looked forward to nibbling my half-eaten, semi-squashed packages of Italian food, and they quizzed me eagerly about what I'd learned to cook.

If my children had no problem accepting the fact that I'd disrupted our family life to do something for me, then why should I?

Slowly I began to get a sense of how much good it was doing me. I found myself, on occasion, feeling as if I deserved special treatment. This made me feel rather pleased with myself. I began to feel important, not as a mom but as a me.

This might be the most important key to these tips on selfism: To feel like a selfist, you have to behave like one first. Because it's so much easier for a woman to do something simple for herself than it is for her to feel as if she really deserves it, the first few steps involve doing. Acting as if something is true will make it so, because beliefs usually follow behavior. If you smile as if you are happy, you'll begin to feel happy. If you pray as if you're a believer, you'll discover faith in a higher power. And if you behave as if you're a selfist, you'll soon think like one.

Doing one thing for yourself can cost a great deal, or it can be virtually free. If you're willing and able to spend money on yourself, by all means do so. Take a class or join a gym. See a therapist or a counselor or make a date to take a friend out for lunch. Rent a videotape or buy a book. Treat yourself to flowers or a plant or a new pair of shoes. Spending some money on yourself is a good first step, because it's tangible proof—to you and to your children and husband—that you believe you are worth it. Sigmund Freud believed, in fact, that patients got better faster if they paid a lot for psychoanalysis. The more they paid, he said, the more motivated they'd be to change.

This doesn't mean, of course, that if you spend $50 instead of $5 to buy yourself some earrings you'll become less sacrificing ten times as fast. More money doesn't mean more selfism. Spending money on yourself should be directly related to how much you earn. If you have disposable income that you would usually lavish on your children or your husband or your cat, try to use some of it for you.

If you simply don't have extra income to spend, or if you just can't bring yourself to spend it, don't let that stop you. Selfism doesn't require pots of money, despite Freud's theory. Instead, do something wonderful for yourself that's free. Take a brisk walk or go for a bicycle ride. Soak in a hot bubble bath or read a library book. Join a chorus or a woman's group. Meet a friend and go for a run. Bake a cake. Light candles and put on some music you love, with the volume turned up really high. Get in bed and watch something you want to see on television. Don't give anyone else the remote, and change the channels twenty-five times every ten minutes if you want.

After you do one thing for yourself, it will make you thirsty for more. The next step, then, is to begin to treat yourself well in a deliberate and planned way. *Set up a plan to spend time alone, to pamper yourself on a regular basis.* Go for a walk every day, no matter what, like the mother in Hawaii who owns a scuba diving business and hikes in the mountains with her two dogs every afternoon. Take time for yourself, even if you have to steal it, as the Chicago mother who locks herself in the bathroom and meditates in the tub every night for ten minutes does.

Scheduling selfist behavior will make taking time for yourself seem mandatory, and it will persuade you that it should be.

One of the healthiest, and most blatant, selfists I've ever met, Claire Sanders of Long Island, New York, is so adept at her pampering program that she's got a fan club of extremely sacrificial mothers who get vicarious pleasure just from hearing about it. A part-time tax attorney at a Manhattan law firm, Claire always looks casually elegant, even if she's just carting her babies to swim class or hanging out at a Mommy and Me class. That's because she devotes nearly as much time to herself as she does to her children. She does aerobics and works out with weights at home for nearly an hour a day, and she's trained her four-year-old daughter not to interrupt her during that time, unless the girl is bleeding from a major appendage, like the head. If the child begs her parents to stay at home, instead of going out together on a Saturday night, Claire firmly refuses, believing that children should not dictate rules to parents on how to live.

At forty-one, Claire has two preschoolers, but only because her husband made her stick to a long-forgotten promise to have children someday. When he insisted that she make good on her pledge, she was so reluctant that she told him, with much trepidation, that she'd try just one.

Claire surprised herself by falling in love with motherhood. She was so smitten that she decided to have one more child. Yet she never, ever, lost sight of herself. She's still at the cutting edge of selfism, even while learning to cope with the half-chewed Cheerios stuck to her bare feet and the baby spit-up down her bra.

Claire knows that when she feels good, she's a better mother. And her daughter learns that Mommy is an important person, whose needs are as significant as everyone else's in the family. The little girl learns that Mom matters.

It's because Claire takes care of herself that she can't help feeling good about herself. And because she feels so satisfied, she can't help doing nice things for herself. On the rare occasion that she's down or feeling some self-pity, she snaps herself out of it, fast.

"There's nothing I don't have," she tells me, explaining the reasoning behind her relentless optimism. "I have a loving husband and two children I'm crazy about. I'm not counting pennies and my family's healthy. If I feel depressed, I know I have nothing to feel bad about, and I think, 'You ungrateful witch!' "

Claire is a perfect example of why selfism is so valuable for mothers. She's a loving and dedicated mother and wife who also has a robust amount of respect for herself. She proves Elizabeth Cady Stanton's statement of more than a hundred years ago, that "self-development is a higher duty than self-sacrifice."

Becoming a selfist, though, doesn't mean that mothers must stop sacrificing forever and focus only on themselves. The goal isn't to become like the wicked stepmother who cares only about her own image in the mirror. Mothers have to learn to balance their sacrifices with self-love and self-interest. For every moment they give to others, they should put in an equal amount of time being good to themselves.

If mothers have to cut back on their sacrifices to make room for themselves, then they have to convince their husbands to take up the slack. That's why step 3 is *sharing the sacrifice*. This is difficult, because a woman has to engage her husband's cooperation. Since raising children requires too much work for just one person to bear, single mothers need to find other single mothers or friends or relatives who can share their sacrifices. And wives must convince their husbands to take on some of the burden, or else they will suffer.

If your husband doesn't see the truth in this, then he may not realize how much you do for your family. Keep a diary for a month, and make a note every time you make a sacrifice. Include the reason you do it and who it's for. Then take a calm, quiet moment and present the evidence to your husband, not in an accusatory way but simply to offer him proof of what you're doing. Talk with him about which of your activities seem unnecessary, which ones you could continue, and which ones he might be able to take on. If he's really interested in improving the quality of your marriage and of your family life, and if he's concerned about your well-being, then he'll give it a try.

It's clear to me, from all of my research, that the best and most successful marriages include couples who share the sacrifices that family life demands. These are what I call "magic marriages," as we'll see in the next chapter. In these unions, husbands do the dishwashing and baby tending and much, much more; they also do a large part of the worrying and the self-denying too. In one such dual-sacrifice marriage, the husband tells me that he never lets a day go by without telling his wife how much he loves her, and he makes sure that he gives the children their baths nearly every night so his wife can rest when she gets home from work. For his wife, combining selfism with sacrifice is a breeze, because she has such a concerned partner.

Unfortunately, though, the large majority of mothers are *not* in a magic marriage or in anything remotely resembling one. For them the idea of creating a magic marriage may seem like an impossible dream. But just discovering that such marriages exist and learning how they work can inspire these women to try to negotiate one of their very own.

*Respect yourself* is the next step. Because this requires a strong inner conviction, self-respect will come gradually, after you have begun to do more things for yourself. Again, *acting* as if you respect yourself will help you come to feel that you really do. If you do things you like every day, if you focus on you, you will prove to yourself that you are worthy of respect and you will come to believe it. A mother who gives herself half an hour a day to read or to watch the news or to bathe will, after a few weeks or months, begin to feel that she deserves that time, that it belongs to her. She will also learn to respect herself, because she gives herself that gift every day, no matter what. When she is able to shower herself with the same affection and attention she showers on her children and her husband, she'll be on the way to feeling true self-respect.

Only when a mother learns to respect herself can she feel genuine respect for her husband and children. If she is proud of who she is, she will be proud of who they are as well. Instead of living her life in the reflected glory of her family, she'll be able to bask in the light of her own accomplishments, and she'll also appreciate theirs more.

A selfist mother from Ohio respects her own wishes as much as she respects those of her four children. She tells me that whatever she does, she gives it her all, because "whatever is worth doing is worth doing well." That's why she graduated at the top of her college class and why she works at the top of her field as a medical assistant, and it's why she lives at the top of her capacity for sexual passion. She takes the time to send her husband sexy printed messages on his pager. She wears lacy lingerie and buys sex toys for their regular hotel trysts. Even though they've been married for fifteen years, they make love at least five times a week, she says, and her heart still skips a beat when he walks into the room. Because she lives her life with so much passion and with such great respect for herself and her own sexual desires, she's got the highest self-esteem imaginable.

*Finding a dream* flows naturally from the ability to respect one's self. If you believe that you deserve a life of your own, if you sense that you have a destiny that encompasses your family but also goes beyond it, then you will understand the importance of seeking your own dream. A selfist mother should feel like an essential and irreplaceable part of her family, but one who also has a sense of herself as a separate human being, one with goals and desires that belong to her alone.

A dream is a realistic vision or a goal that a woman hopes to reach in her lifetime. It's not wanting to become a supermodel or a rock star or a television news anchor, because those are fantasies that just aren't in the realm of possibility for most of us. A dream is something real, something that will satisfy a woman's inner needs, one that will make her feel whole when she finally achieves it. A dream can be as clear-cut as going back to school for a degree, or it can be as undefined as becoming a successful artist or entrepreneur or horse breeder. To find any such dream, a mother has to go beyond her babies. She has to reach deep down inside and discover who she is and what it is that she wants out of life. This can take a lot of time and effort. But it also can pay the biggest dividends.

The last step is to *establish your true self*.

Sacrificial mothers have the greatest difficulty doing this, especially because being sacrificial means that a woman has to be self-effacing. But a woman who is selfist not only confronts but embraces herself. She accepts her weaknesses and flaws as well as her strengths and talents. She pays close attention to her true self, caring for it with as much tenderness as she'd show a newborn baby.

The ultimate goal of selfism, then, is to discover and sustain this true self.

A woman's true self is a colorful and complicated mosaic. It's pieces of who she is, was, and will be at every moment of her life. It's who she was as a young girl and a teenager, as a young adult and as a woman. It's the sum of all of her roles—daughter, sister, wife and mother, lover, friend, worker and neighbor. But her true self is greater than just her ties to loved ones; it's her relationship with her own soul, the essence of her being.

Finding a true self is not easy. Sacrificial mothers might believe that it's a luxury fit only for wealthy executives or movie stars or fashion designers. They are greatly mistaken. Every mother must take the time and the energy and the passion to conceive a self independent of her family. If she does, she'll also become the best mother she can be.

# Seven

# Becoming a Selfist

Here's my idea of pampering.

I pour myself a glass of wine. I make a bag of microwaved popcorn, with butter. I take both downstairs, where I crawl under the comforter that I crocheted when my children were babies, and I recline on our old sofa, the one that's coming apart at the seams. I've rented a videotape; it's a movie that only I want to see. I watch the whole thing, from beginning to end, without a single interruption.

This is my favorite treat after a long week of work.

Every mother needs to close her eyes and envision such a personal Garden of Eden. It can be a simple self-indulgence, like my video session, or it can be as elaborate as taking a course in sign language or becoming an expert in tai chi chuan or doing some birdwatching every morning. The point of this exercise is clear: to nurture yourself as easily and as well as you nurture your family.

Women may have a powerful urge to nurture, whether they're caring for their children, their pets, or their man, but they have an equally strong need to be nurtured themselves. So, in fact, does every human being, according to psychologist Henry Murray. Everyone, he said, needs to nurture and to be nurtured. When he devised his list of the twenty basic human needs over fifty years ago, he included the need for nurturance as well as what he called the need for "succorance," to be consoled, sustained, protected, and cared for by a loving supporter.

Mothers are almost always responsible for most of the family nurturing, whether they enjoy it or not. Just about everyone assumes that mothers should be constantly available to give and give, but mothers also need to receive some nurturing for themselves. In the best of all possible worlds, women will receive that tender nurturing from their husbands. But, unfortunately, most wives live in the real world, where real men don't nurture.

The fact is that the majority of wives simply don't get the affection or attention they deserve from their husbands. It's not necessarily men's fault, but some husbands have no idea how to nurture a woman or are not even aware that she needs nuturing. A wife can try to teach her husband how to pamper her, or she may have to look to someone else for her pampering.

A woman who tells me that her husband doesn't hold her when she's hurting or laugh with her when she's happy often feels lost and alone. She chose to accept some affectionate touching from what she calls "the first bidder," the only man who ever offered her any. But he happens not to be her husband. So she's having an affair, just to be hugged.

Even wives who do have caring and nurturing partners still have to learn how to nurture themselves, if only because most husbands can't or won't do it often enough. Mothers must pamper themselves in the same way they would pamper a sick baby, a seven-year-old celebrating a birthday, or a husband upset about not getting a raise. Being self-indulgent doesn't mean that mothers have to go to wild and crazy extremes. They don't have to rack up thousands of dollars on shopping sprees for leather and jewelry, and they don't have to run off to Los Angeles and try to become music video stars. They don't even have to spend hours at the beauty salon every week. All they have to do is to offer themselves one simple act of kindness every day. They have to treat themselves to something that feels good, something that they feel they deserve.

Mothers also have to learn to pamper themselves without feeling guilty. If you feel guilty while indulging yourself, you ruin the whole effect. Try not to be like the mother in Minneapolis, who spends her precious extra pennies on the porcelain dolls and silver jewelry she loves to collect, but feels horribly guilty every time she buys something. She's not pampering herself, she's just consuming; it's like stuffing her mouth with marshmallows just to have something to chew. A mother in South Florida also invests her extra money to pamper herself with her love of photography. But she doesn't feel guilty, because every time she snaps a picture, she feels a thrill. She's indulging herself without a speck of guilt, because it makes her feel worthy. Photography gives her enormous pleasure, a sense of productivity and competence, and it also provides her with a lasting visual display of her love for her family—twenty-five huge photo albums' worth.

Guilt-free gratification is essential in this prescription for self-indulgence. You're simply not allowed to feel guilty when you nurture yourself. If you do, then you're doing it wrong. If you're indulging yourself but you feel guilty every time you do it, stop right now and pick something else. Look for one small thing you can do that feels good and doesn't inspire guilt. Get rid of the guilt, and you're on your way.

To become a successful selfist, you'll need to progress from doing that one small thing to developing a program of regular pampering. If you take one twenty-minute walk, and you enjoyed it guiltlessly, then start to do it at least two or three times a week. Make sure you go that often, rain or shine, summer or winter. If you like to read at night, then schedule some private reading time for yourself every single day. If you like doing the crossword puzzle in the newspaper, then do it—before anyone else gets to it. If you like manicures, get one when you can afford it and do your own when you can't.

Don't assume that nurturing yourself every once in a while will be enough to make you a selfist. It won't.

You have to learn to treat yourself on a regular basis, over and over again. Pampering yourself has to become habitual so that you feel that you deserve it, that you are worth that special effort. Only when you're convinced that you're worthy of respect will you be able to persuade your husband and children that you are.

All of this might seem ridiculously obvious. Of course mothers should treat themselves well. Of course they deserve to be indulged. Of course they're better off if they pamper themselves.

But the sad truth is that to many mothers, it's not obvious at all.

Mothers have so much trouble pampering themselves, it's as if they think they'll have to walk on hot coals first. Women without children have much less trouble indulging themselves. Mothers with grown children have only some difficulty. But mothers who have children at home seem almost paralyzed by an inability to deem themselves worthy of rewards. It's as if living with children makes them impervious to their own needs and blinds them to what they should be doing for themselves.

Fewer than half of the mothers I've interviewed who have children at home take an hour a day to do something for themselves. Using so much time, sixty whole minutes, on themselves makes them feel queasy, nervous, on edge. They're befuddled if they have to concentrate only on themselves, because they don't really remember how to do it.

Mothers have always had trouble doing things for themselves, in part because they never want to appear too selfish. That's why mothers used to throw themselves into hobbies that kept them focused on home and family. They spent all their spare time doing extra work that was supposed to be fun. They did quilting, sewing, and needlepoint; they grew vegetables and canned and baked; they became engrossed in knitting, crocheting, and doing embroidery. None of these traditional maternal activities was very self-indulgent; all were hidden chores that improved life for husbands and children. Even today, sacrificial mothers who take up knitting hardly ever make themselves sweaters; instead, they churn out baby booties and children's hats. This isn't selfist, it's just more sacrifice, disguised in wool clothing.

Men don't seem nearly as reluctant about indulging themselves as women are, regardless of whether they are fathers or not. Having children at home doesn't seem to affect how most men feel about pampering themselves one way or the other. They do it readily, with or without children around. In part this is because fathers don't worry about looking selfish. They're supposed to indulge themselves, and it doesn't matter if their choice of self-indulgence isn't family-oriented. It's okay if they want to go bowling or to a board meeting at night or to disappear on a Sunday to play golf or tennis. They're allowed to spend hours tinkering with engines or machines and hanging out with friends after work. They're supposed to come home and watch sports on television all night, eagerly changing channels to surf from game to game. It's as if these kinds of self-focused activities are accepted masculine rituals, so husbands and fathers can't be criticized for practicing them.

Why can't a mother be more like a father?

Why can't we try to think like men, to believe that we too have every right in the world to indulge ourselves, to treat ourselves well, to give ourselves a break?

We can. The path to selfism is designed to indoctrinate mothers into believing that they have a right to self-fulfillment and to receiving pleasure outside of their family and children.

## The Power of Pampering

Too many mothers wait for their youngest child to walk out the door before they dare even to think formerly taboo words such as "me," "myself," and "mine." It takes them twenty or twenty-five years to move to the head of the line. When they're on their own, they're deliriously happy that it's finally their turn to go first.

But over an extended period of time, this complete lack of selfism can harm mothers grievously. It can obliterate their self; it can demolish their self-respect and destroy their confidence. It can even damage their physical health.

Sacrificial mothers sometimes fool themselves into believing that they are being self-indulgent when they indulge their children. But they're confusing child-spoiling with self-pampering. When they buy their child a new pair of skates or an expensive pair of jeans, they're as thrilled as if they'd bought themselves diamond earrings or a new watch. When they insist on driving their children to every play date or birthday party or baby gym in the neighborhood, they feel as satisfied as if they'd joined their own exercise class or choral group. But these good deeds are sacrificial, not selfist, so this is not real selfism.

Pampering your children is fine, but it's no substitute for pampering yourself.

Most of us can figure out ways to pamper ourselves on a weekly basis. I find that mothers do indulge themselves, but that their gestures tend to be very modest ones. The most common ways in which women pamper themselves are: reading, taking a long bath or shower, watching television, going to sleep early, getting a haircut or a manicure, going to the movies, getting some exercise, and buying makeup.

It's true that these are relatively superficial, skin-deep ways for women to indulge themselves, but the benefits of these activities can penetrate emotional depths to make women feel better about themselves. When that happens, women are inspired to take risks and to make daring changes in their lives. It gives them the feeling that they deserve to find personal satisfaction in life, and that's what impels them to find the courage to quit a secure job and start a business, or to go back to school or to switch careers.

A thirty-eight-year-old woman from San Francisco I interviewed sometimes has to postpone her hot bath until midnight, because her days are so hectic, but she makes sure to take one every day. She's an obstetrician on a military base who has two preschoolers and almost no free time, so she decided recently to go back to school to become a specialist. That way she'll have more regular hours and she won't have to work nights three or four times a week. She's made this choice so that she can have more time for herself and for her children. She's desperate to be able to spend more time being good to herself, even if it means that "my house is dirtier, my yard less landscaped, and my kids not as immaculately dressed as my neighbors' kids," she says.

I'm pretty sure that she'd be able to appreciate the ultimate pampering adventure, the marathon of self-indulgence—going to a spa. It was only in 1997 that I worked up the nerve and saved up the money to treat myself to a four-day stay at a fancy spa. I went on my spa crusade with a long-time friend from college and three of her friends. Each of us had made elaborate and complex arrangements to sneak away from our families for the weekend; we'd left precooked meals and minute-by-minute schedules for our harried but understanding husbands. For most of us, this trip was the first time in years that we'd ever been away, all alone, for three whole nights.

I felt a bit guilty about condemning my children to their father's cuisine—a diet of greasy fast food and microwaved hot dogs. But that feeling didn't last long. As soon as I let myself go and succumbed to self-indulgence, I was sublimely happy. I had my first massage and rested in a eucalyptus steam room. I went to exercise classes and ate healthful food that somebody else had cooked. By the second day I found myself reclining on a lounge chair in my fluffy white robe and imitating Fred Astaire by singing softly: "Heaven, I'm in heaven . . . "

Part of the reason I felt so serene was that I imagined myself encased in a bubble of luxury. I felt as if I were floating far above the earth, suspended above my everyday worries and fears and troubles. I'd entered an alternate universe in which being self-indulgent was mandatory. I spent four days walking around with a silly smile on my face and a dreamy look in my eyes. I was drunk on pampering.

Spa skeptics should note that even the cartoon character Marge Simpson once visited a health spa, to relax and learn cigar-making and hula dancing, so it's no longer an exclusive province of the rich and/or famous. Even though she's only a drawing, she too had to soak in a hot bath and let down her three-foot-high blue hair to feel good about herself.

If you can't afford a spa, or if you cringe at the idea, pull a temporary disappearing act instead. Some selfist moms vanish for weekend getaways with friends or neighbors, sisters or mothers. They perform their duties faithfully at home 363 days a year without a peep of complaint. But then, for a day or two or three, they give themselves the gift of freedom. One mother tells me that when her children were young, she dared to leave home only for a day and a half at a time. But now that her children are both in double digits, she's "pushed the envelope" and stayed away for two whole nights. Now she has to figure out how to treat herself well during the other fifty-one weeks of the year.

Running away from home can be a great selfism booster, because there are too many reminders in the house of a mother's yet-to-be-made sacrifices: sticky children, needy husband, wet laundry, empty refrigerator. That's why it's so much easier for a woman to relish being pampered when she has to go somewhere else to do it. Escape can be her best option.

The only problem is that sacrificial mothers sometimes have to teach themselves how to behave in public when alone. If they're without children, they feel as if a limb has been amputated. Often being alone completely flusters them, because they've forgotten how to function when they don't have children laughing and tugging, asking questions and making demands. The notion of searching for a bathroom only if she has to go, stopping to look only at things she wants to see, being the only one to make decisions about where to go and when to leave can be devastatingly intoxicating. That's why my spa trip was so delicious—I spent entire days doing precisely what I wanted to do and nothing else.

An activity as simple as shopping can be a challenge for sacrificial mothers. Just getting out of the house, meeting a friend, and walking around together is enough. The point is not really to buy anything, it's just to learn how to be out on your own and not to have thoughts such as "Mommy needs gas" or "Mommy needs to go potty." Learn to think of yourself as separate from your family, at least occasionally.

If you plan to make a purchase, set a limit for yourself so you don't feel unbearably guilty about how much you've spent. Or plan to try, not to buy. Take whatever clothing hits your fancy, try it on, then put it back on the rack. Decide to go "garage-saleing," as some mothers do, to get slightly used clothes at a fraction of the original cost.

A friend of mine who never buys clothes for herself looked at her wardrobe recently and realized that she had a full closet but nothing that she really liked. Every piece of clothing she owned was a gift, from her mother or mother-in-law, her sisters or sisters-in-law. Studying her wardrobe, she felt like a Ghost of Birthdays Past, dragging the chains of every purple sweater she'd ever received. Then and there she promised herself that she'd buy one new item of clothing for herself every other month.

There is one danger for sacrificial mothers who try to shop to pamper themselves, and that's getting sidetracked by things your children want or need. If you deliberately set out to buy something for your children, fine. Otherwise, forbid yourself in advance from even getting near a children's clothing department or a bookstore, or, the most dangerous of all, a toy store. If it's not a birthday or a holiday when you're shopping for yourself, then direct your attention elsewhere.

Exercise is another effective, though sometimes painful, way to take care of yourself. Getting hooked on an aerobic activity forces you to do it on a regular basis. Like bran or celery, it's certainly good for you, although it may not taste so great. Just about every mother who exercises tells me that if she misses it, even for a few days, she suffers, and so does everybody in her family.

Going out for a run is one of the few things I've always done for myself, even when my children were brand-new babies. As soon as my stitches healed, I'd drag myself out of bed and go. A few years later I'd drop them at nursery school and run for a while—setting aside a few extra minutes for coffee and a muffin. When I finally put my youngest on the bus to go to kindergarten, I was still running, only now I was waving good-bye for the day. After years of running alone, I met a group of three other mothers, also runners, going in the opposite direction. We stopped to chat, and soon we were running together every weekend. It's become a treat I give to myself every Saturday and Sunday, no matter what. We go out in the pouring rain and in the driving snow; we run on ice and we run on roads too hot to touch. Because I know they're waiting for me, I have to go. When I don't run, they demand to know why and my children want to know what's wrong with me.

Some women who have babies or toddlers find that it's just too complicated to get out of the house to exercise. So they work out on a machine at home, or exercise to a tape or a television show in the living room. The only problem with at-home exercise is that you have to be really, really motivated to do it, or it can slide off your to-do list as easily as "clean kitchen cabinets" and "organize drawers." If you can't withstand the urge to spend another half an hour in bed instead of exercising, plan to meet a friend and run or to go to a gym together. You'll be much less likely to give up on your exercise scheme if you know that someone else is depending on you to show up. If you know a group of other mothers who want to exercise, arrange a round-robin of baby-sitting, so that one mother watches the children while the rest go out for a walk or a run.

You might consider taking a class. Learning something new, such as yoga or poetry-writing or automobile repairs, will enhance your sense of self. It's also exhilarating to get better at doing something you love. What kind of class you take isn't nearly as important as the fact that you take one. Decide on it, then do it. Don't quit. Pay in advance so that you'll be forced to go every week; otherwise you'll waste all that money.

A friend of mine pays for her dance classes at the beginning of each semester, so she can indulge herself three times a week. Nothing, except a blizzard, prevents her from going to class, because that's the only time she does something purely for herself and not for one of the five other members of her family.

There are a lot more classes for adults available than you might expect, and many aren't that expensive. Check into what's offered at a local community college, YMCA, or town recreation department. Public high schools, dance academies, and community centers also offer evening and early-morning classes. Ask friends and neighbors about any classes they've enjoyed. Check the telephone book. Make a few phone calls to get class offerings and find one that fits your schedule and your budget.

Even after your course is over, claim that night as yours. Now that your family has become accustomed to your absence every week, why not take advantage of it? Invite a friend to go out for coffee or shopping or a movie. Spend a few hours at your local library, walk around a mall, volunteer at a hospital. Find something to do with that block of time every week, and you'll add "Mom's Night Out" to your list of family traditions.

Or sign up for another class.

If you're feeling paralyzed with indecision, or if you don't really feel that you deserve to indulge yourself, it might be a good idea to see a therapist. Paying for a psychotherapist is like hiring a personal cheerleader, someone who's willing to be on your side, no matter what. If your insurance won't cover the cost, try to negotiate the fee downward. Many therapists are flexible about what they charge, and most of them are eager to find new clients. You can even arrange to go every other week, instead of once a week, to cut the cost in half. If nothing else, getting some therapy should open your eyes to the importance of being good to yourself. If it doesn't, then you should find yourself another therapist.

Sometimes, due to circumstances beyond your control, you can't leave your house. If not, then learn to indulge yourself in the comfort of your own home. Make sure, though, that when it comes time to pay attention to yourself, you don't focus on anything else.

If you love to read, read. Buy yourself books or check them out of the library. If you like baths, take a long, hot bath, with bubbles or oil. Light candles and sip a drink. Read a magazine in the tub. Loll around. Lock the door if you have to.

Listen to music you like all by yourself. Get into the habit of tuning into your favorite station on the radio or popping in a tape that you want to hear in the car.

If you enjoy watching television, do it sparingly. Too much television can be a loud and incessant distraction. Television is much more enjoyable if you savor it as a special treat, watching something you really want to see instead of watching for the sake of watching. Sitting in front of a television for hours is not selfist, it's just a passive way to escape from thinking about what you really need. It's hard to learn selfism or to find a dream if you're too busy changing channels.

If you want some inexpensive entertainment, rent a videotape or borrow one from the library. My sister and her friend have a steady date, once a week, to watch a rented movie together. The hostess gets to choose the tape, and it's a treat they look forward to for days.

These are the most obvious forms of pampering for women to adopt, but the list of possibilities is potentially infinite. Women can indulge themselves with whatever they feel passionate about that goes beyond their family. A mother in Ontario, Canada, pampers herself by singing in a barbershop group called the Sweet Adelines. An Ohio mom immerses herself in making genealogy albums and visiting unusual cemeteries. An ambitious Texas mother writes to hundreds of prisoners on death row.

The point is that these mothers have another love in life, a love that has nothing to do with their great love for their children. That's what selfism is all about.

Some mothers, of course, can take selfism to ridiculous extremes. Mothers who spend several hours a day indulging themselves, but never feel as if they have enough time, have crossed over to selfishness. When they view their children as an annoyance, an obstacle that blocks their ability to do whatever they want whenever they want, they've crossed the line. A divorced woman in my neighborhood has gone way beyond selfism. She treats her nine-year-old son as if he's a nuisance, and she seems only vaguely aware that he's there, because she views him as her housekeeper's responsibility. She's much more concerned about her work and her tennis games and her dates than she is about her son. She views motherhood as something she tried for a while, like scuba diving or kick-boxing, but now she's moved on.

Single mothers with children at home who rank their love life as more important than anything else may also be on the verge of extreme self-indulgence. A mother in Idaho tells me that in the course of nine years, she divorced three men and lived with three others, some of whom were abusive. During that time, she says, she paid more attention to her men and her horses than to her two children.

Women who are dedicated to a political or a personal cause can sometimes take that devotion way beyond pampering to obsession. A sixty-year-old woman from New Jersey tells me that while her two children were young, she was deeply involved with a women's rights group. She attended several meetings a week, she picketed, she traveled to Washington, D.C., and she ran a hot line from her house. Looking back, she says she lost sight of her children's needs for the sake of her cause. It saddened her to learn that they never felt they were first in her heart, even though she always believed that they were.

These women all take selfism to a dangerous extreme. While I wholeheartedly advocate pampering, theirs is not the kind of pampering I'm talking about. Mothers must learn how to balance their sacrificing with nurturing, taking care not to make extreme decisions at their children's expense.

A very few lucky mothers don't have to worry about pampering themselves, because they've got husbands who do it for them. Husbands like these, who encourage their wives to be self-indulgent and who sacrifice just as much and as often, are partners in what I call magic marriages.

## Magic Marriages

A man in a magic marriage is a built-in pampering system for his wife. He shares the family sacrifices simply because he doesn't expect her to do them all. He wants her to indulge herself, so he pushes her to become a selfist. If she yearns for some private time, he makes sure that she gets it. While everyone expects a wife to nurture her husband, this man considers it his duty to nurture her as well.

Does he sound like a hero out of a fairy tale, almost too good to be true?

For most wives, he is.

The majority of marriages *don't* include this kind of husband. Most contain a husband more like the one my friend has, a guy who needs to be indulged constantly and who rarely thinks about taking care of her. My friend would love it if her husband would nurture her every so often, but he almost never does. When my friend was in her last month of pregnancy with their third child, she asked her husband to bathe the other two children, because she was having trouble bending over. But he resisted, staying out late so he wouldn't be home in time. She works too, but her husband never cooks dinner or even offers to pick up Chinese food on his way home. Food and laundry and children are her job, as he sees it. Every time she thinks about this, it puts her into a state of righteous fury.

Her anger rears up in the bedroom, too. When her husband calls out, "Oh, hon-neeey!" and starts grabbing her to signal that he wants sex, she locks up as tight as a bank vault on a Sunday. She expresses her rage at him, and her disappointment in their marriage, by feeling almost no interest in sex. She never feels attracted to him anymore, she tells me, and in fact, she wishes he'd leave her alone.

Her reaction isn't very surprising. As I stated earlier, it's quite common for angry, frustrated wives to become sexually frosty. Women who are filled with resentment at their husbands are less likely to fantasize scenes of romance and seduction than they are to envision images of nasty revenge. Many husbands have a lot of trouble understanding this, because they don't react to marital problems the same way. Their sexuality comes in on a completely different channel than their feelings of hurt or rage. Many husbands can be in the middle of a vehement argument and decide that it's time to make love anyway. Then they can't figure out why she's not in the mood.

This obliviousness can make wives even angrier and more sexually belligerent than they were before. It's almost guaranteed, then, that sacrificial, resentful wives won't be in magic marriages, nor will their sex lives be much to brag about.

As discussed in Chapter 4, couples that have the best sex lives include a husband who shares the sacrifices. Because he does more child care and more household chores, his wife does less. Because she isn't doing all the work at home, she isn't forced to be sacrificial. So when she cuddles next to her husband, she's more likely to want to snuggle him than to give him a good slap upside the head.

Shared sacrifices are, in fact, what make marriages magic.

One way to find out if you have this kind of marriage is to think about your level of marital fulfillment at this stage in your life. Give your marriage a grade, from A, the best, to F, the absolute worst. If you can honestly say that your marriage deserves an A or an A+, and if your partner would agree, then you probably have a magic marriage. In my research, fewer than one in five couples describes their marriage this way. About two in five give it a less-than-perfect, but still high, B.

Who are the lucky few who find themselves in a magic marriage?

Couples in a magic marriage aren't any wealthier than average, nor are they younger or closer to the honeymoon stage. Income and age, then, have nothing to do with having a magic marriage, and neither does how many children the couple has or how old those children are. So it's not the external social forces beyond our control that determine who gets this wonderful marriage and who doesn't.

Quite simply, it's the *man* in the marriage who determines if it's magic: A magic marriage almost always includes a terrific husband.

He's someone who's willing to share his wife's sacrifices without being asked. He does more chores at home than other husbands do, and he does them voluntarily. If there's dirt, he vacuums it; if there's laundry, he washes it; if there's no food, he buys it. This is how he shows his wife that he cares, in a way that she can appreciate.

A wife in a magic marriage tells me that there isn't anything in or around the house that her husband won't do. He's not too manly to wipe a child's rear end or too deliberately inept about porcelain to scrub out a dirty toilet. (Many husbands get their face that close to the bowl only when they're vomiting into it.) He remembers the first solid food that each of his three children ever ate. He knows who likes what on their morning toast. He even knows the shoe size of every person in his family, including hers!

Magic marriage husbands also give their wives intangible evidence of their love and devotion. Husbands in these marriages are more thoughtful and considerate of their wives than other husbands are. And I'm not taking their word for it—this is what their *wives* tell me. These men share their feelings more often and they communicate better. They treat their wife with more respect and they're more attuned to her worries. When she's upset, they're truly concerned; they want to know what's wrong and how they can help.

A husband like this would never, ever, dream of not giving his wife a Christmas present, even if he'd just spent his last dime and had to forage in a Dumpster to find one.

These husbands are also fabulous fathers, according to their wives, and they're especially affectionate and gentle with their children. Another mother in a magic marriage says that her children are just as likely to run to their father for comfort as they are to turn to her. She wouldn't hesitate to leave the children alone with him, for an evening or for a month, because she trusts him totally with the little loves of her life. It would never occur to her that she has to protect her children from her husband, as a sacrificial friend of mine does. This woman's husband is so angry and impatient when he comes home from work every day that she has to keep their children quiet, and far away, until he calms down.

That's not a problem for a deliriously happy couple I know. Late bloomers who didn't marry until their mid-thirties, Lou and Jodi fell into a sublimely magic marriage. An unpretentious mail carrier, Lou Ratner lived with his parents until he left home to live with his wife at the age of thirty-five. He was a terrific husband just waiting to emerge from his chrysalis when his future wife plucked him out of confirmed bachelorhood. After they'd been married for only a few months, she knew that he would always be there for her, "1,000 percent." Jodi has no doubt that if she were incapacitated, Lou would never leave her side. He's a father who knows the songs his daughter learns in nursery school so well that he sings along. He even does extra loads of laundry so his little girl can wear her favorite shorts every day.

Jodi boasts that, in their next life, all of her friends in their Florida neighborhood say that they hope they'll get to marry Lou.

Even if you don't have a marriage like this, it's heartening to know that it's in the realm of human possibility. If some couples have it, then maybe the rest of us can hope.

But a magic marriage can't simply be wished into existence, because it takes two partners to make a marriage work. And the first rule of any marriage is that you can't change someone who doesn't want to be changed. A wife who already does most of the sacrificing will certainly be enthusiastic about sharing her sacrifices. But her husband, a man who's gotten away with almost no sacrifices for so long, may be uninterested. Why should he want to rock the boat when he already does so little of the rowing?

There are several reasons why a husband should want a magic marriage as much as his wife does. First of all, if his wife is happier, he will be too. Second, their sex life will improve, perhaps drastically. Third, his children will thrive and he'll become a better father. All of this combined will almost surely make him a better, more contented human being.

Unfortunately, though, there's no guarantee that a wife will be able to convince her husband that this is true. He might dismiss the whole notion of sacrifice as ridiculous, as a subversive lie to make women feel better about themselves and men feel worse. If so, there's not much she can do. I don't have any secret words, no hocus-pocus strategy, that will turn a reluctant husband into a sacrifice-sharer. If he has no interest in having a magic marriage, it will be pretty much impossible to force one on him.

But you can change your expectations of marriage and your hopes for what it could be. Close your eyes and imagine your fantasy husband. I'm not talking about looks, so forget about hunky biceps and piercing blue eyes. Try instead to picture his heart and his soul.

What would your ideal man do around the house? How would he treat you and the children? How would you feel about him if he did? How would you feel about yourself if such a man were yours?

Now open your eyes. Think about the real man you married and how he compares with your fantasy. How close does your real-life marriage come? You may have only a short distance to travel to your ideal marriage goal, or you may be facing a huge gap between the man your husband is and the man you'd like him to be. If so, try to do something about it. Talk to him about why you'd like him to change and how he could do it. Give him realistic suggestions. Don't criticize and attack; be constructive and supportive. It's possible that he has no idea how much you sacrifice. If you let him know, calmly and respectfully, and ask him to help share the sacrifices, he may be perfectly willing to try.

List the sacrifices you make, and ask him to pick a few that he'd like to take on. Men tend to obey concrete directions better than abstract ones, so instead of asking him to worry about the children's health more often, ask him to take them to a weekend doctor's appointment or to change the bandages on the little one's gash. Use your common sense about which sacrifices are appropriate for him to share and which ones aren't. If he can envision sacrifice from your point of view, then he may be more open to sharing it.

Give yourselves a trial period of a few weeks, then make an effort to talk about how successful it was. Praise your husband for even the slightest change in his attitude or behavior. Ask him if those changes made him feel better, and let him know how and why they made you feel. (If none of this made a difference for you, go back to the drawing board and try again.) Ask him if he thinks your sex life has improved. Point out to him how much more sexually receptive you feel, and demonstrate those feelings openly. If you're more sexually alive, then act it.

After another few weeks, assess your workload to make sure that the new sacrifice regime is still in place. If you no longer feel like a martyr to your family and if you've begun taking regular blocks of time just for you, then you'll know it's working.

If simple discussion isn't sufficient, you may have to compromise with your husband. A mother I know in Indiana had to sacrifice more before she could sacrifice less. She'd been in a magic marriage, but it had slowly leaked away, like a soda that's lost its fizz. Her once-cuddly and gentle husband had become so miserable at work that he was no longer the man who willingly shared her sacrifices. He'd become mean and spiteful, yelling at the children and spending silent hours in front of the television set. She insisted that he quit his teaching job, and she volunteered to support the family by turning her part-time work as a librarian into a nearly full-time job. This was a great sacrifice for her, because she never wanted to spend so much time away from her two young children. She hated to be the last one to hear about what happened to her son at kindergarten or about a new word her daughter had said. But to put the magic back into her marriage, she realized that she had no choice.

Her compromise worked. She got back her happy-go-lucky, considerate husband. Not only that, she's finding that she's able to focus more attention on herself. For the first time in six years, she's started to care about how she looks and she's making herself a priority, along with her husband and children.

But don't let her success fool you. Getting your husband to share the sacrifice won't be easy. Magic marriages are rare because they're so difficult to create and to maintain. It's possible that none of these ideas will work, that your husband will simply be unwilling to help you out. As a final step, you might have to resort to threats and intimidation. This is appropriate only if you can no longer bear the weight of your sacrifices, if you feel that the single strand of your sanity is being stretched to the breaking point. In that case, you might have to offer him an ultimatum—share the sacrifices or leave.

A close friend who was desperate did this a while back. She was a sacrificial mother whose husband barely acknowledged her existence, let alone the extent of her work around the house. After ten years of sacrificing for their three children, with no help at all, my friend had had enough. She was hostile and bitter, but her husband didn't have a clue as to the reason. He felt hurt because she no longer seemed to love him; she felt betrayed because he refused to share her chores and responsibilities.

It was only when she threatened to leave him that her husband finally agreed to listen to what she had to say. With the help of a counselor, they learned how to work together as a team, to share family responsibilities and sacrifices. In just a year her husband has undergone a miraculous transformation. Instead of coming home in angry silence every night, he does homework with their children. He helps set the dinner table, he pours the children's milk and cuts their meat. He takes them to movies and local video parlors without being asked. He shows my friend affection, offering small kisses and little surprises. He encourages her to meet a friend for lunch or to buy herself a new jacket. He worries if she doesn't seem happy.

My friend is awestruck that this is the same man she was about to leave, because it's as if all her fantasies of the ideal husband have come to life. If this isn't a suddenly magic marriage, she says, then she doesn't know what is.

Sacrificial mothers like this, who are successful at persuading their husband to share the work, feel a new sense of self-respect and optimism. The next and even more challenging step is for them to find their own dream.

# Eight

# Beyond Babies:
# Finding a Dream

When I turned thirty, I wanted a baby more than anything else in the world. Getting pregnant was my only dream. But several doctors told me that I was physically unable to conceive. How about adoption? they said. This only made me yearn to give birth even more.

Eventually I found a surgeon who didn't write me off as a hopeless case. After endless tests and consultations, I was admitted to the hospital, knocked out, and given three hours of microsurgery. When I woke up, a horde of medical students stood at the end of my bed, wanting to know how many sit-ups I could do, because it had taken so much elbow grease to slice through my abdominal muscles. (Don't be envious; that would definitely not be a problem now.) I spent a week in a hospital bed, flat on my back, and then hobbled home on my husband's arm. I held my breath; I said my silent prayers over and over again. "Just let me be a mother" was my mantra.

Six months later I was pregnant and exquisitely happy. My nearly impossible dream had come true: I was actually going to be a mother! The miracle of my daughter's birth convinced me that my life was truly complete; she was all I needed to have a sense of meaning and purpose. I'd come so close to suffering the lifelong pain and sorrow of never becoming a mother that all I wanted was to be able to spend the rest of my days raising my baby.

So that's what I did, along with steady part-time work. I had no other dream for myself, except to be a terrific mother. Most of the time I didn't live up to that ideal, but life zipped along in a blur anyway, including the birth of my son. Every day seemed to have a hundred hours in it, the time went by so excruciatingly slowly. But at the same time, the years were gone in a flash. One week I looked up and noticed that both of my children were gone—in school all day long. It was then that I realized I had to reclaim my life, for me.

I was unnerved to discover that I wanted to be more than just a mother, because I'd worked so hard, and hoped so hard, for motherhood. But I had to admit that I felt too young to have finished dreaming, that I was unwilling to sacrifice the entire second half of my life for my children's sake. Although I'd fallen into the very common trap of assuming that I was obliged to abandon my own dreams when I became a mother, I pulled myself out before it was too late. I was like so many women who use motherhood as an excuse, a noble reason for not wanting to do or be anything other than a mother. But being without a personal dream, without a sense of purpose in life other than mothering, can leave a woman feeling empty and devoid of direction. It can result not only in emotional troubles but in real physical ailments. Mothers without a goal for themselves tell me they feel obliterated or on hold, as if they're treading water, stalled out. They're adrift. They lack confidence, and they often feel anxious or depressed. In voices that are sometimes wistful, sometimes full of regret or slightly bitter, mothers who have sacrificed their own dream for their children's sake try to convince me—and themselves—that they've made the right choice. The essence of what they're saying is that they're hoping to forget they ever wanted anything else for themselves, because motherhood has become their all-encompassing, substitute vision in life.

While this might seem to be the most honorable and admirable path, it's not.

It's actually a sacrificial mother's lazy alternative, a socially acceptable way to avoid a duty to one's self.

It's relatively easy for a woman to rest on her maternal laurels. She can say, with pride, "I've had a baby, so I don't need to accomplish anything else." Being a mother becomes the last dream she forms, and the only one that matters. It confirms her sense of femininity, it makes her feel like a real woman, which is partly why even a superstar like Madonna, a celebrity with gargantuan goals of her own, still feels a need to become a mother. But because so many women don't feel like good enough mothers, they always have a niggling sense of anxiety, a suspicion that they are not doing their job well enough. So a woman's maternal dream is naturally flawed, because it's almost guaranteed that she'll feel as if she's failed; she'll have a nagging sense that she didn't do her best. This is how a mother's feelings of self-confidence and self-respect can slowly erode over the passing years. Tiny droplets of maternal doubt wear down her sense of motherly competence, one by one by one. Drip, drip, drip.

This isn't her fault, though. It's a natural outcome of maternal sacrifice and of her refusal to acknowledge that she has a right to have a dream for herself. A mother who insists that children are all she needs will almost always suffer in the end. She may never gain the sense of self-respect she deserves.

I know a woman who is exactly like this. A high school graduate, she was lucky enough to get a secretarial job that involved travel all over Europe. When she decided to marry, she quit the job—not to have children, but to help her husband live out his life goals. They moved wherever his job took them. When they finally had a baby, she was convinced that her life's work was over. She tried for years to have another child, but several efforts to bear a test-tube baby failed, as did a few disastrous attempts to adopt privately. Her son is now a teenager, and she's become the Mother Who Drives. She drives him anywhere, any distance, for any purpose; even if her son isn't going, she drives other people's children wherever they need to go. She claims to be happy, but she's been convinced for a long time that she's not smart enough to get another job, not slim enough to be attractive, not a good enough soprano to solo in her choir.

She's a mother without a vision for herself, a woman who doesn't even realize what she's missing.

Unlike this friend, it took me only a few years to realize that something wasn't right. I had the insight that children are not enough—not even my ultra-precious children, the ones who were never supposed to have been born. Even though I'm grateful to have them, I know that I need more. I need something that will make me feel like a complete human being, or I'll end up like this woman, a maternal blankness.

I often struggle with this feeling, my resistance to motherhood, because it makes me feel a little ashamed, as if I'm betraying my children. I begin to feel like a selfish wretch, somebody who should remember to be eternally thankful to be a mother. Don't I realize that children are the most gratifying, rewarding, and lovely gifts a woman could ever want?

Yes, of course I know that. But I also understand that *children are not enough*.

Even if they might not express this thought openly, deep in their hearts many mothers know this to be true. Almost all mothers sense that children provide equal parts delicious pleasure and fulfillment as well as exquisite pain and frustration, according to my research. More than a few mothers also admit that raising a child is satisfying, but it's simply not enough to keep a woman totally absorbed. The implication here is obvious: Some savvy mothers sense that they need to keep a piece of themselves separate, theirs alone. The fragment that is segregated from their children's needs and demands is the one that will be able to find a dream.

A mother who respects herself will always find a way to define that self above and beyond her role as a mother. Motherhood will always be a great part of who she is—even one of her best parts—but it's *not* all of her. Every woman can be, and should be, more than a mother. To prove that to herself, and to everyone else, she needs to find a way to define herself with something that is hers alone. She has to find a unique passion and make it hers. Having a dream gives a woman a focal point other than motherhood, a place on which to fix her attention so she doesn't lose herself completely.

A mother with a strong enough vision will never falter, because her dream can't be destroyed or diminished by motherhood. A young mother from Kentucky, for instance, has such a powerful dream that it steers her course through life. She has a passion for writing fiction and is determined to have her work published someday. Although she has two children under the age of two and no help at home, she manages to write every single day, sometimes for hours at a time. She has to scrounge and scrape for the luxury to write, but she does it no matter what. She tests scraps of dialogue in her head while doing the Stairmaster; she jots down ideas with her free arm while nursing her six-month-old; she writes furiously during precisely coordinated double naps. She doesn't let anything or anyone prevent her from focusing on her goal.

This is exactly what every mother has to find: an enduring and passionate dream of her own that she has the determination to pursue.

## Women Need to Have a Dream

A dream offers a woman a reason for living, because it gives her a goal that is exclusively hers. A dream is her vision of who she will be or can be; it's her version of her best self. It's something that she can fantasize about, long for, and then strive for.

Explain this to your husband, and it's quite possible that he'll scoff. I know, because my own husband did.

"Oh, please, what's the big deal?" he asks me. "Just get on with your life."

Many men just don't understand how important it is for a woman to have a dream, in part because they take the ability to have one for granted. When they're little, boys dream about becoming major-league baseball heroes or basketball stars; they fantasize about growing up to be super-rich computer jocks or presidents of something. By the time they are mature, most men have more realistic dreams, but they don't stop dreaming. And it might never occur to them to put aside their dream for a while so that their wife could achieve one of her own.

It's clear to me that men are simply more comfortable about having a private vision than women are. In fact, my surveys show that more men than women have one, probably because having a personal dream comes more easily to them.

There is, perhaps, one exception to this rule. When they're

young, almost all women have one special goal—a vision of true love. As soon as girls become teenagers and through their early twenties and ever after, almost all of them want to find real love, timeless romance, everlasting bliss with the man of their daytime fantasies and nighttime dreams. Amorous goals like these are perfectly natural, probably because we're all equipped with a strong biological urge that directs us to find a man and to reproduce with him. It shouldn't be surprising, then, that psychologists think that finding an intimate attachment is one of the first, and most important, tasks that every young adult, woman or man, has to accomplish. Searching for intimacy, they say, is a basic human need, just as vital as seeking nourishment and a place to live.

But the dreams I'm talking about are not about intimacy. You can seek my kind of dream, a goal for the soul, only after you've met your other, minimum human requirements—for food and shelter and love. This kind of dream is a luxury; it's for women who already have all of the basics.

What personal visions do mothers form?

It would be impossible for me to provide a list here of every potential dream that women have, since each woman has to fashion one that's right for her. One woman tells me that she envisions running a sanctuary for wounded owls; another wants to learn to play the organ; yet another hopes to buy a boat and put out to sea. But even idiosyncratic dreams like these can be put into general categories, just like the more mundane dreams of becoming an accountant or learning to play the flute. In my research, I've found nearly a dozen different types of dreams. These are: family, love, spiritual, career, education, artistic, humanitarian, personal, financial, entrepreneurial, and pipe dreams.

Dreams of family and love are like Old Faithful—they bubble up every so often, no matter what. These are the longings women have about finding Mr. Right and falling in love and about raising happy, healthy children. Sadly, some women stop here and never manage to find another goal for the rest of their lives. But this kind of dream is rarely a catalyst for selfism, because rather than encouraging a healthy attention to self, it fosters more and more sacrifice.

Spiritual dreams, though, can be quite conducive to selfism.

These visions give women a sense of inner peace and a connection with a higher power. Mothers with spiritual dreams talk about living their faith every day, about being active members of a religious community, or of trying to make it to heaven by living well right now. A mother of three in Pennsylvania even tells me that she's achieved her goal of becoming a Wiccan priestess, a sort of laid-back millennial witch. She and her family hold ceremonies on the full moon, praying to the goddess of the verdant plain.

Although less dramatic and ardent than spiritual dreams, career goals also help mothers become more selfist. Mothers like this yearn to get a promotion or a better job; they dream of becoming a nurse or a minister or a dentist. Others want to switch careers completely by becoming a hospital chaplain, a computer programmer, or a high school principal. Still others plan to start their own company. Whatever glorious new career they hold in their imagination, women with this vision spend years working toward a challenging goal that will lead them to selfism.

Education dreams serve two purposes. To some women, the dream is the end in itself—they want to prove how smart or talented they are by getting a degree. Other women, though, look on their education as a means to a specific end, so that they'll be able to find a more challenging or better-paying job. They want to go to business school so they can become an auditor; they want to finish a nursing degree so they can get a job in an intensive care unit. For these moms, going to school is the direction they take to lead them to a long-hoped-for goal.

An artistic dream often involves great passion and endless hours of creative work. Mothers with a goal like this tell me that they want to write science fiction or to become an artist whose work is shown in galleries. They want to play guitar in a rock-and-roll band. These mothers are often quite driven and have little problem being selfist, because they're so confident about their artistic talents. Their goals are endlessly renewable too, because there's always another story to write or another drawing to sketch.

Humanitarian dreamers want to save the world, usually through a political or social cause. One mother with a vision like this tells me she wants to do more for the homeless; another hopes to open a recreation center for the elderly. A mother in Maryland yearns to become an alcohol and drug abuse counselor, because her father had a serious drinking problem. Women who envision helping other people often plunge into their crusade so fiercely that they end up sacrificing too much for their cause. They don't put their family first, but they don't put themselves first either. Instead, the rest of the world comes first.

Personal dreams are simple and totally self-centered. Mothers with such a goal want to lose sixty pounds or to get in shape or to become a better person. Once they achieve what they want, selfist mothers know how to move on. But sacrificial mothers can spend decades trying to achieve a personal goal without ever coming close. These are mothers who are forever trying to lose weight or to fix themselves up. They'll never realize these dreams, though, because they don't know how to focus on themselves.

Financial dreams are often vague and sometimes border on being pipe dreams. Mothers with visions of money hanker after great wealth, but they don't necessarily want to work hard for it. They long to be financially secure, to save money, to get money, but they don't have a clue as to how. Dreaming about money in this way is childish, because it's a magical belief by women who have no idea how to reach that goal. Still, realistic thoughts about earning more money can be very valuable. Many women harbor entrepreneurial dreams, for instance. Mothers with this kind of goal plan to work for wealth by opening their own businesses. They aren't necessarily doctors and lawyers, either. Women who dream of being self-employed tell me that they want to run a mini-farm or to own a horse ranch. They'd like to open a Hallmark card shop or start a house-cleaning service. They seem to sense that they can balance selfism and sacrifice by becoming their own boss. Entrepreneurs expect to have their own goals and to earn a living, but they also hope to be able to show up at their children's spring concerts and class parties.

Finally, there are pipe dreams, visions that are ridiculously unlikely. They are almost always unreachable and impossible, and therefore they are terribly frustrating for the women who have them. Mothers who cling to pipe dreams seem to be hoping that a fairy godmother will descend from the sky and grant them the ability to live happily ever after. A woman with this kind of goal might as well just fall asleep and dream.

How can you tell if your dream is a pipe dream? Listen to some of the examples I've heard: to win an Oscar, to be in the Olympics, to bowl 300, to strike it rich. If you're really a working actress or an athlete in training, a great bowler or an oil prospector, then these visions might just possibly be realistic. If not, then your goals are feathery wisps spun in the air, like cotton candy that melts at a tongue's touch. Any dream that seems completely out of the realm of possibility, something you can't really try to achieve, is a pipe dream.

As long as a dream is even partly feasible, though, it doesn't matter what kind it is. What counts is that a mother has a dream at all, because it forces her to focus attention on herself. A dream gives a woman her own song, it helps her to sing her own lyrics. Because the song belongs to her alone, having a vision gives a woman a liberating sense of self-respect. It also helps her to avoid being overwhelmed by "shoulds." This plague afflicts mothers who become so desperate to please their family or husband or children that they're afraid to do anything other than what everyone tells them they "should."

A friend of mine spent almost thirty-five years going around and around in an increasingly frustrating circle of shoulds until she finally whipped herself out of that infinite loop. As a young girl, she'd dreamed of becoming a sculptor, and when she left home after high school, she attended a school of visual arts. She was so fond of her first sculpture, a bronze of a woman on a ladder, that it made her eyes fill with tears of pride every time she looked at it. But my friend's family thought she should become an actress, because they were all in show business. She listened to their shoulds and quit art school to act. Yet she carried that bronze piece in her pocket, to every audition and to every performance, because it was the only thing she'd ever done that gave her confidence and made her feel strong, even fifteen years after she'd created it.

Eventually my friend married and had three children. At first, she earned more money than her husband did, but as she got older, she began to earn less. That's when her husband told her she should quit work and stay at home. This was the "should" that broke the camel's back. She was so incensed by his demand that she met with a lawyer and drew up divorce papers.

A week later, waiting to audition for a television sitcom with thoughts of divorce raging in her breast, she suddenly had a dramatic change of heart. She didn't want to live her mother's dream anymore; she was fed up with being an actress. She left the audition before she'd opened her mouth and flew home to her husband and children, tearing up the legal papers and vowing to become the perfect wife and mother. She made elaborate breakfasts, hung curtains, and drove her kids to every swim practice and tennis class and baseball game they wanted. A year of this never-ending charade made her realize that she needed to find a new dream. Almost by accident, she wandered into a sculpture class and rediscovered her passion for art. She'd come back to the goal she'd kept alive by clutching that small bronze piece in her hand for so many years. Now she does her art every day, and she's even sold some pieces to nearby galleries. She'll probably never make as much money as she did before, but she's finally following her vision for personal happiness.

Like my friend, some women have to stumble before they latch onto the dream that's right for them. Others identify it early on and never let go, even if it takes decades to fulfill. A woman in New Mexico told me that she'd always longed to build her own home, but it wasn't until she was fifty-five that she could finally afford to buy a cement mixer and take the time to gather stones from the desert, sift sand for mortar, and do it. The process took nearly two years, but she constructed her own "earth shelter" with eighteen-inch-thick walls. She lives in it now, with her thirty-six-year-old second husband.

A woman's dream should be fluid and mercurial, not rigid and unchanging. Like any desire or fantasy, it should mature and grow along with the woman who nurtures it. Most mothers, it seems to me, rarely keep the same ideal vision over a lifetime. My artistic friend was perceptive enough to revive her girlhood dream, but only after she let it go into hibernation for nearly two decades.

After they become mothers, for example, women almost always alter their dreams. They learn to reshape and reinvent them, along with their vision of who they are. What a young girl fantasizes about at the age of fourteen or twenty-one is usually not feasible, or even desirable, by the time she reaches thirty-five or forty-five. When she was young, a woman I know used to plan exotic climbing trips, and she traveled all over the world in her search for adventure. Now that she's a mother in her mid-thirties, though, she's scaled down her vision—literally. She teaches rock climbing and leads Scout troops on hiking trips. By the time she hits forty-five, she says, she'll be ready to make another, maybe more adventurous, life plan.

Mothers can and should have more than one dream in a lifetime. A woman can switch in midstream if one becomes too difficult or another seems more appealing. Or she can use one goal as a stepping-stone to another. A mother I spoke to whose first plan was just to finish college did so at the age of forty-one. Now she'd like to go to law school. A mother in Tennessee wanted to lose some weight, but she was so successful at it that she began to compete in statewide body-building competitions. Now she dreams of winning a national title.

It's important that women never lose sight of their dream when they become mothers. Babies fulfill a very deep need, but babies are not enough to satisfy a woman's equally powerful need to work toward a future goal. It's so easy to give up and to give in, to let children smother your dream. While I agree that it's difficult to build a house or to climb a mountain if you're caring for a baby, you can keep your vision alive by letting it simmer on a mental back burner.

The sad reality is that most mothers don't bother to do this. As soon as they have children, they drop their own personal goals as readily as they ditch a dirty diaper. Just about every young woman between the ages of eighteen and twenty-four has at least one special dream, a big, important goal to work toward, my research shows. But by the time women marry and have children, usually when they reach their late twenties and thirties, the number who still have a secret goal drops dramatically, and it continues to decrease, decade by decade. It's as if maternal sacrifice sucks women dry, draining all of the spark and vitality and hope from their lives. When women lose their self-respect, they also lose their incentive to find a dream beyond motherhood.

This might not matter much, except that mothers need to nurture their own visions. Those who do are emotionally and physically healthier than those who don't, according to my surveys. They're also a lot more positive about life. They have hope. Mothers with a dream believe that they can do better, climb higher, achieve more. They view themselves as creative and courageous. They feel that setbacks in life only make them stronger and more determined. Mothers without a goal tend to be complaisant and resigned. They settle for what is rather than aiming for what could be. They live with little intensity or purpose; they lack passion.

A woman I used to know was just like this. She lived for her husband's career and for their church activities, but she was bitter and deeply resentful of mothers who were lucky enough to have their own dreams. She envied other women's careers, their new babies, even their renovated kitchens and new wallpaper. Her strict religious beliefs prohibited her from having a dream and so did her stern, egotistical husband. No wonder she was so desperate and frustrated.

If my former friend had been poverty-stricken, unable to feed or clothe her children, her lack of a goal would be understandable, even justified. But as it happens, she was quite well-to-do, so she didn't have an economic excuse. In fact, my research shows that having a dream isn't related at all to how much money a woman has. Some very wealthy women who should have endless opportunities don't have even one simple goal for themselves, while others who are barely getting by financially do.

There are a few mothers, though, who make sure that their goals rule their lives every moment of every day. Mothers who live their vision have to be teeth-grittingly determined. I've met only a few women like this, one of them with a dream so powerful that it has taken over her entire family—husband and six children included.

As a young wife, Catherine Mattison wanted to be the most efficient, cautiously frugal woman in the West. She canned peaches, pears, beans, and tomatoes from her own half-acre garden. She stripped and refinished all her own furniture. She made blue jeans out of yards of denim, because she couldn't afford to buy real Levi's for her six children. She was Idaho's answer to Martha Stewart, except that she did Martha a decade before Martha did.

But after plunging herself into this sacrificial dream for more than ten years, Catherine decided to find a dream just for her. Her goal: to direct her ever-widening tornado of passion into her own business. She had a few false starts, including a business plan that never got off the ground and a truck-washing business that she had to sell. But then Catherine zeroed in on what seemed to be a perfect fit. Because she had a degree in nutrition and a great love and talent for cooking, she decided to open a bakery. She found a building to house the store that was only a block from her home, so she could walk to work. All six of her children helped out every day; a few baked doughnuts at dawn, the others worked the counter after school. Catherine made everything from scratch: hundreds of loaves of white, whole wheat, and sourdough bread; and enough rolls, muffins, cakes, pies, doughnuts, eclairs, and cinnamon buns to feed every police officer in the state. At first the business was wildly successful, and she was making more money than she could handle.

But Catherine's baked goodies turned out to be a little too good for her own good. She became personally responsible for fattening up nearly everybody in her tiny Idaho town. Pretty soon most of her regular customers were on a diet, and although they didn't mean to be cruel, they in essence began to boycott her bakery. Her revenues plummeted, and she had to fire almost all of her employees. To top it off, she had to dump everybody the week before Christmas. Doing all the work by herself, Catherine began each day in a flood of tears, overwhelmed by exasperation and frustration. She knew that a successful business was within her reach, but she just couldn't make it work financially. When her banker began to pester her about filing for bankruptcy, she knew she was in trouble.

But Catherine refused to concede defeat. She was so obstinate about not failing that she decided to fashion another dream for herself, even if it had to be from the ashes of the old one. In thinking about her problem with her too-successful bakery, she realized that if people were trying to avoid cholesterol and fatty food, she'd invent a way for them to eat sweets without the harmful side effects. She brainstormed a solution, then puttered, tested, and tasted for weeks, until she'd formulated a low-fat, low-calorie baking butter that tasted just as good as the high-fat, high-calorie real thing. When she used her invention to bake moist, chewy brownies that she gave out at a local grocery store, no one believed that the sweet was low-fat. When she used it in croissants, her neighbors were amazed by how silky and buttery the pastry seemed.

Sensing that she had success in the palm of her hands, Catherine and her husband decided to sell their product directly. First, though, they had to manufacture the stuff. The whole family gathered at the bakery to stir up the mixture in huge vats, working until after midnight to pack the butter into hundreds and hundreds of containers. They'd come home bleary with fatigue and with two inches of sticky goop caked into their sneakers. But the fake butter was an instant success. In Catherine's first appearance on a television shopping network, she sold all 5,000 buckets of the stuff in six minutes. The product even won several food-industry contests.

Catherine's second dream has now turned into a thriving business, one that employs her entire family. It's also become an infinitely renewable source of self-respect for her. Although her success may seem inevitable, it was anything but. Catherine is a faithful Mormon wife, and she has a substantial tradition of female subservience to overcome. She became a selfist against all odds, only because she had got enough grit and spunk to stick to her convictions and to respect herself. She did this despite setbacks, hardship, and self-doubt. She did it despite having a clan of children to tend to, a skeptical banker to persuade, and a dubious husband to train not to expect to be served supper at six every night.

This kind of life-focusing dream used to be a man's prerogative. Fathers had a right to set off on a quest for selfhood, and everyone else in the family was supposed to cheer along the way. Finding a dream in which they see themselves as heroic is an expected stage of life for men, according to Daniel Levinson, a psychologist who in the 1970s studied how men change during adulthood. Men have to begin life with a search for a meaningful purpose in life, usually before the age of thirty or so, he said. Women don't really need or want their own dream, according to Levinson, since their job is to help their husband realize his.

That attitude may have been appropriate several decades ago, but it hardly rings true at the turn of the millennium. In the 1980s,

Levinson decided to study women's lives, and ultimately he recanted his original theory. Because women's lives are now so similar to men's, he said, they're just as likely to need and want their own dream.

But if both partners now expect to have their own far-reaching goals in life, two-dream couples can have unforeseen marital problems. Because each person needs to be a hero, neither is willing to be the sidekick, the supporting character who was traditionally the wife. Both want to be Superman; neither one wants to be Lois Lane. Either they have to take turns fulfilling their goals, or one has to step aside and let the other's dream dominate, as Catherine's husband did.

Not all wives are lucky enough to have a husband willing to play second fiddle. When they give up waiting for this to happen, some choose to leave the marriage to seek their own vision. One woman I know waited until two marriages had ended and five children were raised before she finally set off on her own quest. She had a simple personal dream: to live for herself, by herself. To pursue that goal, she sold most of her possessions and got a half-year job as a fire lookout on a mountaintop in Arizona. And now she lives her dream, sitting in a tiny room at the top of a tall tower, far from any town. She's like Rapunzel, only she's got a solar-powered laptop, and she's certainly not waiting to be rescued by any prince. Watching for wisps of smoke among thousands of Ponderosa pines, she uses her computer to write the biography of her mountain. When her tower is hit by lightning, the hair on her arms stands straight up and she feels invincible, she says.

## How to Find a Dream

A woman like this, who feels invigorated rather than terrified when she's struck by lightning, must have an enormous amount of self-confidence. She's also not afraid to put herself first, and she's convinced that she deserves to have a dream of her own. Granted that her way of earning self-respect—living like a sky-high hermit six months a year—is just this side of sane. But there are plenty of mothers like her, women who need to take extreme measures to be able to believe in themselves. They have to be kicked and prodded into finding a goal outside of their family. That's why some therapists make a habit of escorting women on biking trips in China, backpacking treks in Tanzania, and cliff-climbing expeditions in Utah. They use these trials-by-fire to persuade women to respect themselves. If you can ride the length of the Great Wall of China or scale a sheer precipice, they figure, then you'll conclude that you're a fairly capable and special person. It's an "if I can do something terrific, then I must be terrific" technique, and it works quite well for those who can afford it.

For most of us, though, the idea of investing so much time and money to test ourselves seems preposterous. We don't have to go to the ends of the earth to prove that we're worthy of self-respect. I've got a friend who earns her sense of respect by running a marathon once or twice a year. Another one dyes her hair an exotic new shade of blonde every few months. When I want to feel good about myself, I try to shove my knees down lower on the mat in yoga class.

Pounding some self-respect into your soul doesn't have to take elaborate planning or a lot of money. All you have to do is to give yourself small tests of courage and competence a few times a week. Run a little farther, walk a bit faster. Do something unexpected or innovative at work. Finish a project you've been postponing. Learn a computer language. I can't offer a standard plan of seven or twelve foolproof ways to prove yourself to yourself. You'll just have to use whatever methods are right for *you*, whatever will convince *you* that you deserve respect and a round of applause.

Don't make the mistake of trying to demonstrate your worth by focusing on your family. Even if you really need to spend more time with your husband or to read to your children more often, do it on family time, not on self time. These good deeds will make you a better wife and mother, but they won't necessarily make you a better you. You'll have to prove your worth on your own terms, by engaging in something that challenges you as an independent human being.

Another way to inspire self-respect is to volunteer in your community. Community members don't sleep in your house, but they surround you and live in your neighborhood. They're a potential second family. Show your concern by heading a fund-raising effort at a local school or church, volunteering to visit the elderly in a nearby nursing home, counseling troubled teenagers, or tutoring adults who can't read. Getting involved in selfless activities like these will, surprisingly, help you learn to focus on yourself. Finding out that you have the ability to comfort or teach a stranger will give you an amazing feeling of mastery. You'll learn that you can make a difference in the world, the world outside of family. Nurturing people who aren't your children or your husband will help you to nurture yourself.

Planting seeds of self-respect like this will help you to cultivate a dream for yourself. Only when you begin to respect yourself, when you feel confident about your abilities and talents, will you be emotionally ready and able to find your own vision. Possessing a core of inner strength is just as essential to support a dream as having the talent or skill to make it happen. A woman I know can draw gorgeous illustrations, paintings of little girls in gardens that pulse with colors and textures so vibrant that the people seem ready to get up and walk off the page. But she has so little confidence in her ability that she has never gotten close to realizing her lifelong goal—to write and illustrate children's books. It's clear that she has an extraordinary artistic facility, but she doesn't have the self-respect and ambition essential to realize her dream. It's as if she has a car but can't find a key for the ignition, so she'll never be able to back it out of the garage.

Still, she has to be admired for keeping her dream alive after she had children, an accomplishment in itself. So many mothers lack a clear-cut, strong vision, a purpose that doesn't dim with motherhood or disappear as they grow older. That's why I don't want to mislead mothers by telling them that they have to *follow* their dream. First, they have to be able to forge one; they have to force themselves to imagine what it is they want most and, only then, to figure out a way to get it.

A dream has to go beyond motherhood, a concept that many sacrificial mothers simply can't grasp. But this dream doesn't have to burst out fully formed, like a newborn who emerges walking and talking. A dream almost always has to begin as a vague feeling of what you'd like to accomplish, a hazy vision of what you want out of life.

If this process confuses you, here's another way to think about it. Imagine yourself as a grizzled granny. You're looking back on your life, on everything you've ever done and said, everyone you've ever known. What would you like to be able to say was your purpose for being alive? Other than having so many wonderful children and grandchildren and great-grandchildren, what did you accomplish in your long life?

If you can answer these questions, then you're on your way to forming a dream.

If you try again and again but still can't fix on a goal for yourself that doesn't include the words "wife" and "mother," think back to how you were as a young girl. Most children and adolescents have a great talent for concocting elaborate plans for what they want to be when they grow up. My daughter, who's only eleven, already has a dream for herself. She wants to be a professional ballerina, and she imagines quite vividly what it will be like to be a dancer and live in New York City. Little girls like her carry so many possible future selves in their head that there's often no room for a present self. At this time of life, becoming a grown-up feels light-years away. Adulthood is a rumor, a fantasy world, and imagining it is like picturing what it would be like to live on the moon. For young girls, dreaming is as easy and as fun as playing with dolls or painting their fingernails. If you've lost touch with your ability to play and fantasize, try to reimagine yourself as a girl. Remember a time when having a dream in the day was nearly as easy as having one in the night.

If you want to re-create a heady, childlike state of mind, you'll have to use all of your powers of imagination. Try to conjure up a fantasy of yourself ten or twenty years from now. Picture this "possible self." If you're having trouble, practice first on images of disaster, of terrible future selves. Unfortunately, most of us are fairly adept at doing this. We can easily imagine ourselves ending up as a bag lady or an alcoholic, as someone who's crippled or who can't find work. After you take this path to a scary, awful dream, remember that if you can picture the bad, you can also picture the good. All you have to do is believe that anything is possible. Move on to the next step by imagining a happy and successful possible self. Close your eyes and envision your face on the front page of the newspaper. You've won the lottery! How about this: You're going to medical school or you lost twenty pounds or you're going to be an astronaut or you're going to perform on Broadway.

To create a possible self, you have to think like this, in very specific, realistic, and deliberately optimistic terms. Fill in all the details to make your dream come to life, piece by piece, bit by bit. If you're an art teacher, like my sister, you might build a vision in which you begin to take on private students and eventually open your own art academy. If you're like my lawyer friend who bakes delicious powdered-sugar walnut buttons, you might dream about starting a business with an army of cookie carts in New York City.

After you fantasize your best possible self, you'll have to figure out how to make her come alive. To do this, you have to take action to bring your dream closer to reality. Some mothers won't be able to do this alone. If you can't, don't be afraid to ask for help. Explain to your husband and children what you're trying to do, and ask for their cooperation. If you need some quiet time, even if only to think and plan, arrange to get it. If you need to go out every Saturday afternoon, find a way to make it possible. This is not pampering yourself, because pampering should be the means to this end. You should already be an expert in self-indulgence, so by now you should have confidence about asking for help to achieve your goals. If your family and friends understand how important this is for you, they'll be willing to help you find a way.

The most difficult part of self-realization is trying not to cut yourself off from your family while immersing yourself in your dream. If you're close to realizing your goal but you have become completely unavailable to your husband and children, then you've taken selfism beyond the point of no return—to complete selfishness. You have to learn the toughest trick of all, to balance your needs and the demands of your dream with the needs of the people you love. It's rough, but it's not impossible.

When Catherine, the bakery mother, was struggling to keep her business afloat, she recognized that she could rejuvenate it if she'd relocate to a booming tourist village five hours from her hometown.

The upscale skiers and vacationers who cram the village all year long would go crazy for her fresh, homemade goodies. But she also knew that she'd be working nonstop and that she'd get to see her children only on Sundays. So rather than move her failing bakery to Wyoming, she shut down the retail part of it and found herself an alternate goal. That was how she balanced her need to dream with her need to be available for her children.

Even now, Catherine fights a never-ending battle to balance her needs with those of her family. Although her fake-butter business is constantly expanding, she and her husband never work past 5:00 P.M., and she limits her travel to two or three days a month, so that she won't lose touch with her family. She has never seen her dream as a way to exclude her children; she always expected it to be a perfect way to teach them practical business skills firsthand. Her bakery still turns out 568 loaves of poppy seed bread every day for a local restaurant, and her fifteen-year-old son does all the baking. Her ten-year-old twins bag the bread every day too. Her vision has given all of her children an intimate understanding of what it means to invest in oneself, and they've learned how important it is for a mother to have goals of her own.

Catherine's dream has also taken her on a path to discovering her true self.

# Nine

# Finding Balance

Here's my version of a familiar Old Testament phrase: "To every thing there is a season, and a time to every purpose under the heaven. A time to be sacrificial and a time to be good to yourself." The hardest part, of course, is knowing which time is which.

My baking-butter mom has a knack for this kind of knowledge. That's because she always recognizes the distinction between what it is that she needs and what it is that her family needs, and she gives equal weight to both. She holds on tight to her sense of self by never losing sight of her own dream. She's constantly trying out new ideas for her business, to expand on and reimagine it. She wrote a cookbook of recipes for her butter that she sells on her monthly television shopping network appearances. She invented a low-calorie baking sugar and a low-fat sauté butter, both of which she's testing, so that she can sell them someday, along with her other products.

Although part of her mind is always on her work, Catherine makes herself available to all six of her children. She sits with her twins while they do their homework. She consoles and encourages her adolescent daughter, so the girl can survive a hellish year of junior high school taunting. A while ago she supervised her oldest son as he filled out his college application forms, and she organized his effort to get into a prestigious military academy, where he just finished his first year.

This mom is proud of her children, and she'll brag about them from morning to midnight if you let her. But she's just as proud of her own achievements. She'll give you a blow-by-blow description of her bakery traumas and triumphs over tea and Western omelettes (made with only a drop of oil), and she'll tell you what happened when she met with the president of the famous shopping network she appears on. It doesn't really bother her that some of her neighbors disapprove of her ambition or that a few members of her church envy her financial success. She knows who she is and what she wants out of life, and as long as she and her children are doing well, that's all that matters to her.

A mother like this, a woman with a strong sense of self, doesn't need the approval of other people to feel good about herself. Her sense of who she is comes from within, and it belongs to her *no matter what*. No one can give it to her, and no one can take it away from her either. If people disparage her choices or criticize her, the abuse doesn't lessen her opinion of herself. And if they praise her, the flattery doesn't enhance her view of herself either. She's self-contained, self-possessed, and self-motivated. She's a woman with a firm and unwavering sense of self.

Mothers who have a true self don't necessarily neglect or forget their children. It isn't an either/or situation; it isn't us or them. In fact, many mothers are able to pay attention to themselves and to their children simultaneously, as the wealthy mom who reads to her four-year-old son while she's getting her legs waxed at home does. She's certainly an extreme, even a kooky example, but she's definitely attempting balance. Balance is mothers' ability to attend to their family's needs but also to recognize their own needs and to be able to switch their attention back and forth between the two.

The fact that women almost always have to deal with two or three or five things at once isn't necessarily a handicap. Unlike men, we rarely get a chance to be single-minded about anything, because there are too many people depending on us for too many things. Women have always "tended to live with ambiguity and multiplicity," writes Mary Catherine Bateson. And this is good, she says, not bad, because it enables us to cope with the complexity of real life.

Balance is this ability to juggle three balls at once—self, children, husband—without dropping any one of them too often. It might not be possible to keep all those balls in the air all the time, but you can certainly try.

When I'm engrossed in work, I'm still thinking of my children, though they're tucked away in a far corner of my mind. All it takes is a phone call from a teacher or the school nurse to bring them looming into the foreground. And when there's an urgent need, I drop what I'm doing in a flash. A while ago I decided to stop work in mid-deadline so I could go to school and watch my daughter compete in a spelling bee. I held my breath, my heart racing, as I saw her standing at the front of the stage. She had her hands clenched behind her back and a look of terror in her eyes, but she spoke each letter loud and clear. I gritted my teeth as I listened to her spell the word "agriculture."

"A-G-R-A-C-U-L-T-U-R-E," she said.

My stomach dropped. But only one other fourth grader spelled it correctly, so she took second place, and I felt myself melting with relief. As I drove back to work, giddy with feelings of pride, I switched gears and focused on myself and my own work for the rest of the afternoon.

My children's accomplishments have always given me a special thrill, but I also need to achieve on my own, to do things just for me that satisfy only me. I try to cherish myself nearly as often as I cherish them. That's why I run, why I take yoga classes, why I go to the movies by myself, why I work so hard. I create my own private life that happens outside of my family limits.

This doesn't mean that I can't get enormous pleasure from doing things for my family; in fact, I do, because that's how I show them I care. For many mothers, including me, food is "the currency of care," as Bateson puts it, and I make special efforts to buy them what they like to eat. When I go grocery shopping, I look for the gooey pudding cups my children like and the offensive dehydrated instant coffee my husband prefers to drink. On my son's birthday, I went to three stores before I found just the right present, and I made elaborate plans and arranged complicated equipment rentals for his video game party at home. I had to rent two video systems and two new games, and I had to finagle an extra television set from a neighbor.

I sacrifice to do these things, but in the worldwide family of mothers, I'm doing only what's expected. If I were a member of the !Kung, a tribe of African nomads who still hunt and gather all their food, I'd have had to *carry* my children all day long. Not just when they were infants either, but until they turned four or five; and I'd have been carrying them every step of the way for 1,500 miles, the distance the tribe travels every year. I'd also have to help gather the tribe's food too.

The extent of the sacrifices that mothers in industrial societies are expected to make aren't as extreme as the !Kung's, but there is a lot of social pressure for mothers to do more and more for their children while they're also helping to support the family. In a way, we too have to carry our children while we also gather and cook the food. And we do all of this while earning a living too.

Why haven't we advanced far beyond this stage? Why are we still stuck in these old habits, entrenched in a pattern of self-denial and sacrifice that we find so difficult to escape? Why do people in nearly every country, on nearly every continent, assume that sacrifice is what women are born to do, what they're meant for?

Is there no escape for women from the biology and psychology of sacrifice?

There must be, and soon.

It's unfair, immoral, and just plain wrong to expect women to continue to make most of the family sacrifices, as if their lives haven't changed since prehistoric times. Mothers can no longer make these enormous, backbreaking sacrifices, as if we all belonged to an aboriginal band of hunter-gatherers. Mothers have to take charge of their lives. They have to expect more from themselves and from their families. They have to learn to demand self-respect and to devote some nurturing to themselves. They have to feel waves of fondness for themselves, as they do for their family. They have to find a purpose in life outside of family, and to stick with it. And, finally, they have to create a true self and carry it with them.

## The Elusive True Self

For a lot of mothers, finding a true self can be terribly frustrating. Uncovering it is like searching for oil that's been buried under thousands of feet of sediment and bedrock for millions of years. A woman's true self can also be hidden beneath layers of her obligations to people and her responsibilities as a mother and wife, daughter and sister. She's got to work as hard to unearth this self as a geologist prospecting for crude oil.

It's taken me years to see this for a fact and to realize that I would have to probe my own past in order to understand my future. As I look back at myself as a young woman, I see someone who was incredibly adventurous and full of naive self-confidence. I was brash and impertinent and proud of it. I said exactly what I thought and I didn't take grief from anybody. One summer I hitchhiked across England, Wales, and Spain with a friend. A few years later I worked my way across Europe and the Middle East, on my own, and I lived in Israel during a major war. Then I moved to New York City by myself, subletting apartments and juggling boyfriends and part-time jobs and graduate school.

But when I became a wife and mother, I turned into a completely different woman, one who was infinitely more cautious and not nearly as self-assured. I became a woman whose idea of adventure was to drive around the neighborhood without wearing a seat belt, whose concept of daring was to order an "everything" bagel or to stay up past midnight on a Saturday.

Where did that bold, enthusiastic, vivacious young woman go?

She was engulfed by waves of motherly duty and sacrifice. She was replaced by an older and wiser woman, one who was often tired. This new woman couldn't sustain that girlish effervescence and all that self-focused enthusiasm. She figured that to be a good mother, she'd have to give up her quest for thrills. She faced the fact that her responsibility to her children was more urgent than the call of being wild. She was somebody who felt happy only when her children and her husband were happy.

But after living as a self-righteous sacrificial mother for more than ten years, I began to understand that I had to go back and find one small kernel of the former me to hang on to. I needed this missing link to forge my new true self, to combine the me I am now with the me who used to be. I had to remember the best parts of my old self and find a place for them in my heart. I wanted my true self to include that risk-taking, spontaneous me as well as the careful and worried sacrificial mother and the determined-to-be-more-selfist woman. To turn back time and find the young me, I had to take a few lessons from that old self. I had to relearn how to be self-centered, how to take chances, how to enjoy myself as much as I enjoy my children. And I had to warn the former me about the dangers of becoming too sacrificial.

This sounds as if it should have been relatively easy, but it wasn't. It was one of the hardest things I've ever tried to do, so I'm incredibly proud that I've nearly succeeded.

Like me, most mothers have a nearly forgotten self, a woman they used to be, once upon a time. This old self is important, a precious relic of a woman's past life, one that demands to be preserved. Her true self should be an intricate mosaic of who she was as a teenager and a young woman as well as who she is as a wife and a lover and a mother. All of these shards of self are part of who a woman is right now.

The only way for a woman to achieve a balance in her life is to use all of these disparate pieces to lead her to her true self. It's also the best way for her to prove to her daughters that a mother can be, and must be, more than just sacrificial.

The search for a true self can take years and years, or it can be accomplished in a heartbeat. The time it takes depends mostly on what inspires a woman to begin her quest in the first place. If her search for self is triggered by a quirk of fate or an important life event, it's possible that her progress will come at lightning speed. When all of her children leave home, for example, and she's no longer a mother every minute, she'll have an obvious incentive to find herself fast. When her parents die and she's no longer someone's daughter, she may feel a terrible and urgent longing to find out who she is. If she gets divorced or becomes widowed, she might be ripe for an immediate and serious bout of soul-searching. If she suffers the loss of a close friend or relative, or if she herself becomes seriously ill, she might be propelled, like a human cannon-ball, from sacrificial blindness into self-aware clarity.

It wasn't until her husband died of AIDS, a mother of two little boys tells me, that she realized that she needed to establish a firm sense of self. She's still mourning her husband, but his death has taught her that she has to do things for herself right now, while she still has time. So she's going back to school for a degree; she's taking a dance class; she's buying tickets to see the ballet at Lincoln Center for the first time in her life. Her husband's tragic and premature death has forced her into a quest for self—she wants to value her role as a mother, but she also needs to focus on her worth as a person with important needs and desires of her own.

The search for self can become a prolonged odyssey for mothers who don't have an external event to inspire them. If they live with a mysterious inner longing, they may find themselves at an emotional crossroads, with a nagging and inexplicable yearning that won't go away. Perhaps they've reached a certain age or their baby boy has just started to shave. Maybe they looked into the mirror and saw a woman they no longer recognize. It doesn't really matter why, but as long as mothers are driven to reassess their lives and their feelings about who they are, they're beginning the journey to discovering a true self.

This life passage can occur when a woman is twenty-five or forty-five, but it's probably not her first experience with a search for self. Women almost always battle with the searing question of "Who am I?" as teenagers. This is when young women struggle to gain independence from their family and it's when they're most likely to have an initial identity crisis. This psychological rite of passage is nearly as predictable as puberty. Teenage girls wrestle to figure out who they are, apart from their mother's daughter or their brother's sister, and they agonize about how they will find their way in the world. Unfortunately, though, many teenagers are handicapped by having a false self, so their emotional battle ends as soon as it begins. They're confused about who they are and what they want, because they've been so thoroughly brainwashed to be nice, friendly, polite, and accommodating. They put on a fixed mask of complaisant cooperation, trying to become ultra-feminine, everyone's idea of a good girl.

But good girls don't have a true self; they have a self that mirrors other people's expectations. It's not genuine, it's a reflection. And the longer they keep up this false front, the harder it will be to shake loose.

Women who fail to outgrow this false self take it along for the ride when they become mothers. They present it to their children and husband, and they never reveal how they really feel or think, even to the people they love. They're always more considerate than they'd like to be, more self-denying than they want, and a lot more sacrificial than is good for them. Women who put up a false front for decades may never be able to achieve a balance between sacrifice and selfism.

To find her true self, a sacrificial mother has to have self-respect, and she also has to create a dream for herself. It's pretty much impossible for her to do any of this without a certain amount of introspection. She has to be able to think about herself. She has to be able to figure out what assets she possesses and which ones she needs to rediscover. This isn't easy, because self-examination demands a willingness to shut others out as well as a certain amount of quiet and solitude. It's hard enough for a woman to face her deepest flaws and fears, but it's even more stressful if she's got to do it amid thousands of everyday distractions. If her life is noisy, filled to the brim with children's whines and cries, a husband's groans and complaints, a boss's demands and needs, then she's got no quiet space for herself. That's why she needs to isolate herself, to take the time and make the effort to be alone. It's only by looking inside that a mother will be able to see herself as she is now and figure out a way to acquire a new, more balanced version of herself. She has to go on a kind of internal safari to penetrate to that other, secret self, one that's hidden in the dense, lush jungle of the psyche.

Unfortunately, I can't tell mothers exactly what it is they need to find, because there are no right answers. Every woman must discover her true self for herself; and only she will know when she succeeds. But I can tell mothers how to put themselves on the proper path to balance. Here are a few suggestions.

## Find a padded cell

I don't mean this literally, of course, though I have spoken to mothers who have locked themselves into bathrooms, closets, and garages to be able to think their own thoughts. What I do mean is that you should find yourself a private and quiet place to go. Mothers are hardly ever alone, and rarely cocooned in silence, so they never have a chance to sit and indulge themselves in thoughts of self. If this is your problem, make it your goal to find time every day to be alone, in silence. If you have to, force yourself to get up half an hour before the rest of the family or to go to bed after everyone else is asleep. Figure out a way to use this time for your own benefit—to focus on yourself, to think about who you are, where you've been, and where you're going. Call it meditation or quiet time or solitude, but make it yours. Learn to relax and to listen to your inner self. Even if you don't hear anything, try to reflect on who you are right now and who you want to be in the next phase of your life. Think of yourself not as a mother or a wife or a daughter, but as you, a separate human being who has to face the world on her own.

## Let go

When you get sick, give in to the illness. *Be sick.* Stay in bed and let your family take care of you. Don't martyr yourself by doing the food shopping with a fever or finishing the laundry with a strep infection. You're only undermining yourself this way. Give your husband and children a chance to see what it feels like to be the one who takes care of instead of the one who is cared for. Let them have a chance to sacrifice for you: Give them a crash lesson in being sacrificial. Let your family see that you too can fall apart and that sometimes you need attention and caring. Teach them that you're a human being, not a sacrifice robot. This might even help you to unlearn your own sacrifice habit, at least for a while.

You don't have to wait until you get sick to let go, either. A friend of mine found herself so exhausted one night that her eyes ached and her limbs were leaden. She fell asleep fully dressed, shoes included, because she was too tired to put on a nightgown. Up at six the next morning, she still didn't feel refreshed, so she decided to give in to her fatigue. She announced to her family that she'd spend the next week relaxing, that she wouldn't pick up anything from the floor or do any serious cooking or jump up every time one of her three children asked for a glass of milk. She informed her husband and children to think of it as a mom strike and to be ready to make adjustments. And they did. It worked out so well that now she considers herself on a semistrike almost all the time.

## Your family is not you

Remember this well. Force yourself to say "My family is not me" at least several times a day. Your children and your husband are very special; they're a sacred part of who you are. But they're not all of you. There is more to you than motherhood or wifedom. "The power of the womb, marvelous as it is, does not have the wattage to light up a lifetime," as Anne Roiphe writes. You are worth so much more to your children as a complete, well-balanced person than as an automaton dedicated only to their well-being. It may seem like a paradox, but by giving more to yourself, ultimately you will give more to them.

## Dig up your past

Try to recall who you were and what your dreams were when you were young. If you have trouble remembering your history, do some investigating. Talk to your mother or your aunts or your sisters. Ask them what you used to be like, how you were different from who you are now. Call a high school friend and reminisce about the old days. Sift your life for the gold nuggets that were the best parts of you in the past and incorporate them into your present self.

## Dive into the dull and boring

It may sound silly, but it can work. If you take on some monotonous, repetitive activities, they'll force you to think about your inner life. You'll have to do some introspection, if only to keep yourself from going crazy. Go for a long walk or a run or a hike. Take the same route and travel the same distance each time. Ride a stationary bike or swim or walk on a treadmill. Wash the kitchen floor or vacuum the house. Put your body on automatic so your mind can be free to wander. Direct your thoughts to yourself, to thinking about who you are and who you'd like to become. Don't make the mistake of boring yourself by watching television or listening to the radio. Both can certainly be dull, but they're much too distracting. They'll take you out of yourself, not deeper into yourself. You need to find something to do that will free your mind, not weigh it down.

How will you be able to tell if any of this works, if you have, in fact, come close to finding your true self?

You might not, at least at first.

Don't expect any miraculous, heavenly interventions. Bells won't ring; angels won't hover over your head. Your children won't be filled with sudden respect and gratitude for your gracious and self-denying ability to sacrifice for them. But you might find that your outlook on life has undergone some subtle changes. You'll still give to your children, but you'll know when to stop, when enough is enough. You'll still feel gratified by your children's successes, but you'll feel an equal pleasure in your own achievements. You'll still accommodate yourself to your children's needs, but you'll find that you can pick and choose your sacrifices much more carefully. You'll feel happy when they are, but you'll be able to find pleasure for yourself too. Finally, you'll probably still feel anxious about your choices, about whether it's okay to pay more attention to yourself and less to your children. But you'll have learned about the importance of balance, the ability to steady the yin of sacrifice with the yang of selfism.

## Maintaining Balance

By now my message should be loud and clear: Mothers have to offset their sacrifices with an equal focus on self—not to replace sacrifice, just to temper it with some self-focus. A healthy balance between the two is the only way for women to retain their humanity.

I'm certainly *not* saying that mothers should give in to the troubling and persistent impluse to do whatever they want whenever they want. I'm *not* telling mothers that it's okay to neglect their children and feel free to do their own thing. My prescription for selfism doesn't make every night New Year's Eve, an exclusive event to which children aren't invited. Children will always need a certain amount of adult sacrifice, but it doesn't really matter if it's Mom or Dad doing the sacrificing.

It's especially important for mothers with daughters to practice balance so that they can offer their daughters an example of the benefits of having a true self. Teenage girls wage a tough battle to find this true self, and they need all the allies they can get. A mother who's not afraid to have a life of her own can be their most powerful protector and model. Boys also benefit by having a mother who balances selfism and sacrifice, because they see that women who value themselves not only exist but thrive. These boys might even become husbands who share the give and take with their wives, instead of husbands who expect only to take and take.

A well-balanced, selfist mother can become a role model for the next generation and a conscientious guardian of her own well-being. But the road to maternal balance isn't always easy, or even simple and direct. Sometimes when mothers try to balance their needs with their children's, the plan backfires.

You might think that the anthropologist Margaret Mead would have been an ideal model of balance for a daughter. Mead was a famous author and world traveler by her mid-forties, as well as a frequently photographed doting mother of a little girl. But when Mead's daughter, Mary Catherine Bateson, grew up, she revealed that she never fully absorbed the nonsacrificial lesson of her mother's life. In fact, Bateson admitted that she spent several decades putting her own needs last, giving her husband's career top priority. She simply "never questioned" what she called the "culturally supported attitude toward women."

If Margaret Mead couldn't raise a nonsacrificial daughter with a firm sense of self, it must be harder than we can imagine. That's why I now make a conscious effort to talk to my children about what I'm doing for myself as well as what I'm doing for them. When I took my weekend spa trip, I couldn't be there to put my daughter's hair in a bun for dance class, nor could I attend my son's Sunday basketball game. I apologized, but I also let them know how excited I felt to be going away for such a special treat. They understood how much it meant to me, even though they bellyached about all the sacrifices they were making for me!

Some mothers, though, are so deeply sacrificial that they will never be able to find balance. A single mother I know from Barbados sacrificed everything to provide for her children, only to realize that she'd never given them what they really needed. To earn a living, she had to abandon her young children to find work in the United States. She had to give her seven-year-old daughter to the girl's grandmother to raise, and she paid a neighbor to keep her four-year-old son. Working as a housekeeper and a nanny for other women's babies for the next twelve years, she carefully hoarded all of her extra money to send home to her own children. But in all that time, she never once saw or held her own daughter and son; she knew them only from letters and phone calls. It wasn't until her son was a senior in high school that she could finally afford to bring both of them, nearly grown, to live with her in New York. By then both children were strangers to her. She'd provided for them financially, but they grew up without a mother to talk to at bedtime or to kiss away their hurts.

She sacrificed her life, and she never considered balance to be a possibility.

Luckier mothers, those who are blessed with more financial options than she had, can seek balance in many ways. A few, like a neighbor who's so self-involved she doesn't know the name of her son's third-grade teacher, might need to remove some selfism and add more sacrifice. But most women, like me, may need to find ways to sacrifice less.

I knew I'd managed to discard some sacrifice the day I left for my spa weekend without a backward glance or an ounce of guilt in my heart. I truly felt that it was my turn, and so did my family. Because I've achieved a kind of delicate balance, I feel so much less anxious and I'm much more relaxed. I enjoy my children more too. They're more independent and confident than ever, and they take more pride in themselves. My relationship with my husband has deepened and prospered as well. We're much more affectionate and caring, and even when we bicker, it's more in fondness than in anger. He's learned how to show us he cares, and he expresses his concern by calling home two or three times a day. He even threw me a surprise party, the only one I've ever had, inviting all of my friends to a sumptuous lunch at a restaurant along the Hudson River. Before we began to eat, he led a champagne toast to me. My eyes misted with tears as I felt a kind of vindication of my renunciation of sacrifice. It had worked! We celebrated that day, and nearly every day since.

If I can shed my overly sacrificial cloak, anybody can. To find out how close you are to true balance, ask yourself a few key questions.

- *Do you make sacrifices for your family, yet are you sufficiently good to yourself?*

- *Do you have a dream?*

- *Do you feel confident and secure about who you are?*

If you can honestly say yes to all of these questions, then you've achieved a balance between doing for others and doing for yourself.

If you're coming up with no or even maybe, you might have to try to reorganize your life. Pare down your household responsibilities and duties. Share chores with your husband and older children or pay an employee to do them. If you can afford it, hire someone to clean or to shop or to do laundry. Banish all of your unnecessary chores. Instead of changing sheets every week, do it every two or three weeks. Wash towels once or twice a month. Set aside time for your children, and then plan some time for you—and make sure those two times don't overlap.

If you can, try to cut back on your paid work too. Instead of putting in forty or fifty hours a week, try to work only thirty or twenty-five. You'll earn less, but you'll have more time. Fewer hours of work outside the home will mean that you have more time to spend with your family, but you'll also have more time for yourself. Once you manage to grasp that precious time, make sure that you use some of it wisely and for your own good.

Think of the words "part time" as your new motto. If you're lucky enough to find a good part-time job, you can still be a valuable breadwinner for your family. Working part time can give you the best of two worlds: an outside life of your own and a life at home with your family.

If all of this seems too impractical, or if you can't afford to earn less money, aim for a simpler solution to the problem of balancing your life. Think about repossessing your sexuality, for example. This simple step will help you focus on yourself and on your marriage, and it can also teach you to be good to yourself more often. Take yourself back to a time before your belly was stretched, before you became a household servant, before your life revolved around toys and tapes, birthday parties and play dates. Go back to a time when sex was gloriously simple and deliciously relaxing. Remember the days when you and your husband could languish in bed all weekend, getting up only to go to the bathroom and find some food?

Reminisce fondly about those days for thirty seconds. Then forget them. Those days are as gone as silent movies and the telegraph; they're not coming back either. But you don't have to re-create your lost youth to be able to resurrect your sensuality. Instead, change your expectations to fit the reality of your older, parental self. Find sixty minutes of quiet on a Saturday night or a Sunday afternoon, and cram every bit of sensual pleasure you can into that single precious hour. Even thirty minutes can do the trick. Be grateful for small sexual favors, whenever and wherever you can find them.

Even if reviving your sex life doesn't help you with balance, at least you won't have lost anything.

Another way to seek balance is to go out and have some fun. Sacrificial mothers sometimes become so dead serious about their role as the emotional backbone of the next generation that they forget how important it is to loosen up and have fun. Fun is what you had in the days when you had no responsibilities, no cares in the world but what you'd do next. Fun is taking the time to wallow in little pleasures, small delights, tiny moments of pure pleasure. It's possible to be a selfist, balanced mother and also to have fun; in fact, having fun is essential.

When you take your children ice-skating, rent skates for yourself. When you go to the park, join in their baseball game. When they're flying a kite, take a turn; when you're at the beach, build a sand castle. Feel the exhilaration of being a child with your own children.

Don't take life so seriously.

Learn to live for right now, to have fun in this moment. If you adopt this outlook on life, you'll be inspired to attain more balance.

Most important of all, perhaps, is to try to change your instinctive disapproval of women who don't put themselves last all the time. A friend remembers that when her mother and grandmother really wanted to insult a woman, they'd say, "She really knows how to take care of herself." My goal is to make that statement the new ultimate *compliment* for a woman, so that mothers can feel proud of being good to themselves.

## Some Final Words

I'll say this one last time.

Mothers can't give up all their sacrifices, because sacrifice is one of the things that makes motherhood so sweet and bittersweet. Giving of yourself for your children's sake is part of what it means to be a mother, whether you're an octopus or an elephant or a human being. Only human mothers, though, can revel in the deep joys of self-denial. And only they can take action to balance that feeling with an equal zest for self-indulgence.

If this secret passion for sacrifice gives mothers an intense and heart-swelling rapture, what can be so bad about it? After all, most women spend about twenty to twenty-five years raising children, so if they live to be eighty, that's only a quarter of their lifetime. Why *not* devote those years to the children?

Because extreme sacrifice will make them sick and miserable and insecure for the duration, and perhaps for a long time after.

Because while it may give their husbands an easier life, it won't help their marriage, and it may even damage their sex life, not just for one or two decades but for always.

And because, in the end, it won't really help their children very much.

Too much sacrifice isn't healthy, it isn't smart, and it just isn't fair.

The nearly universal social rules that force women to engage in excessive and unnecessary sacrifice are equally unfair. So is the social pressure put on mothers to be the primary family sacrificers. Women give and give and give some more because they know they are the only ones who will. When men are overloaded with responsibility, when they're faced with a chance to sacrifice, many of them often turn the other cheek. They can't face the pressures and hardships of obligation. That's why divorced fathers often abandon their children rather than trying to fit a former family into a new life. That's why so many husbands refuse to do extra chores around the house, why they're unwilling to learn how to operate a washing machine or how to prepare a decent meal. It's not that these men are cruel or incompetent or evil, it's just that they simply cannot cope; they literally can't manage. As a friend's husband tells her with great exasperation when she asks him why he won't vacuum the family room: "I need one *less* thing to think of, not one *more* thing."

So it is that mothers walk a sacrificial path on which most men would clearly stumble and fall. It's not that some men don't want to sacrifice, it's just that they *can't.*

A society that depends on mothers' excessive sacrifices to fuel families, though, exploits and damages mothers. This is a culture that approves of women who are family servants, and it creates insurmountable obstacles to mothers' feelings of self-respect and self-confidence. When a group encourages extreme maternal sacrifice, it fosters a family structure in which mothers are bound to be subservient and deferential, insecure and unfocused. This arrangement almost guarantees that vague but troubling emotional problems will plague women for years.

The immense power of society to demand and foster maternal sacrifice is what makes that trait so difficult to subdue. The habit of self-denial may seem as if it comes from within, a voluntary act on the part of dedicated mothers, but it's also a result of virulent social expectations.

Although so many mothers in industrial nations now earn a substantial part of the family income, they're still expected to be sole sacrificers, as if sacrifice were their highest duty. It doesn't matter that women's lives have begun to resemble men's lives in so many ways that their roles have become nearly identical. Fathers work for pay, and so do mothers. Mothers cuddle their children, and so do fathers.

Why, then, must it be only mothers who sacrifice so faithfully?

It must not be. Overzealous maternal sacrifice has to be rejected by the mothers who are doomed to indulge in it and to suffer from it. The buck must stop with women themselves.

Sacrificial mothers everywhere must start a revolution, an upheaval that will end the caste system that uses them so carelessly, so harshly, and so dangerously. They have to start that rebellion in their own home—as if their life is on the line, because it truly is. Mothers who don't put up a fight will enter the millennium with an invisible handicap that they'll surely pass on to their daughters and granddaughters. The time to do something about it is not later but right now; to do something not halfway but all the way.

Don't try to teach men how to be better fathers; teach all parents how to be good mothers. Both men and women must learn how to sacrifice, when necessary, for their children, how to deny themselves, when necessary, for their children, and how to love, cherish, and support their children. But they must also learn, together, how to care for themselves, as separate human beings and as a cooperative team in the game of life. They have to learn to collaborate in their caring.

When this happens, mothers will no longer have to worry about being overly sacrificial. Every parent—mother and father alike—will yearn to sacrifice for family and to focus on self. To make this happen, mothers have to change their sacrificial ways. Once they do, the men in their lives will have to change as well. Eventually, women's protest will force the social rules for sacrifice to crumble and fall away.

There will be no other choice.

# Notes

## 1. Women and the Tradition of Self-Denial

**Page 11:**

"the Susan Smiths of the world": The Union, South Carolina, mother who drowned her two young sons in 1995. In a *Newsweek* poll released on July 29, 63 percent of Americans said she should receive the death penalty for her crime. Instead she was sentenced to life in prison. "No Casting of Stones," *Newsweek*, August 7, 1995, p. 31.

**Page 12:**

"The vast majority of mothers": In my 1996 *Family Circle* Sacrifice Survey, 50 percent of mothers give up being alone as often as they'd like, 47 percent sacrifice spending money the way they want, 44 percent give up reading, 41 percent of mothers say they give up getting enough sleep, and 40 percent give up socializing. *Family Circle* mailed this survey to a random sample of married couples with at least one child living at home in November 1995. The survey was answered by 600 women and men; 245 of them are couples married to each other. The report, "Surprising Secrets of Great Marriages," appeared in the October 9, 1996, issue of *Family Circle*. In my list of twenty-three possible sacrifices, fully half of mothers say they give up at least four. The complete list of sacrifices includes: watching as much television as I'd like, reading as much as I'd like, spending money the way I want, raising our children the way I prefer, playing sports or exercising as often as I'd like, watching as much sports on TV as I'd like, attending live sports events as often as I'd like, socializing as often as I'd like, being alone, having sex as often as I'd like, having the kind of sex I enjoy, going to the movies or theater, doing the kind of work I'd prefer, having a career, being able to travel, spending time with my own parents and family, keeping up with my friends, going to college, being the kind of person I'd like to be, getting enough sleep, taking care of myself, buying the kind of clothes I like, reaching a personal goal.

"about eight in ten mothers say they often sacrifice": In my 1996 *Family Circle* Sacrifice Survey, 78 percent of mothers say they often sacrifice their needs and desires for their children; 58 percent believe that it's a mother's duty to sacrifice for her children.

**Page 15:**

"most mothers with children under the age of eighteen": 67 percent of mothers with children under the age of eighteen have little time for self-fulfillment, according to my 1993 *New Woman* Relationship Survey. This was a random national telephone survey conducted by the Roper Organization in May 1993 for *New Woman* magazine. Roper interviewed 764 women between the ages of seventeen and sixty. The report on the survey, "The Joy of Relationships," appeared in the October 1993 issue of *New Woman*. Also, according to my 1993 *New Woman* Infidelity Survey, I found that 92 percent of women say most wives sacrifice their personal pleasure for their family, but only 16 percent believe that husbands do the same. "The Infidelity Survey" appeared in the August 1993 *New Woman*, and 7,000 women responded. The report, "The 1994 *New Woman* Infidelity Report," appeared in March 1994.

**Page 16:**

"A great many women actually *expect* to lose themselves": Of the women who answered the 1993 *New Woman* Infidelity Survey, 83 percent say that "in marriage, most women submerge a vital part of themselves."

"I take better care of my family's needs than my own needs": This is from the 1992 *New Woman* Self-Esteem Survey, a random national telephone survey conducted by The Telephone Center in March 1992 for *New Woman*. They interviewed 1,202 women and men ages eighteen and over. The report, "*New Woman* Report on Self-Esteem," appeared in the October 1992 issue of *New Woman*. My results show that women are more more likely than men to agree that they take better care of their family's needs than of their own.

"think of their husband as 'just another child'": According to my 1996 *Family Circle* Sacrifice Survey, 46 percent of women agree with this statement. But only 15 percent of husbands describe their wives this way.

**Page 20:**

"Wanda Holloway's seedy sacrificial story": Early in 1991 Wanda Holloway made a down payment of a pair of diamond earrings to have her neighbor, Verna Heath, murdered. Heath's thirteen-year-old daughter, Amber, had twice won a spot on the cheerleading squad that Holloway hoped would go to her own daughter, Shanna Harper. Holloway was caught and sentenced to fifteen years in prison. See "Verdict Is Guilty in Cheerleading Trial," *New York Times*, September 4, 1991, p. A18.

**Page 20:**

"she had set five forest fires": See "A Mother's Love Runs to Arson, Police Say," *New York Times*, August 6, 1995, p. 26.

"the doctor who spent two years": Elizabeth Morgan claimed that her husband had raped their five-year-old daughter during court-sanctioned visits. She sent the child to live with her parents in New Zealand and went to jail instead of revealing her daughter's location. See "Who's to Judge," *New York Times Magazine*, May 21, 1989, p. 28.

**Page 21:**

"federal judge who promised to give up her seat": See "Judge Agrees to Step Aside to Aid Her Son," *New York Times*, May 8, 1996, p. B11.

"refusing aggressive chemotherapy": See "Out of Death, a Cherished Life," *Washington Post*, March 12, 1995, p. A1.

"the mother in South Carolina who was chained": See "Judge Orders Delinquent Girl to Be Chained to Her Mother," *New York Times*, December 15, 1995, p. A28. Also see "Tethered to Daughter, 15, a Mother Pays," *New York Times*, December 22, 1995, p. A26. In a terrible postscript to this story, the mother, Deborah Harter, was killed in an auto accident after visiting her daughter, who had been sent back to juvenile prison. "Mother in Tethering Case Is Killed in Car Accident," *New York Times*, September 24, 1996, p. A16.

Patti Smith: "Poet, Singer, Mother: Patti Smith Is Back," *New York Times*, December 12, 1995, p. C17.

**Page 22:**

Annie Lennox: "Domesticated Diva," *People*, August 7, 1995, pp. 103–104.

Susan Sarandon: "Labor of Love," *Entertainment Weekly*, March 22, 1996, p. 26.

Susan Butcher: See "Far from the Limelight, It's Mush, Mush, Mush," *New York Times*, February 13, 1996, p. B11.

Marcia Clark: See "Trials of a Female Lawyer: Should Marcia Clark Be in Court or in the Kitchen?" *Washington Post*, March 3, 1995, p. B1. Also see "Demands of Simpson Case Land Prosecutor in Custody Fight," *New York Times*, March 3, 1995, p. B8.

"More judges in divorce cases": See "Courts Reshape Image of 'The Good Mother,'" *APA Monitor*, December, 1995, p. 31.

**Page 23:**

"Sacrificial movie mothers": For a psychoanalytic view of maternal melodramas, see Ilsa J. Bick, "Stella Dallas: Maternal Melodrama and

Feminine Sacrifice," *Psychoanalytic Review*, vol. 79, no. 1 (1992), pp. 121–145.

**Page 24:**

"potential sacrifice hormone, oxytocin": For background on this research, see C. Sue Carter, "Patterns of Infant Feeding, the Mother-Infant Interaction and Stress Management," in Tiffany M. Field, P. M. McCabe, and N. Schneiderman (eds.), *Stress and Coping Across Development* (Hillsdale, N.J.: Erlbaum, 1988). Also see Cort A. Pedersen, "The Psychiatric Significance of Oxytocin," in C. B. Nemeroff (ed.), *Neuropeptides and Psychiatric Disorder. Progress in Psychiatry*, vol. 29 (Washington, D.C.: American Psychiatric Press, 1991). For an overview of some of this research, see *New York Times*, "Illuminating How Bodies Are Built for Sociability," April 30, 1996, p. C1. Quotes from C. Sue Carter are from personal interview, May 1996.

**Page 25:**

"a single gene they call fosB": See "Gene May Be Clue to Nature of Nurturing," *New York Times*, July 26, 1996, p. A21.

"a mother cat risked her life": This story was on the wire services and had national coverage in newspapers and on television. See "8 Lives Left, 5 Cats Get New Homes," *New York Times*, June 28, 1996, p. B6.

"to save her nestlings": For bird research, see David Barash, *Sociobiology and Behavior*, 2nd ed. (New York: Elsevier, 1982).

**Page 26:**

"an Indian elephant and her three-month-old calf": As described in Jeffrey Moussaieff Masson and Susan McCarthy, *When Elephants Weep: The Emotional Lives of Animals* (New York: Delacorte Press, 1995), pp. 64–65.

"A herd of giraffes": Masson and McCarthy, *When Elephants Weep*, p. 70.

"A mother octopus": This story appears in David P. Barash, *The Whisperings Within: Evolution and the Origin of Human Nature* (New York: Harper & Row, 1979), pp. 95–96.

"mothers' death-defying devotion is genetic": One of the best presentations of the idea that parental love is selfish love can be found in Barash, *The Whisperings Within*, p. 94.

**Page 27:**

"a Russian peasant woman": These figures are from *The Guinness Book of World Records, 1996* (New York: Facts On File, 1996).

"Older gulls make more feeding trips": From David Barash, *Socio-

*biology and Behavior,* 2nd ed., p. 303. Speculations about human parallels are from a personal interview with Barash in February 1996.

**Page 29:**

"Most mammal mothers": These ideas are from Frans De Waal, *Good Natured: The Origins of Right and Wrong in Humans and Other Animals* (Cambridge, Mass.: Harvard University Press, 1996). The phrase "emotional umbilical cord" appears on p. 122.

"every standard test of femininity": Empathy is included as a feminine trait in the Bem Sex Role Inventory and the Personal Attributes Questionnaire, both measures of gender identity. They are summarized in John Robinson, Phillip R. Shaver, and Lawrence Wrightsman (eds.), *Measures of Personality and Social Psychological Attitudes* (New York: Academic Press, 1991).

**Page 30:**

"girls define themselves by their ability to feel for other people": From Nancy Chodorow, *The Reproduction of Mothering* (Berkeley: University of California Press, 1978), p. 167.

"In my research": About seven in ten women find it very easy to feel sympathy for other people, compared to barely five in ten men, according to my 1992 *New Woman* Self-Esteem Survey. Yet only 16 percent of women say they find it very easy to feel sympathy for themselves.

"When women or men need a shoulder to cry on": For a convincing study of how people seek out women for emotional support, see Harry Reis, "Gender Effects in Social Participation: Intimacy, Loneliness and the Conduct of Social Interaction," in R. Gilmour and Stephen Duck (eds.), *The Emerging Field of Personal Relationships* (Hillsdale, N.J.: Erlbaum, 1986).

**Page 31:**

"among two-year-old children": See Carolyn Zahn-Waxler, Pamela M. Cole, and Karen Caplovitz Barrett, "Guilt and Empathy: Sex Differences and Implications for the Development of Depression," in J. Garber and K. S. Dodge (eds.), *The Development of Emotion Regulation and Dysregulation* (Cambridge: Cambridge University Press, 1991). Quotes from Zahn-Waxler are from a personal interview, May 1996.

"by the age of thirteen or fourteen, more girls than boys are depressed": See Susan Harter, "Causes and Consequences of Low Self-Esteem in Children and Adolescents," in R. F. Baumeister (ed.), *Self-Esteem: The Puzzle of Low Self-Regard* (New York: Plenum, 1990).

"Twice as many grown women": Susan Nolen-Hoeksema and Joan S.

Girgus, "The Emergence of Gender Differences in Depression During Adolescence," *Psychological Bulletin*, vol. 115, no. 3 (1994), pp. 424–443.

**Page 35:**

"By the age of two or three": Girls develop a talent for self-denial early on. See Eleanor Maccoby, "Gender as a Social Category," *Developmental Psychology*, vol. 24, no. 6 (1988), pp. 755–765.

"By the age of ten or twelve": From the work of Carol Gilligan, *In a Different Voice* (Cambridge, Mass.: Harvard University Press, 1982). Also see Carol Gilligan, Nona P. Lyons, and Trudy J. Hanmer (eds.), *Making Connections: The Relational Worlds of Adolescent Girls at Emma Willard School* (Cambridge, Mass.: Harvard University Press, 1990).

"self-esteem plummets between fourth and tenth grades": From a study of 3,000 children in grades 4 to 10. See the report "Shortchanging Girls, Shortchanging America," American Association of University Women (AAUW Education Foundation, 1992).

"girls are much more negative": Susan Harter, "Self and Identity Development," in S. Shirley Feldman and Glen R. Elliott (eds.), *At the Threshold: The Developing Adolescent* (Cambridge, Mass.: Harvard University Press, 1990).

"Parents reinforce their daughters' insecurities": For a study comparing how parents get teenagers to do chores, see Jacqueline J. Goodnow, "Children's Household Work: Its Nature and Functions," *Psychological Bulletin*, vol. 103 (1988), pp. 5–26.

**Page 36:**

Mary Pipher: See Mary Pipher, *Reviving Ophelia: Saving the Selves of Adolescent Girls* (New York: G.P. Putnam's Sons, 1994), pp. 255–256.

"'False self' behavior": This is from a fascinating group of studies by Susan Harter. See, for example, "The Personal Self in Social Context: Barriers to Authenticity," in R. Ashmore and L. Jussim (eds.), *Self and Identity: Fundamental Issues* (New York: Oxford University Press, 1997). Also see "Lack of Voice as a Manifestation of False Self Behavior Among Adolescents: The School Setting as a Salient Stage Upon Which the Drama of Authenticity Is Enacted," *Educational Psychology*, vol. 32 (1997), pp. 153–173.

## 2. Making a Habit of Sacrifice

**Page 39:**

"Half of mothers fall in love with their baby": In my 1990 *Parenting*

Baby Survey, half of mothers say they fell in love with their baby before it was born and another 30 percent fell in love at the birth. In addition, 57 percent of mothers say the intensity of that love is overwhelming, compared to 37 percent of fathers who say so. This survey appeared in the October 1989 issue of *Parenting* ("That's My Baby"); 9,000 mothers and fathers responded. The report, "That's My Baby," appeared in April 1990.

"a mother's relationship with her children": In my 1993 *New Woman* Relationship Survey, 81 percent of mothers with a child under 18 say that having a good relationship with children is most important to them. Nearly every mother—93 percent—says that motherhood is more fulfilling than she ever thought possible. Even more, 96 percent, say that it gives them a great deal of personal satisfaction, and just as many say it teaches them a lot about life.

**Page 40:**

"Their need for their child": Three in four mothers say that they need their children the most, more than their husband, their friends, or their own parents, according to women who answered my 1993 *New Woman* Relationship Survey.

"Mothers admit that they devote": In my 1993 *New Woman* Relationship Survey, eight in ten mothers say they give a great deal of emotional energy to their children, compared to 71 percent who give that much to their husband, 52 percent who give as much to their mother, and 47 percent who give that much to a friend.

**Page 42:**

"I give women a test to find out": The following test is adapted from my 1996 *Family Circle* Sacrifice Survey and has a reliability of $r = 0.71$.

Decide how much you agree or disagree with each of the following statements, then add up the numbers that correspond with your answers.

If you **Strongly Agree**, give yourself a **4**

If you **Agree**, give yourself a **3**

If you **Disagree**, give yourself a **2**

If you **Strongly Disagree**, give yourself a **1**

1. I feel I often sacrifice my needs and desires for my spouse.
2. I feel I often sacrifice my needs and desires for my children.
3. It's a mother's job to sacrifice for her children.
4. It's a father's job to sacrifice for his children.
5. Sometimes I think of my spouse as just another child.

After you add the five numbers, your score should total between 5 and 20. A woman who gets an 11 or lower is not very sacrificial. She's what I call a light sacrificer. If she gets a 12, she's right in the middle, a medium sacrificer. A woman who scores 13 or above, though, is an extreme sacrificer. Mothers score significantly higher on this test than fathers do. The three groups of sacrificers, light, medium, and extreme, are based on the answers of the 303 women who answered this survey.

"there aren't special demographic characteristics": In comparing the mothers who score lowest (light sacrificers) on this scale with those who score highest (extreme sacrificers), I find there are no significant differences between the two groups in education, income, marital status, or whether they work outside the home or not.

"Mothers of newborns and toddlers are definitely the most sacrificing": In comparing the sacrifice scores of mothers based on the age of their youngest child, I found significant differences between those with a preschooler (younger than six), those with a seven- to seventeen-year-old, and those whose youngest is eighteen or older. As their child's age increases, mothers had successively lower sacrifice scores. In the 1996 *Family Circle* Sacrifice Survey, I also found that mothers with a young child sacrifice about eight things; those with a child seven to seventeen sacrifice five things; those with a child at least eighteen give up, on average, only two things.

Page 44:

"An enormous number of mothers with young children are deeply troubled": In my 1992 *New Woman* Self-Esteem Survey, I compared mothers with a child younger than six to all other mothers. I found that mothers of young children are least happy and most likely to be depressed; they also feel most insecure about their ability to be good mothers. They're less satisfied with their lives overall and, in particular, with their work and friendships. They are most likely to believe that they are not using their talents to the fullest. In my 1994 *New Woman* Beauty Survey, I compared women with a young child (five or younger) and found that they feel ugly most often and are most unhappy about the way they look. This was a random national telephone survey conducted by Yankelovich Partners in May 1994 for *New Woman*, in which they interviewed 800 women between the ages of eighteen and fifty-nine. The report, "Through the Looking Glass," appeared in the October 1994 *New Woman*.

"new mothers are intimidated, terrified, frustrated": Seven in ten new mothers say they find newborns intimidating, according to my 1990 *Parenting* Baby Survey. For an overview of other research on this topic, see my article "The Baby Bomb," *New York Times Good Health Magazine*, October 8, 1989, p. 34.

"Rates of depression for mothers of one- and two-year-olds": See Ardis L. Olson and Lisa A. DiBrigida, "Depressive Symptoms and Work Role Satisfaction in Mothers of Toddlers," *Pediatrics*, vol. 94, no. 3 (September 1994), pp. 363–367.

"it makes them want to scream with frustration": See Mary Georgina Boulton, *On Being a Mother: A Study of Women with Pre-School Children* (London: Tavistock Publications, 1983).

"Children are a mother's greatest source of stress and worry": In my 1993 *New Woman* Relationship Survey, I found that 86 percent of mothers with children under age eighteen say the relationship is "often a source of stress," 87 percent say it's a lot more work than other relationships, and 71 percent say it's more frustrating than they ever expected.

**Page 45:**
"More than half of couples": An excellent study of the effects of parenthood on marriage is in Carolyn Pape Cowan and Philip A. Cowan, *When Partners Become Parents* (New York: Basic Books, 1992). Another source for this research is Jay Belsky and John Kelly, *The Transition to Parenthood: How a First Child Changes a Marriage* (New York: Delacorte Press, 1994).

"New mothers complain": Almost all the research about marriage before and after parenthood finds these differences. In a survey I did for *Parenting* on sex after baby, I found that women say they get less attention and affection from their husband but that he argues more. The figure showing that only one in five marriages improves after the birth of a first child comes from research by Cowan and Cowan, *When Partners Become Parents*. See also Carin Rubenstein, "Sex After Baby," *Parenting* (May 1988), p. 76.

"mothers are less happy about their marriage": From the results of my 1993 *New Woman* Relationship Survey and also from the 1990 *New Woman* Gender Survey. This was a random national telephone survey conducted by Yankelovich Clancy Shulman in March 1990 for *New Woman*. They interviewed 1,201 women and men. The two-part report, "A Brave New World" and "Getting What We Want," appeared in the October and November 1990 issues of *New Woman*.

**Page 46:**

"more wives than husbands wish their spouse appreciated them more": In my 1992 *New Woman* Self-Esteem Survey, I found that 53 percent of wives wish their spouse appreciated them more and 65 percent wish he listened to them more. This is especially true for mothers. Only 77 percent of wives feel their husband listens when they have something "really important to say," but 91 percent of husbands feel that their wife listens.

**Page 48:**

"During their first year with a firstborn": In my 1990 *Parenting* Baby Survey, I found that after their first child's first birthday, eight in ten mothers have never been away for a weekend and more than half wait six months before going out for several hours in the evening.

"new mothers become baby obsessed": These findings are also from the 1990 *Parenting* Baby Survey, in which 24 percent of mothers say they worry constantly and another 38 percent worry "much of the time." For my 1992 *Parenting* Parents Survey, I designed a Baby Obsession Test. This survey appeared in the March 1992 *Parenting* ("Could You Be a Better Parent?"), and 6,000 mothers and fathers responded. The report, "The Way We Worry," appeared in the September 1992 *Parenting*.

To take this test, answer the following 7 questions:

How nervous were you, are you, or will you be about the following?

If you are **Not at All Nervous**, give yourself a **1**

If you are **Somewhat Nervous**, give yourself a **2**

If you are **Very Nervous**, give yourself a **3**

     A. Your ability to care for a newborn

     B. Dropping your baby

     C. Your baby's eating habits

     D. Your child starting school

     E. Your child getting AIDS

     F. Your child drinking alcohol or taking drugs

     G. Your child having teen sex

Now add up your score. It should be between 7 and 21. If your total is 14 or above, you are a high anxiety mother, as are 40 percent of the women who answered the 1992 *Parenting* Parents Survey. If you scored 12 or 13, you're in the middle. Anything 11 or below, and you are among the lowest-anxiety mothers.

Page 49:

"baby-obsessed moms seem to have the most troublesome tots":

Those in the high anxiety group, the ones who are baby obsessed, are most likely to call their baby noisy (46 percent), a poor sleeper (37 percent), and cantankerous (23 percent).

**Page 50:**

Dr. Benjamin Spock: His book *Baby and Child Care* was first published in 1946. So far it has sold more than 43 million copies. This discussion of Spock-inspired mother-blaming is drawn from Shari L. Thurer, *The Myths of Motherhood: How Culture Reinvents the Good Mother* (Boston: Houghton Mifflin Company, 1994).

**Page 51:**

"'The guilties'": This is from Mary Kay Blakely, *American Mom* (Chapel Hill, N.C.: Algonquin Books, 1994), p. 10.

Erma Bombeck: From an article that appeared after Bombeck's death, "A Thank You to a Suburban Lifesaver," *New York Times*, May 1, 1996, p. C10.

**Page 52:**

"During their first baby's first year": In my 1990 *Parenting* Baby Survey, I found that 44 percent of new mothers feel guilty about being too tired, 33 percent about spending more time with the baby than their mate, 30 percent about not spending enough time with the baby, and 27 percent about not playing with the baby enough. About nine in ten mothers (89 percent) say they feel guilty about at least one thing. In addition, half of mothers, 54 percent, say they yelled at their baby during that first year.

"Working mothers": This is from my 1990 *Working Mother* Guilt Survey, in which a majority of mothers with school-age children say they feel "very" or "somewhat" guilty about all of the following: not being there when the kids come home from school; being flabby and out of shape; not spending enough time alone with husband; losing my sexual desire; not being able to go to my children's trips or school events during the day; not going out often enough with my husband; not being active in the PTA; having a dirty house; not entertaining enough; having to wake up my children to get them to day care. This survey appeared in the October 1990 *Working Mother* ("Guilty or Not Guilty"); 3,000 women responded. The report, "Guilty or Not Guilty," appeared in May 1991. For this survey, I devised a guilt test for mothers who work outside the home. Here is an abbreviated version of that test:

Decide how guilty you feel about each of these seven possibilities. Then add the numbers you pick for each one. (This test applies *only* to mothers who work *outside* the home.)

How guilty do you feel?

If you feel **Not Guilty**, give yourself a **1**

If you feel **Somewhat Guilty**, give yourself a **2**

If you feel **Very Guilty**, give yourself a **3**

> 1. I don't spend enough time with my children.
> 2. My caregiver spends more time with them than I do.
> 3. I can't be there when they come home from school.
> 4. I can't go to parties, plays, or field trips during regular work hours as often as I'd like.
> 5. I'm not home to create special activities for my kids or take them to lessons.
> 6. I have to wake them so early to get them to day care.
> 7. My children eat too much junk or fast food.

Your score should total between 7 and 21. If your score is 12 or less, you are among the minor guilt mothers, which consists of about one-third of the working mothers who answered the 1990 *Working Mother Guilt Survey*. If your score is 13 or 14, you have middling guilt. If your score is 15 or above, you are among the four in ten working mothers who feel major guilt.

**Page 55:**

"When I ask women what they think of a mother who stays at home": In my 1990 *New Woman* Gender Survey, I asked women how they would feel about a woman who stayed home with her children while her husband works; 73 percent say they'd respect her more. But 62 percent also say that "raising a child provides many rewards, but as a full-time job raising children cannot keep most women satisfied."

"a majority of wives feel that it's their responsibility": In my 1990 *New Woman* Gender Survey, 56 percent of women agreed that "when it comes down to basics, both the man and the woman should have equal responsibility for earning a living." Among women who work full time, nearly seven in ten agree that they should be equally responsible to earn a living. Also, in my 1994 *New Woman* Money Survey, half of mothers say their husband and children depend on them financially. This survey appeared in the February 1994 *New Woman* ("The Money Survey"); 6,000 women responded. The report, "The Money in Your Life," appeared in November 1994.

**Page 57:**

Betty Friedan: See Betty Friedan, *The Feminine Mystique* (New York: Dell, 1963).

"Half of married women even earn as much as their husbands do": This result is from a random survey of 1,502 women ages eighteen to fifty-five, two-thirds of whom work outside the home, conducted by Louis Harris and sponsored by the Families and Work Institute. See "Women: The New Providers," Whirlpool Foundation Study (May 1995). This study also shows that nine in ten women who work also feel responsible for taking care of their family. In my 1993 *Working Mother* Work Survey, I also found that working mothers tend to see themselves as providers, that it's their responsibility to help support the family. This was a random national telephone survey conducted by the Gallup Organization in October 1993 for *Working Mother*; Gallup interviewed 1,000 working mothers with a child under the age of eighteen. My report, "The Confident Generation," appeared in May 1994.

**Page 58:**

"Mothers now do a second shift of chores at home": This has been documented in just about every study on who does what at home. The term "second shift" was coined by Arlie Hochschild, *The Second Shift* (New York: Viking, 1989).

"Among mothers who work full time": This is from my 1990 *Working Mother* Guilt Survey, in which only 8 percent of working mothers say their husband shares child care and household chores. About six in ten say he does less than one-quarter of what needs to be done around the house.

**Page 59:**

"Most mothers now say that if they had a choice": In a *Parents* magazine survey that included 18,000 parents, 61 percent of mothers said that if they could do whatever they wanted, they'd work part time. See Richard Louv, "What Do Mothers Really Want?" *Parents* (May 1996), p. 38.

"In my research": In my 1990 *New Woman* Gender Survey, I found that the largest proportion of women say that the best life is to be married, have children, and work part time. Among part-time workers in this survey, 75 percent say that the ideal life includes part-time work; so do 45 percent of those working full time and even 41 percent of mothers who are at home.

"mothers who work part time are in better emotional health": This is from my 1990 *New Woman* Gender Survey. When I compared mothers who work part time with those who work full time, I found that the part-timers are significantly happier with their marriages, their work, and how their lives are going.

"Women who work part time are less likely to call it a career": In the 1990 *New Woman* Gender Survey, 55 percent of those who work full time consider their job a career, compared to only 33 percent of those who work part time.

"Part-time workers are usually paid less": See Jill Smolowe, "The Stalled Revolution," *Time*, May 6, 1996, p. 63, which documents the growing trend in part-time work.

**Page 60:**

"Young women now defer getting married": From Arlene Saluter, "Marital Status and Living Arrangements: March 1994," Current Population Reports, U.S. Department of Commerce, Bureau of the Census, Washington, D.C., P20–484. Also, 42 percent of women ages fifteen to forty-four have never had a child, according to Amara Bachu, "Fertility of American Women: June 1994," Current Population Reports, U.S. Department of Commerce, Bureau of the Census, Washington, D.C., P20–482.

**Page 61:**

"A fairly large group of women in their twenties": From my 1990 *Glamour* Adulthood Survey, in which the average age of respondents was twenty-six. Among these women, 33 percent say they don't feel grown up yet. This survey appeared in November 1990 *Glamour* ("New Signs of Adulthood"), and 9,000 women responded. The report, "The New Adulthood," appeared in April 1991.

"They want to finish school": These figures are also from the 1990 *Glamour* Adulthood Survey.

**Page 62:**

"When I compare mothers in their twenties": This is from my 1996 *Family Circle* Sacrifice Survey, in which I compared mothers between the ages of twenty-four and thirty-four with those thirty-five and older. The younger mothers scored significantly higher on my Sacrifice Test.

**Page 63:**

"Mothers in their twenties are much more unhappy about their lives": This is also from the 1996 *Family Circle* Sacrifice Survey. The younger mothers have lower self-esteem and score higher on a test of self-loathing. They feel less satisfied with their lives and feel they've been less successful with their lives. For a more detailed description of these measures of self-esteem and self-loathing, see the notes for Chapter 3.

## 3. The Sacrifice Syndrome

**Page 66:**

"they feel so much less successful as wives and mothers": When I compared the extreme sacrificers who answered my 1996 *Family Circle* Sacrifice Survey (a group of 97 women) with the women who sacrifice the least (a total of 117 women), I found that they rate themselves as significantly less successful as a wife and as a mother. So they give up more but feel they get less. These wives are also least satisfied with their marriage and with their sex life.

"They feel they put so much more effort into their marriage": The most sacrificial wives in the 1996 *Family Circle* Sacrifice Survey say they put more effort into their marriage, but they also feel less satisfied with how much their husband appreciates them.

"Sacrificial mothers do more for their husbands": In my 1996 *Family Circle* Sacrifice Survey, the extremely sacrificial wives say they give up an average of six things for their husband, compared to only three things for the least sacrificial wives. This is from a list of twenty-three possible sacrifices.

"They come to begrudge the fact he never gives as much as he gets": The extremely sacrificial wives in my 1996 *Family Circle* Marriage Survey say that their husband contributes significantly less intimacy, support, respect, and understanding than less sacrificial wives say their husbands do.

**Page 69:**

"women always score lower on tests of self-esteem": For a summary of these findings, see Carin Rubenstein, "*New Woman*'s Report on Self Esteem," *New Woman* (October 1992), p. 58.

"when I separate the extremely sacrificial mothers": In a comparison of most and least sacrificial women from the 1996 *Family Circle* Sacrifice Survey, the ones who sacrifice most have significantly lower self-esteem than the others.

"Every other woman—one in every two": In my 1992 *New Woman* Self-Esteem Survey, 32 percent of women agree that "At times I think I am no good at all," compared to 20 percent of men (a statistically significant difference). In addition, 48 percent of women agree that "Every so often, I really feel disgusted with myself." Only 36 percent of men agree with this statement.

"Some women, for instance, get into a habit of calling themselves names": In my 1992 *New Woman* Self-Esteem Survey, 33 percent of women call themselves sloppy, fatso, or stupid.

**Page 70:**

"Sacrificial mothers are most self-loathing of all": The most sacrificial women score significantly higher on a test of self-loathing adapted from the 1996 *Family Circle* Sacrifice Survey.

To find out how you would score on both the Self-Esteem Test and the Self-Loathing Test, answer the following six questions. These scores are based on how women in my *Family Circle* survey answered similar questions.

Decide how much you agree with each statement, then add up the numbers that correspond with your answers.

If you **Strongly Disagree**, give yourself a **1**

If you **Disagree**, give yourself a **2**

If you **Agree**, give yourself a **3**

If you **Strongly Agree**, give yourself a **4**

1. I take a positive attitude toward myself.
2. On the whole, I am satisfied with myself.
3. I feel I am a person of worth, on an equal basis with others.

Subtotal: add your score: _____

4. At times I think I am no good at all.
5. I feel I do not have much to be proud of.
6. Every so often, I feel really disgusted with myself.

Subtotal: add your score: _____

The first subtotal is your self-esteem score, which should fall between 3 and 12. If it's 8 or less, you have low self-esteem. If it's a 9 or 10, you have average self-esteem. If it's 11 or 12, you have high self-esteem. In the *Family Circle* survey, 17 percent of women fall into the low self-esteem category, 51 percent fall into the middle, and 31 percent are in the high self-esteem group.

The second subtotal is your self-loathing score. It, too, should fall between 3 and 12. If your subtotal is 6 or less, you are a low self-loather. If it's a 7, you are about average in self-loathing. If your total is 8 or higher, you fall into the most self-loathing group. In the *Family Circle* Survey, 56 percent of the women who answered are in the low self-loather category; 19 percent are in the middle; 25 percent fall into the highest self-loathing group.

**Page 71:**

"a woman can't like herself if she doesn't like the way she looks":

Some of the popular books that explore this theory include Gloria Steinem, *Revolution from Within* (New York: Little, Brown, 1992); Naomi Wolf, *The Beauty Myth* (New York: William Morrow, 1991); Nancy Friday, *The Power of Beauty* (New York: HarperCollins, 1996). There is also a great deal of academic research on this topic. For a comprehensive summary of this research, see Elaine Hatfield and Susan Sprecher, *Mirror, Mirror: The Importance of Looks in Everyday Life* (Albany: State University of New York Press, 1986).

"from the age of twelve or thirteen on, girls are more negative than boys about their appearance": See Susan Harter, "Self and Identity Development," in S. Shirley Feldman and Glen R. Elliot (eds.), *At the Threshold: The Developing Adolescent* (Cambridge, Mass.: Harvard University Press, 1990). This finding is also reported in "Shortchanging Girls, Shortchanging America," American Association of University Women (AAUW Education Foundation, 1992).

"grown women are also more negative than men about their appearance": For an overview of research in this area, see Linda A. Jackson, *Physical Appearance and Gender: Sociobiological and Sociocultural Perspectives* (Albany: State University of New York Press, 1992).

"I decided to ask women about their bodily features": In my 1994 *New Woman* Beauty Survey, one of the questions I asked was: "Which do you feel is your best feature from the shoulders up?" I found that 59 percent love their eyes, 15 percent adore their hair, 5 percent like their lips best, and the rest prefer the shape of their face, their complexion, cheeks, nose, or neck.

"mothers are least happy about their physical appearance": From my 1993 *New Woman* Relationship Survey.

**Page 72:**

"sacrificial mothers are most distressed of all about their looks": In my 1996 *Family Circle* Sacrifice Survey, the women in the extreme sacrificer group were significantly less satisfied with their body and physical appearance than other mothers.

"Mothers spend less time than other women on their appearance": In my 1994 *New Woman* Beauty Survey, I found that significantly more mothers than childless women agree that they can't be bothered spending time on their appearance. While childless women spend nearly 50 minutes in the morning grooming themselves, mothers spend about 43 minutes (a statistically significant difference).

**Page 73:**

"Extremely sacrificial mothers have *twice as many* psychological problems": In my 1996 *Family Circle* Sacrifice Survey, I compared the psychological and health symptoms of the extreme sacrificers with those of the light sacrificers. The differences were striking. Some examples of the differences in psychological problems:

|  | Extreme Sacrificers | Light Sacrificers |
|---|---|---|
| Which of the following have bothered you in the past year? |  |  |
| Tiring easily | 60% | 33% |
| Feeling irritable | 54% | 22% |
| Feeling depressed, blue | 50% | 15% |
| Insomnia | 36% | 28% |
| Trouble concentrating | 34% | 11% |
| Often feeling guilty | 33% | 11% |
| Often feeling lonely | 31% | 12% |

"They feel less successful in life than other mothers": Also in the 1996 *Family Circle* Sacrifice Survey, I found that the extreme sacrificers feel less successful as wives and mothers and are significantly less satisfied with their friends, their work, and the way their lives are going.

**Page 74:**

"Empathic mothers tend to be depressed mothers": See Carolyn Zahn-Waxler, Pamela M. Cole, and Karen Caplovitz Barrett, "Guilt and Empathy: Sex Differences and Implications for the Development of Depression," in J. Garber and K. S. Dodge (eds.), *The Development of Emotion Regulation and Dysregulation* (Cambridge: Cambridge University Press, 1991). Also, in my 1996 *Family Circle* Sacrifice Survey, I found that 50 percent of the extreme sacrificers have felt depressed or blue during the past twelve months, compared to only 15 percent of the low sacrificers.

"other-focused women suffer from the same problems as sacrificial mothers": For a presentation of her theory about women who are "other-focused," see Susan Harter, Patricia Waters, Lisa Pettitt, Nancy Whitesell, and Jennifer Kofkin, "Autonomy and Connectedness as Dimensions of Relationship Styles in Adult Men and Women," *Journal of Social and Personal Relationships*, vol. 14 (1997), pp.145–164. Quotes from Harter are drawn from a personal interview, April 1996.

**Page 76:**

"Adults who take care of a senile spouse": From Janice Kiecolt-Glaser, Jason Dura, Carl Speicher, O. Joseph Trask, and Ronald Glaser,

"Spousal Caregivers of Dementia Victims: Longitudinal Changes in Immunity and Health," *Psychosomatic Medicine*, vol. 53 (1991), pp. 345–362.

"*All* women have more emotional and physical problems than men do": I've come up with this finding in every survey I've done for the past fifteen years, just as Gove did twenty years ago. See Walter R. Gove and Michael Hughes, "Possible Causes of the Apparent Sex Differences in Physical Health," *American Sociological Review*, vol. 44 (February 1979), pp. 126–146.

In my research, it doesn't matter how the survey was done, if it's by telephone or in a magazine, if it includes a random national sample or if it involves readers who answer a questionnaire that appears in a magazine. Women always admit to having more problems than men do. Here is the list of twenty psychological symptoms and health problems that I include in most of my surveys; this one is taken from my 1996 *Family Circle* Sacrifice Survey:

Which of the following have bothered you in the past twelve months?

1. High blood pressure
2. Frequent headaches
3. Indigestions or upset stomach
4. Muscular aches and pains
5. Lower back pain
6. Feeling fat or gaining weight
7. Allergies
8. Heart or chest pain
9. Dizzy spells
10. Trouble falling or staying asleep
11. Tiring easily
12. Trouble concentrating
13. Often feeling guilty
14. Often feeling lonely
15. Irrational fears
16. Loss of interest in sex
17. Feeling irritable or angry
18. Feeling depressed or blue
19. Crying spells
20. Disabling accident

In this survey, women said they have, on average, about five of these problems; men said they're troubled by three.

"vast gender gap in emotional health": For a discussion of the value of using magazine surveys to get at this kind of gender difference, see Phillip Shaver and Carin Rubenstein, "Research Potential of Newspaper and Magazine Surveys," in Harry T. Reis (ed.), *Naturalistic Approaches to Studying Social Interaction*, New Directions for Methodology of Social and Behavioral Science no.15 (San Francisco: Jossey-Bass, 1983).

**Page 77:**

"Women's lives are more difficult than men's": Other researchers also have come to this conclusion. See, for example, Joseph Veroff, Elizabeth Douvan, and Richard A. Kulka, *The Inner American* (New York: Basic Books, 1981).

"[Parenthood is] most distressing and painful for mothers": Some experts now say that it's a "social fact" that children have a negative impact on the well-being of mothers. In my 1993 *New Woman* Aging Survey, for instance, I found that mothers have more psychological problems and physical symptoms than childless wives do. This survey appeared in the January 1993 *New Woman* ("Women Growing Older"); 6,000 women answered. The report, *"New Woman's* Aging Survey Report," appeared in November 1993. In this survey, mothers were also more likely than child-less wives to suffer from insomnia, trouble concentrating, heart palpita-tions, and dizziness. While 49 percent of mothers said they are happy about their lives, 63 percent of childless wives are. See also Debra Umberson and Walter R. Gove, "Parenthood and Psychological Well-Being," *Journal of Family Issues*, vol. 10, no. 4 (December 1989), pp. 440–462; Sara McLana-han and Julia Adams, "Parenthood and Psychological Well-Being," *Annual Review of Immunology*, vol. 5 (1987), pp. 237–257.

"Mothers are even more *angry* than fathers": From Catherine E. Ross and Marieke Van Willigen, "Gender, Parenthood, and Anger," *Journal of Marriage and the Family*, vol. 58 (August 1996), pp. 1–13.

**Page 78:**

"sacrificial mothers are sexually frustrated": In my 1996 *Family Circle* Sacrifice Survey, I found that the most sacrificial women are much less satisfied with their sex lives than the least sacrificial women and fewer say they are in passionate love with their husband (40 percent are, com-pared to 61 percent of the least sacrificial women). In the 1996 *New Woman* Passion Survey, I found exactly the same: The extremely sacrifi-cial mothers are significantly less satisfied with their sex lives than are the least sacrificial ones.

**Page 80:**

"Six months to a year after the birth": Eighty percent of couples agree that "after they become parents, most couples' sex lives suffer," according to new parents who answered a survey I wrote called "Is There Sex After Parenthood?" in *Parenting* (November 1987). In that survey, half of new parents say that they are having sex less often than usual a year after the birth. One working mother told me that she thinks of sex as "another wifely chore, like cleaning the bathroom."

"one in three mothers suffer from an ongoing and persistent loss of interest in sex": 30 percent of wives in the 1996 *Family Circle* Sacrifice Survey say they have lost interest in sex, as have 30 percent of women who responded to my 1993 *New Woman* Aging Survey.

"one in ten fathers has the same problem": About 13 percent of the men in my 1996 *Family Circle* Sacrifice Survey say they've felt a loss of interest in sex during the past year.

**Page 82:**

"Sacrificial mothers are sick mothers": In my 1996 *Family Circle* Sacrifice Survey, the most sacrificial women have more of the health problems on the list of twenty than the least sacrificial group. On average, they have about six problems, while other women have fewer than four. They also visit the doctor more often—five times a year—compared to three times a year for the least sacrificial mothers. And they're significantly less satisfied with their health and physical well-being. Some other differences in physical problems, taken from the *Family Circle* Survey:

|  | Extreme Sacrificers | Light Sacrificers |
|---|---|---|
| Which of the following have bothered you in the past year? | | |
| Tiring easily | 60% | 33% |
| Indigestion | 35% | 19% |
| Allergies | 35% | 25% |
| Frequent headaches | 37% | 31% |
| Muscle aches, pains | 32% | 25% |
| Lower back pain | 43% | 23% |
| Heart, chest pain | 10% | 4% |
| Dizzy spells | 10% | 5% |

Page 83:

"The wives take care of sick husbands": When I ask husbands who looks after them when they're sick in bed with a high fever, the majority (60 percent) say their wives do, according to my 1996 *Family Circle* survey. But when wives are just as sick, the majority—62 percent—say they are usually the ones who have to take care of themselves.

"because women neglect their own health": See Walter R. Gove, "Gender Differences in Mental and Physical Illness: The Effects of Fixed Roles and Nurturant Roles," *Social Science Medicine*, vol. 19, no. 2 (1984), pp. 77–91. Also see Lois M. Verbrugge, "Role Burdens and Physical Health of Women and Men," in *Women & Health*, vol. 11, no. 1 (1986), pp. 47–77.

Most national health surveys, such as the National Health Interview Survey conducted by the National Center for Health Statistics, have similar findings. The most recent one shows that women visit the doctor, on average, about seven times a year; men go about five times. See P. F. Adams and M. A. Marano, "Current Estimates from the National Health Interview Survey, 1994." National Center for Health Statistics, Vital Health Statistics, Series 10, no. 193, 1995. In my 1996 *Family Circle* Sacrifice Survey, I found that women have an average of five health problems, while men have only about three. In that study, women said they visit the doctor nearly four times a year, compared to about two times for men.

"Single women . . . are just as healthy as bachelors": From Gove and Hughes, "Possible Causes of the Apparent Sex Differences in Physical Health, 1979."

## 4. How Sacrifice Helps Men

Page 88:

"there are now 'host clubs'": From "Clubs Where, for a Price, Japanese Men Are Nice to Women," *New York Times*, September 8, 1996, p. 149.

Page 89:

"It gives them a sense of meaning in life": From Linda Waite, "Does Marriage Matter?" *Demography*, vol. 32, no. 4 (November 1995), pp. 483–507.

"Married men are actually healthier, happier": From David Popenoe, *Life Without Father* (New York: The Free Press, 1996).

**Page 90:**

"They sense that their husbands give them less intimacy and caring": From statistical analyses comparing the most and least sacrificial mothers who answered my 1996 *Family Circle* Marriage Survey.

"husbands live a lot longer than single men": From Waite, "Does Marriage Matter?"

"divorced men are especially likely to succumb": From Yoav Ben-Shlomo, George Davey Smith, Martin Shipley, and M. G. Marmot, "Magnitude and Causes of Mortality Differences Between Married and Unmarried Men," *Journal of Epidemiology and Community Health*, vol. 47 (1993), pp. 200–205.

**Page 91:**

"Many wives protect men from themselves": See Waite, "Does Marriage Matter?"

**Page 92:**

"husbands don't engage in as much . . . risky behavior": From Debra Umberson, "Gender, Marital Status and the Social Control of Health Behavior," *Social Science and Medicine*, vol. 34, no. 8 (1992), pp. 907–917.

*New Yorker* cartoon: From *The New Yorker*, September 16, 1996, p. 72.

"for a man to be truly happy": In my 1990 *New Woman* Gender Survey, 67 percent of men say that for a man to be truly happy, he needs to have a woman around.

**Page 93:**

"husbands are significantly happier": See Waite, "Does Marriage Matter?" Also, in my 1992 *New Woman* Self-Esteem Survey, I found that husbands are significantly happier than single men about their life in general as well as with their work, their children, their body, their friendships, and the way they spend their free time. For an excellent study on the effects of marriage and attachment on well-being, see Catherine E. Ross, "Reconceptualizing Marital Status as a Continuum of Social Attachment," *Journal of Marriage and the Family*, vol. 57 (February 1995), pp. 129–140.

"a woman needs a man to be truly happy": In my 1990 *New Woman* Gender Survey, only 31 percent of women say that a woman needs a man to be truly happy.

"Married men are depressed less often": In my 1992 *New Woman*

Self-Esteem Survey, I found that single men are depressed more often than husbands, although there is no similar difference for single and married women.

**Page 94:**

"Husbands feel best when they're snug at home": Researchers discovered this by asking couples to carry pagers that would beep at random intervals. Couples had to rate their feelings about how happy they felt, how cheerful or irritable, how friendly or angry at that moment. See Reed W. Larson, Maryse H. Richards, and Maureen Perry-Jenkins, "Divergent Worlds: The Daily Emotional Experience of Mothers and Fathers in the Domestic and Public Spheres," *Journal of Personality and Social Psychology*, vol. 67, no. 6 (1994), pp. 1034–1046.

"husbands reap a sexual bonanza from marriage": There is an excellent discussion of these research findings in Waite, "Does Marriage Matter?" and also in Popenoe, *Life Without Father* .

**Page 95:**

"smiling makes people feel happy": See Paul Ekman and Richard J. Davidson, "Voluntary Smiling Changes Regional Brain Activity," *Psychological Science*, vol. 4, no. 5 (September 1993), pp. 342–345.

**Page 98:**

"A Russian cosmonaut": She is Yelena Kondakova; see "Perspectives," *Newsweek*, September 16, 1996, p. 35.

Shannon Lucid: See "Spacewoman Tells of Her Readjusting to Earth," *New York Times*, October 25, 1996, p. A22.

**Page 99:**

"husbands believe they should be doing more at home": This is a common finding in many surveys on the topic, according to James Levine, director of the Fatherhood Project of the Families and Work Institute; personal interview, September 1996.

**Page 102:**

"husbands make a mental 'love map'": This is according to John Gottman, codirector of the Seattle Marital and Family Institute, in a personal interview, August 1996. See also John Gottman, *Why Marriages Succeed or Fail . . . And How You Can Make Yours Last* (New York: Simon and Schuster, 1994).

"Men approach a kind of personal best": See Waite, "Does Marriage Matter?"

**Page 103:**

"Men who are fathers are simply more satisfied": See Popenoe, *Life Without Father*. Also, in my 1990 *New Woman* Gender Survey, I compared a random sample of 79 married men with no children to 302 married fathers, excluding those who'd ever been separated, divorced, or widowed. Here are a few differences:

|                                      | Nonfathers | Fathers |
| ------------------------------------ | ---------- | ------- |
| Very happy about marriage            | 68%        | 81%     |
| Feel both partners work at marriage  | 62%        | 78%     |
| Very happy about how life is going   | 56%        | 67%     |
| Feel more masculine that other men   | 49%        | 58%     |
| Very happy about work                | 42%        | 58%     |
| Feel many women respect them         | 23%        | 32%     |

**Page 104:**

"a burly Manhattan bus driver": See "Metropolitan Diary," *New York Times*, September 18, 1996, p. C2.

"parenthood may actually be more beneficial for men": My analysis of the differential benefits of parenthood for men and women comes especially from two random national surveys, the *New Woman* Self-Esteem Survey and the *New Woman* Gender Survey, in which I compared married but childless men and women to married parents, excluding those who had been separated, divorced, or widowed. More childless wives are very happy with their marriage than mothers—77 percent versus 72 percent—but the reverse is true for men. While 78 percent of childless wives say both partners work to keep their marriage running smoothly, only 71 percent of mothers say so; again, the reverse is true for men. These differences, though small, are statistically significant. And 88 percent of childless wives feel their husband spends enough time with the family, but only 76 percent of mothers agree. Among men, there are no differences between childless husbands and fathers, 88 percent of both saying that their partner spends enough time with the family. While only 36 percent of childless wives wish their husband appreciated them more, 54 percent of mothers say so; 66 percent of childless wives say they have real power at home very often, compared to 54 percent of mothers. Finally, 47 percent of childless wives are very happy these days, compared to 39 percent of mothers.

**Page 105:**

"fathers spend so much less time with their children than mothers do":

This is from a study supervised by the High/Scope Educational Research Foundation and written by David P. Weikart and Patricia P. Olmsted, *Families Speak: Early Childhood and Education in 11 Countries* (Ypsilanti, Mich.: High/Scope Press, 1994). They studied more than 20,000 parents with a four-year-old child in eleven countries: Belgium, China, Finland, Germany, Hong Kong, Italy, Nigeria, Portugal, Spain, Thailand, and the United States. The researchers found that American mothers spend an average of 10.7 hours a day alone with their child, the highest of all. German and Nigerian mothers came in second; they spend an average of 10 hours a day. In China, where 98 percent of the mothers work outside the home for pay, the researchers surveyed 12,835 Chinese parents.

**Page 106:**

"An extraordinary number of fathers simply leave their children behind": In studies of post-divorce couples, researchers found that about one in five fathers hasn't seen his children for a year after the divorce; half have seen their children only a few times. See Popenoe, *Life Without Father*, p. 31.

"fathers feel so much less parental stress and strain": From Jacqueline Scott and Duane F. Alwin, "Gender Differences in Parental Strain," *Journal of Family Issues*, vol. 10, no. 4 (December 1989), pp. 482–503.


## 5. Children Don't Need a Sacrificial Mother

**Page 107:**

"If she sacrifices, they benefit": In my 1996 *Family Circle* Sacrifice Survey, 66 percent of mothers say that the reason they sacrifice is because it makes their children happier. Half also believe that it makes their husband happier and their marriage better.

"her great passion for her children": This is from results of my 1996 *New Woman* Passion Survey, in which I compared the most and the least sacrificial mothers. The most sacrificial mothers are significantly more passionate about their children and their husband, and 70 percent say they give up their passions because other people's needs come first. Only 8 percent of the least sacrificial mothers say so. This survey appeared in the July 1996 *New Woman* ("What Lights Your Fire?"); 2,000 women responded. The report, "Your True Passions," appeared in February 1997.

**Page 108:**

"They feel a gnawing inner absence": In the Passion Survey, significantly fewer of the most sacrificial mothers feel they have a purpose in life, and they're less passionate about their body and their health and their personal growth. Slightly more than half confess that they have a secret passion in a fantasy life.

**Page 108:**
"Sacrificial mothers tend their secret garden of fantasies": This is from a question in the 1996 *New Woman* Passion Survey, in which I asked respondents to write about a passion they fantasize about.

**Page 110:**
"a Georgia mother of twins": See "For Twins, Double Jackpot on the S.A.T.," *New York Times*, November 10, 1996, p. A16.

**Page 111:**
"will set a course for the child's emotional well-being": This is the gist of nearly all of the hundreds of articles written and studies conducted about attachment during the past several decades. One line of research even connects the nature of the mother-infant bond to the ways in which an adult falls in love. See Kim Bartholomew and Leonard M. Horowitz, "Attachment Styles Among Young Adults: A Test of a Four-Category Model," *Journal of Personality and Social Psychology*, vol. 61, no. 2 (1991), pp. 226–244. See also Phillip R. Shaver and Cindy Hazan, "Adult Romantic Attachment: Theory and Evidence," *Advances in Personal Relationships*, vol. 4 (1993), pp. 29–70.

**Page 112:**
"Strange Situation Test." This is described in detail in Diane Eyer, *Motherguilt: How Our Culture Blames Mothers for What's Wrong With Society* (New York: Times Books, 1996). The test is being used in a current government study of infant day care conducted by the National Institute of Child Health and Human Development. See NICHHD Early Child Care Research Network, "The Effects of Infant Child Care on Infant-Mother Attachment Security: Results of the NICHHD Study of Early Child Care," Unpublished manuscript (1996).

"hundreds of researchers have spent decades": For a discussion of the inherent flaws in this logic, see Sandra Scarr, *Mother Care/Other Care* (New York: Basic Books, 1984).

"psychology's dirty little secret": See, for example, Jerome Kagan, *The Nature of the Child* (New York: Basic Books, 1984), and Jerome Kagan, "Three Pleasing Ideas," *American Psychologist*, vol. 51, no. 9 (September 1996), pp. 901–908. One researcher, Everett Waters, and his colleagues at the State University of New York at Stony Brook have managed to track down babies after they grew up to retest their attachment. But Waters was mostly interested in whether they'd stayed in the same type or not. From a personal interview, Phillip Shaver, January 1997.

**Page 113:**

"imbue that relationship with great magic": The seeds of this idea are from Kagan, "Three Pleasing Ideas."

"Men are what their mothers made them": Ralph Waldo Emerson, *The Conduct of Life*, "Fate," first published in 1860.

**Page 114:**

"a child inherits a disposition that determines how he sees the world": Auke Tellegen, David T. Lykken, Thomas J. Bouchard, Jr., Kimerly J. Wilcox, Stephen Rich, and Nancy L. Segal, "Personality Similarity in Twins Reared Apart and Together," *Journal of Personality and Social Psychology*, vol. 54, no. 6 (1988), pp. 1031–1039.

"Identical twins are twice as similar genetically as fraternal twins": Robert Plomin and Denise Daniels, "Why Are Children in the Same Family So Different from One Another?" *Behavioral and Brain Sciences*, vol. 10, no. 1 (March 1987), pp. 1–16.

"In a story": Described in a fascinating article by Lawrence Wright, "Double Mystery," *The New Yorker*, August 7, 1995, pp. 45–62, and based in part on research by Peter Neubauer at New York University.

**Page 115:**

"hundreds of sixty-year-old twins": This is from a study of 99 pairs of identical twins reared apart, 229 pairs of fraternal twins reared apart, 160 pairs of identical twins reared together, and 212 pairs of fraternal twins reared together. The average age of these twins is fifty-nine. From Robert Plomin, G. E. McClearn, Nancy L. Pedersen, John R. Nesselroade, and C. S. Bergeman, "Genetic Influence on Childhood Family Environment Perceived Retrospectively from the Last Half of the Life Span," *Developmental Psychology*, vol. 24, no. 5 (1988), pp. 738–745.

"the genes sing a prehistoric song'": From Thomas J. Bouchard, Jr., David T. Lykken, Matthew McGue, Nancy L. Segal, and Auke Tellegen, "Sources of Human Psychological Differences: The Minnesota Study of Twins Reared Apart," *Science*, October 12, 1990, pp. 223–228. (The quote appears on p. 228.)

"half of the differences in human personality": From Bouchard et al., "Sources of Human Psychological Differences."

"The other half of personality": From Plomin and Daniels, "Why Are Children in the Same Family So Different . . . ?"

"two boys raised in the same upper-middle-class family": This example is cited in Plomin and Daniels, "Why Are Children in the Same Family So Different . . . ?" p. 15.

**Page 116:**

"children raised in the same house": In fact, most children are aware of being treated differently by their parents. See Plomin and Daniels, "Why Are Children in the Same Family So Different . . . ?"

"The way my children are now": I was convinced of this by a fascinating paper on how "genes drive experience," by Sandra Scarr and Kathleen McCartney, "How People Make Their Own Environments: A Theory of Genotype-Environment Effects," *Child Development*, vol. 54 (1983), pp. 424–435.

**Page 117:**

"Identical twins . . . have nearly identical feelings of contentment": David Lykken and Auke Tellegen, "Happiness Is a Stochastic Phenomenon," *Psychological Science*, vol. 7, no. 3 (May 1996), pp. 186–189.

"About one in three children is incredibly resilient." See Emmy E. Werner and Ruth S. Smith, *Vulnerable But Invincible: A Longitudinal Study of Resilient Children and Youth* (New York: McGraw-Hill, 1982).

**Page 118:**

"Growing up very poor, with a single mother": These results are presented in Sara McLanahan and Gary Sandefur, *Growing Up with a Single Parent: What Hurts, What Helps* (Cambridge, Mass.: Harvard University Press, 1994).

"Her standard of living": Judith Seltzer, "Consequences of Marital Dissolution for Children," *Annual Review of Sociology*, vol. 20 (1994), pp. 235–226.

"After a divorce, about half of fathers": From David Popenoe, *Life Without Father* (New York: The Free Press, 1996).

"frequent moves under these circumstances": From McLanahan and Sandefur, *Growing Up with a Single Parent*.

**Page 125:**

"Mothers do not retain sole ownership of their children": A thoughtful debunking of the myth of motherhood appears in Louise B. Silverstein, "Transforming the Debate About Child Care and Maternal Employment," *American Psychologist*, vol. 46, no. 10 (October 1991), pp. 1025–1032.

Ruth De Kanter: A description of several children's collectives appears in Ruth De Kanter, "The Children's Home: An Alternative in Childrearing Practices in the Netherlands," in Beverly Birns and D. F. Hay (eds.), *The Different Faces of Motherhood* (New York: Plenum Press, 1988).

**Page 127:**

"In the happiest marriages, husbands willingly share the sacrifices": This comes from several of my surveys about marriage. See notes for Chapter 7.

## 6. Be Good to Yourself

**Page 129:**

"I call this talent selfism": The word "selfism" appears in *Webster's Third New International Dictionary*. It's defined as "concentration on self-interest."

"A woman is a selfist": In the 1992 *New Woman* Self-Esteem Survey, I asked women "How comfortable do you feel about making yourself happy and doing things for your own personal pleasure?" Those who said "very comfortable" I called selfist; those who said "pretty" or "not too comfortable" I called not selfist. In the 1996 *Family Circle* Sacrifice Survey, I combined answers to three questions for a selfism scale. Women had to say how strongly they agreed or disagreed with these statements: "I consider myself first," "My needs come first," and "I make sure I have time to myself every day." Finally, in the 1996 *New Woman* Passion Survey, I considered women selfist if they said that this statement was true: "I usually take about an hour a day to do something for myself."

"Using this definition": The one-in-three figure comes from the *New Woman* Self-Esteem Survey, since it includes a random national sample of women.

**Page 130:**

Oscar Wilde: He said, "Self-sacrifice is a thing that should be put down by law." From Rudolf Flesch (ed.), *The New Book of Unusual Quotations* (New York: Harper & Row, 1966).

**Page 132:**

"Mothers who are crack addicts": Social scientists studied sixty-eight mothers addicted to crack cocaine, though, and found that these mothers don't view themselves as selfish. They rationalize their drug use and try to protect their children from it so they can view themselves as good mothers. See Margaret H. Kearney, Sheigla Murphy, and Marsha Rosenbaum, "Mothering on Crack Cocaine: A Grounded Theory Analysis," *Social Science Medicine*, vol. 38, no. 2 (1994), pp. 351–361.

**Page 133:**

"Selfist mothers are happier and healthier": All of these results come from three surveys, and almost all of the findings are repeated in each one. The surveys are the 1992 *New Woman* Self-Esteem Survey, the 1996 *Family Circle* Sacrifice Survey, and the 1996 *New Woman* Passion Survey.

George Bernard Shaw: Also cited in Flesch, *The New Book of Unusual Quotations*.

**Page 134:**

"selfist mothers also have the . . . greatest amount of self-confidence." From a self-confidence test included in my 1992 *New Woman* Self-Esteem Survey.

**Page 136:**

"Older women are almost always more selfist": In all three surveys, selfist women are significantly older than the nonselfist women.

"There is something about being in midlife": This thought is based on material from Daniel J. Levinson, *The Seasons of a Woman's Life* (New York: Alfred A. Knopf, 1996).

**Page 137:**

"My research shows that women's income doesn't seem to make a difference": In all three surveys, when I compare the selfist women with those who are not selfist, there is no difference in their income levels.

"selfist women tend to have better marriages": In the 1992 *New Woman* Self-Esteem Survey, selfist women rate themselves as better wives. The nonselfist women were significantly more likely to wish they got more appreciation from their husbands. In the 1996 *Family Circle* Sacrifice Survey, more selfist than nonselfist wives have 50/50 marriages. And in the 1996 *New Woman* Passion Survey, selfist wives are more satisfied with their relationship with their husband.

"Almost half of mothers are in a marriage": These figures are from my 1993 *New Woman* Infidelity Survey, in which 50 percent of women say their husband shows them affection a few times a month or hardly ever; 47 percent say they hardly ever have intimate conversations with him, and another 26 percent say they do only a few times a month. Fifty-five percent describe their marriages as difficult or bad, although only 22 percent describe their lives this way.

Because this survey was focused on unfaithfulness, it's possible that more women with unhappy marriages answered it than would have otherwise. On the other hand, the kind of harsh and honest questions about marriage that I asked are rarely posed in other major national surveys. So it's possible that we received more honest answers than usual, albeit much more negative ones.

**Page 139:**

"My research indicates that nearly three in ten mothers": This is from the 1993 *New Woman* Infidelity Survey. It includes only married women with a child under the age of eighteen living at home.

**Page 142:**

"Sigmund Freud believed": See Carin Rubenstein, "A Consumer's Guide to Psychotherapy," in Carol Tavris (ed.), *EveryWoman's Emotional Well-Being* (Garden City, N.Y.: Doubleday & Company, 1986).

**Page 144:**

"Elizabeth Cady Stanton's statement": She made this comment to a reporter and instructed that it be printed in capital letters. See David P. Barash, *The Hare and the Tortoise: Culture, Biology, and Human Nature* (New York: Viking, 1986), p. 112.


## 7. Becoming a Selfist

**Page 149:**

Henry Murray: Murray did most of his work in mid-century, and although he wasn't a psychoanalyst, he was strongly influenced by Sigmund Freud. Some of the other needs he proposed include the need for achievement, affiliation, autonomy, dominance, play, sex, and understanding. For a simple overview of his theory, see Calvin S. Hall and Gardner Lindzey, *Theories of Personality* (New York: John Wiley & Sons, 1970).

**Page 152:**

"Women without children have much less trouble": While half of wives without children say they feel very comfortable making themselves happy (49 percent), only 33 percent of mothers do, according to the 1992 *New Woman* Self-Esteem Survey.

"Fewer than half of the mothers I've interviewed": In the 1996 *New Woman* Passion Survey, about 45 percent of mothers say they usually take an hour a day to do something for themselves, compared to 63 percent of women with no children.

"Men don't seem nearly as reluctant about indulging themselves": In the 1992 *New Woman* Self-Esteem Survey, the same number of men, both childless husbands and fathers, say they find it very easy to make themselves happy: about four in ten.

**Page 154:**

"The most common ways in which women pamper themselves": In the *New Woman* Passion Survey, women say they do an average of four or five things to pamper themselves.

Here is what women say they do to pamper themselves:

| | |
|---|---|
| Read | 69% |
| Take a long bath, shower | 65% |
| Watch television, rent tape | 52% |
| Go to sleep early, wake up late | 51% |
| Get a haircut | 46% |
| Go to the movies | 37% |
| Get some exercise | 34% |
| Buy makeup | 33% |
| Get a massage | 31% |
| Get a manicure | 27% |
| Take an exercise class | 11% |

**Page 162:**

"it's quite common for angry, frustrated wives": The idea that a woman's anger at her husband can turn into sexual frigidity is standard among many sexuality experts. See, for example, the discussion of this issue in Rosalind C. Barnett and Caryl Rivers, *She Works/He Works: How Two-Income Families Are Happier, Healthier, and Better Off* (New York: HarperCollins, 1996).

"Couples that have the best sex lives include a husband who shares the sacrifices": The fact that husbands who do more household chores have better marriages has become widely accepted among marriage researchers, according to John Gottman, a psychologist at the University of Washington in Seattle. He says that men who do more housework are better off, are more emotionally engaged in their marriage, and have more respect for their wives. They're even in better physical health, he says, and they have better sex lives. From a personal interview, August 1996.

"Who are the lucky few": Most of the information about magic marriages comes from my 1991 *Child* Marriage Survey, in which 19 percent of the wives who answered gave their marriage a 5 out of 5 and another 38 percent gave it a 4. There are no age or income differences between those with a top-rated marriage and others. But wives with a 5 marriage are significantly more likely to say that their husband is more thoughtful and considerate, that he communicates better and shares their feelings more, and that he treats them with more respect. They also say that he is a better father. This survey appeared in the October 1991 *Child* ("When Kids Happen to a Marriage"). In all, 700 mothers and fathers responded. The report, "Married, With Children," appeared in October 1991.

## 8. Beyond Babies: Finding a Dream

**Page 172:**
"Almost all mothers sense that children provide": In my 1993 *New Woman* Relationship Survey, 95 percent of mothers say that motherhood gives them a great deal of personal satisfaction; the same number say it teaches them a lot about life. Ninety percent also say that being a mother is more fulfilling than they ever expected. But nearly as many admit that it's often a source of great stress and more frustrating than they expected.

"More than a few mothers also admit": In my 1990 *New Woman* Gender Survey, I found that six in ten mothers agree that: "Raising a child provides many rewards, but as a full-time job, raising children cannot keep most women satisfied."

**Page 173:**
"my surveys show that more men than women have one": In my 1992 *New Woman* Self-Esteem Survey, 62 percent of men say they have a special dream of their own, compared to 55 percent of women, a statistically significant difference.

**Page 174:**
"psychologists think that finding an intimate attachment": Searching for intimacy is a basic human need, according to most developmental psychologists. It's also a commonly accepted stage of adult life; see Daniel J. Levinson, *The Seasons of a Man's Life* (New York: Alfred A. Knopf, 1978).

"In my research, I've found nearly a dozen types of dreams": This analysis comes from my 1992 *New Woman* Self-Esteem Survey, in which men and women answered the following question: "Did you or do you have a special dream for yourself in life, a big, important goal to work toward? If so, what is it?" People described their dream in a few words or sentences, and their answers were categorized.

**Page 179:**
"As soon as they have children, they drop their own personal goals": In the *New Woman* Self-Esteem Survey, 64 percent of women who are not mothers say that they have a dream, but only 52 percent of mothers do.

"continues to decrease, decade by decade": While 81 percent of those between eighteen and twenty-four have a dream, 67 percent of those twenty-five to thirty-four do; 58 percent of those thirty-five to forty-four do and 42 percent of those forty-five to fifty-four have one. Finally, only 33 percent of women fifty-five and older still have a dream.

**Page 180:**
"mothers need to nurture their own visions": When I compare mothers who have a dream to those who don't, I find very striking differences. In the 1992 *New Woman* Self-Esteem survey, mothers with one are significantly more likely to agree that they're capable of more than they have achieved and to say that they grow stronger from their setbacks in life. They wish they had a better job and a better marriage; they yearn to be better mothers and to earn more money. More of them than dreamless moms feel creative, and more of them have risked a job by speaking out.

"my research shows that having a dream": When I compare women with a dream to those without, there's no difference in income between the two groups.

**Page 182:**
"Finding a dream in which they see themselves as heroic": This is from Levinson, *The Seasons of a Man's Life*.

"Women don't really need or want their own dream": It's a wife's job to help her husband realize his dream, according to Levinson, *The Seasons of a Man's Life*, p. 110.

**Page 183:**
"recanted on his original theory": See Daniel J. Levinson, *The Seasons of a Woman's Life* (New York: Alfred A. Knopf, 1996).

**Page 184:**
"That's why some therapists make a habit": From a personal interview

with Marilyn J. Mason, January 1993. See Marilyn J. Mason, *Making Our Lives Our Own: A Woman's Guide to the Six Challenges of Personal Change* (New York: HarperCollins, 1991).

**Page 186:**
"so many possible future selves": For research on this idea, see Hazel Markus and Paula Nurius, "Possible Selves," *American Psychologist*, vol. 41, no. 9 (September 1986), pp. 954–969 and Susan Cross and Hazel Markus, "Possible Selves Across the Life Span," *Human Development*, vol. 34 (1991), pp. 230–255.

## 9. Finding Balance

**Page 189:**
"a familiar Old Testament phrase": From Ecclesiastes 3:1–8, which begins: "To every thing there is a season, and a time to every purpose under the heaven: A time to be born, and a time to die."

**Page 190:**
Mary Catherine Bateson: See Mary Catherine Bateson, *Composing a Life* (New York: Plume, 1990), p. 184.

**Page 191:**
"the currency of care": Also from Bateson, *Composing a Life*, p. 128.

**Page 192:**
"a member of the !Kung": From Sarah Hall Sternglanz and Alison Nash, "Ethological Contributions to the Study of Human Motherhood," in Beverly Birns and Dale F. Hay (eds.), *The Different Faces of Motherhood* (New York: Plenum Press, 1988).

**Page 195:**
"many teenagers are handicapped by having a false self": For a discussion of the problem of false self for teenage girls, see Chapter 1.

**Page 198:**
"The power of the womb": See Anne Roiphe, *Fruitful: A Real Mother in the Modern World* (Boston: Houghton Mifflin Company, 1996), p. 151.

**Page 200:**
"Bateson admitted that she spent": From Bateson, *Composing a Life*, p. 40. For a moving description of the birth of her daughter, see Margaret Mead, *Blackberry Winter* (New York: William Morrow, 1972).

**Page 201:**

"A single mother I know from Barbados": It's quite common for mothers from Caribbean islands to leave their children to work in the United States; they send food and clothing in big barrels once or twice a year. See "The Barrel Children," *Newsweek*, February 19, 1996, p. 45.